DOING GLOBAL URBAN RESEARCH

Sara Miller McCune founded SAGE Publishing in 1965 to support the dissemination of usable knowledge and educate a global community. SAGE publishes more than 1000 journals and over 800 new books each year, spanning a wide range of subject areas. Our growing selection of library products includes archives, data, case studies and video. SAGE remains majority owned by our founder and after her lifetime will become owned by a charitable trust that secures the company's continued independence.

Los Angeles | London | New Delhi | Singapore | Washington DC | Melbourne

DOING GLOBAL URBAN RESEARCH

EDITED BY
JOHN HARRISON & MICHAEL HOYLER

Los Angeles | London | New Delhi
Singapore | Washington DC | Melbourne

Los Angeles | London | New Delhi
Singapore | Washington DC | Melbourne

SAGE Publications Ltd
1 Oliver's Yard
55 City Road
London EC1Y 1SP

SAGE Publications Inc.
2455 Teller Road
Thousand Oaks, California 91320

SAGE Publications India Pvt Ltd
B 1/I 1 Mohan Cooperative Industrial Area
Mathura Road
New Delhi 110 044

SAGE Publications Asia-Pacific Pte Ltd
3 Church Street
#10-04 Samsung Hub
Singapore 049483

Editor: Robert Rojek
Editorial assistant: Catriona McMullen
Production editor: Katherine Haw
Copyeditor: Catja Pafort
Proofreader: Neil Dowden
Indexer: Martin Hargreaves
Marketing manager: Susheel Gokarakonda
Cover design: Stephanie Guyaz
Typeset by: C&M Digitals (P) Ltd, Chennai, India
Printed in the UK

First published 2018

Library of Congress Control Number: 2017950860

British Library Cataloguing in Publication data

A catalogue record for this book is available from the British Library

ISBN 978-1-4739-7856-0
ISBN 978-1-4739-7857-7 (pbk)

'In the exciting recent whirl of theorising cities and urbanisation through new globalised and planetary configurations, empirical underpinnings have often struggled to keep pace. This much needed collection addresses this issue head-on offering a carefully assembled and importantly pluralistic set of tools, techniques and insights to guide and inspire new and enhanced routes into global urban research.'

Andrew Harris, Co-director of UCL Urban Lab and Senior Lecturer in Geography and Urban Studies, University College London

'This agenda-setting volume provides a cohesive, candid, and conceptually rich perspective on global urban research. Emerging and established scholars share insights about their methods, ethics, and research practices. These interdisciplinary perspectives make *Doing Global Urban Research* a valuable and provocative resource for researchers interested in global urban analysis.'

Michael Glass, Senior Lecturer of Urban Studies, University of Pittsburgh

'This is a landmark volume addressing the issue of the cumulative global significance and impacts of the majority of the world's population livingin cities.

Under Harrison and Hoyler's leadership, *Doing Global Urban Research* unlocks new intellectual and political territory to reconfigure the debates on why and how cities matter now and into the future.'

Susan Parnell, Professor of Environmental & Geographical Science, African Centre for Cities, University of Cape Town

'The cities of the world and the world of cities have transformed rather dramatically in the past half century. Instead of offering rather frictionless theorizing on these changes, this volume offers a very useful and highly reflective guide to do actual empirical research on a wide range of topics related to global urban studies.'

Robert C. Kloosterman, Professor of Economic Geography and Planning, University of Amsterdam

'Although there are myriad texts about cities, very few provide useful guidance on how and why to research them. Harrison and Hoyler's *Doing Global Urban Research* does just that: it provides novice and seasoned scholars alike with a range of approaches to researching cross-cutting urban themes at the global scale. Highly recommended to those interested in researching cities from geographical, sociological, historical, and/or planning disciplinary lenses, particularly as looking "across" methodological and theoretical perspectives has great potential to enhance research bridging the global and urban scales.'

Thomas Sigler, Senior Lecturer in Human Geography, The University of Queensland

'While globalization has become a common subject of the social sciences, the practice of doing global urban studies has been neglected so far. This book provides a good sense of how to deal with this, both for students and researchers.'

Markus Hesse, Professor of Urban Studies, University of Luxembourg

CONTENTS

LIST OF FIGURES AND TABLES

Figures

Tables

ABOUT THE EDITORS

John Harrison is Reader in Human Geography at Loughborough University and an Associate Director of the Globalization and World Cities (GaWC) research network. He is an urban-regional geographer interested in how large urban and regional spaces are conceptualized and mobilized politically. His recent publications have focused on global urban and regional governance. He is also co-editor of *Planning and Governance of Cities in Globalization* (Routledge, 2013), *Megaregions: Globalization's New Urban Form?* (Edward Elgar, 2015) and the *Handbook on the Geographies of Regions and Territories* (Edward Elgar, 2018), as well as an editor of the journal *Regional Studies*.

Michael Hoyler is Reader in Human Geography at Loughborough University and an Associate Director of the Globalization and World Cities (GaWC) research network. He is an urban geographer interested in the transformation of cities and metropolitan regions in contemporary globalization. His recent publications have focused on (world) city and city-regional network formation. He is also co-editor of *Global Urban Analysis* (Earthscan, 2011), the *International Handbook of Globalization and World Cities* (Edward Elgar, 2012), *Cities in Globalization* (Routledge, 2013), *Megaregions: Globalization's New Urban Form?* (Edward Elgar, 2015) and *Global City Makers* (Edward Elgar, 2018).

ABOUT THE CONTRIBUTORS

Michele Acuto is Professor of Urban Politics in the Melbourne School of Design, University of Melbourne, and visiting professor in the City Leadership Lab in the Department of Science, Technology, Engineering and Public Policy (STEaPP) at University College London. He is an international relations and urban studies researcher interested in the interplay between global and urban politics. His recent publications have focused on city networking and diplomacy as well as the links between urban science and policy. He is the author of *Global Cities, Governance and Diplomacy: The Urban Link* (Routledge, 2013), and co-editor of *Global City Challenges* (Palgrave Macmillan, 2013) and *Reassembling International Theory* (Palgrave Macmillan, 2014).

Tim Bunnell is Associate Professor in Geography and Chair of the Global Urban Studies research cluster at the National University of Singapore. He is a human geographer who works on urban transformation in Southeast Asia and that region's wider constitutive linkages. His recent publications have focused on relational geographies of urban and social change. He is the author of *From World City to the World in One City: Liverpool Through Malay Lives* (Wiley-Blackwell, 2016) and co-editor of *Urban Asias: Essays on Futurity Past and Present* (Jovis, 2018).

Mariana Dantas is Associate Professor of History at Ohio University. She was the Co-Investigator of the AHRC-funded International Research Network 'The Global City: Past and Present' and is a founding member of the Global Urban History Project. Her research focuses on early modern urban slavery and African diasporic communities in the Americas. Her recent publications examine slave women, families of mixed descent and gender in the colonial towns of Minas Gerais, Brazil. She is the author of *Black Townsmen: Urban Slavery and Freedom in the Eighteenth-Century Americas* (Palgrave Macmillan, 2008).

Ben Derudder is Professor in Human Geography at Ghent University and an Associate Director of the Globalization and World Cities (GaWC) research network. He is an urban geographer interested in settlement systems in general and their emergence at the global scale through inter-city networking in particular. His recent publications have focused on world city network formation and polycentric urban regions. He is the co-author of the second edition of *World City Network: A Global Urban Analysis* (Routledge, 2016), and co-editor of *Global Urban Analysis* (Earthscan, 2011) and the *International Handbook of Globalization and World Cities* (Edward Elgar, 2012).

Christopher Gaffney is Senior Research Fellow in the Department of Geography at the University of Zürich. He is an urban geographer whose research focuses on the urban and social impacts of sports mega-events. His recent publications examine the ways in which event coalitions produce changes in the political economy of urban regions. He is the author of *Temples of the Earthbound Gods* (University of Texas Press, 2008) and editor of the *Journal of Latin American Geography.*

Katherine V. Gough is Professor of Human Geography at Loughborough University. She is an urban social geographer interested in the transformation of housing, employment and mobility in low-income settlements in the Global South, with a particular emphasis on comparative and longitudinal studies. Her recent publications have focused on youth employment and entrepreneurship in sub-Saharan Africa. She is co-editor of *Rural–Urban Dynamics: Livelihoods, Mobility and Markets in African and Asian Frontiers* (Routledge, 2010) and *Young Entrepreneurs in Sub-Saharan Africa* (Routledge, 2016), as well as an editor of the journal *International Development Planning Review.*

Emma Hart is Senior Lecturer in Modern History at the University of St Andrews. From 2015–16 she was Principal Investigator of the AHRC International Research Network 'The Global City: Past and Present' and she is a founding member of the Global Urban History Project (GUHP). She is a historian of British colonial North America, interested in urban history and the history of economic life. She is the author of *Building Charleston: Town and Society in the Eighteenth-Century British Atlantic World* (University of Virginia Press, 2010), as well as of numerous articles on the economic and social development of Britain's North American colonies before 1783.

Nikos Katsikis is an urbanist working at the intersection of urbanization theory, design and geospatial analysis. He holds a Doctor of Design from the Harvard Graduate School of Design (GSD) and is currently a Postdoctoral Fellow at the University of Luxembourg and a Research Affiliate at the Urban Theory Lab, GSD. He is co-editor of *New Geographies 06: Grounding Metabolism* (Harvard University Press, 2014) and co-author, with Neil Brenner, of the forthcoming *Is the World Urban? Towards a Critique of Geospatial Ideology.*

Roger Keil is York Research Chair in Global Sub/Urban Studies, Faculty of Environmental Studies, York University in Toronto. He researches global suburbanization, urban political ecology and regional governance and is the Principal Investigator of the Major Collaborative Research Initiative on Global Suburbanisms (2010–18). He is the author of *Suburban Planet* (Polity, 2018), editor of *Suburban Constellations* (Jovis, 2013), and co-editor of *Suburban*

Governance: A Global View (University of Toronto Press, 2015), *Governing Cities Through Regions* (Wilfrid Laurier University Press, 2017) and *The Globalizing Cities Reader* (Routledge, 2018).

John Lauermann is a Assistant Professor of Geography at Medgar Evers College, City University of New York. He is an urban geographer interested in the political economy of large land investment projects. His recent publications have focused on mega-event planning, appearing in *Environment and Planning A*, *Journal of the American Planning Association*, *Urban Geography* and *Urban Studies*. He is co-author of *Failed Olympic Bids and the Transformation of Urban Space* (Palgrave Macmillan, 2017).

Donald McNeill is Professor of Urban and Cultural Geography at Western Sydney University. He is interested in the production of urban space, with a particular focus on the corporate and professional practices that structure different spatial types, such as airports, hotels, office buildings and central business districts. His most recent books, *The Global Architect: Firms, Fame and Urban Form* (Routledge, 2009) and *Global Cities and Urban Theory* (Sage, 2017), have focused on the relationship between global practices, firms and the built environment.

Martin Müller is Swiss National Science Foundation Professor at the University of Lausanne. He is a human geographer working on the planning and impacts of mega-events and contributing to conceptual debates regarding actor-network theory and assemblage thinking. His recent publications have developed the concepts of 'hazardous planning' and 'improvisation' in the context of planning mega-events. His work on mega-events has been published in, among others, *Journal of the American Planning Association*, *Regional Studies* and *Environment and Planning A*.

Zachary P. Neal is Associate Professor in Psychology and Global Urban Studies at Michigan State University, an Associate Director of the Globalization and World Cities (GaWC) research network, and an Associate Editor at *Journal of Urban Affairs*, *Evidence and Policy* and *Global Networks*. He is a network researcher whose interests span urban geography, public education, research utilization and quantitative methodology. His recent publications have focused on techniques for inferring network structure from affiliation data. He is also author of *The Connected City: How Networks are Shaping the Modern Metropolis* (Routledge, 2013) and editor of the *Handbook of Applied System Science* (Routledge, 2016).

Andrea Pollio is a doctoral student at the Institute for Culture and Society, Western Sydney University. He is interested in the relationship between cities and techno-entrepreneurial cultures. His research focuses on the performativity of economic and humanitarian knowledge in the making of Cape Town's start-up scene. His previous publications address questions of technocratic expertise around the introduction of smart city policies in Italy.

Hyun Bang Shin is Associate Professor of Geography and Urban Studies at the London School of Economics and Political Science. His research focuses on the critical analysis of the political economic dynamics of speculative urbanization, with particular attention to Asian cities. He is co-editor of *Global Gentrifications: Uneven Development and Displacement* (Policy Press, 2015) and co-author of *Planetary Gentrification* (Polity Press, 2016). He is currently writing a monograph *Making China Urban* (Routledge), and co-editing *Contesting Urban Space in East Asia* (Palgrave Macmillan) and *The Political Economy of Mega Projects in Asia: Globalization and Urban Transformation* (Routledge).

Peter J. Taylor is Emeritus Professor at Northumbria and Loughborough Universities and Director of the Globalization and World Cities (GaWC) research network. He is a world-systems analyst rewriting political and urban geographies. His recent publications focus on city/state relations in a trans-modern framing from urban origins to anthropogenic climate change and include *Extraordinary Cities: Millennia of Moral Syndromes, World-Systems and City/State Relations* (Edward Elgar, 2013), as well as the co-authored *World City Network: A Global Urban Analysis* (2nd edition, Routledge, 2016), *Working, Housing: Urbanizing* (Springer, 2016) and *Political Geography: World-Economy, Nation-State, Locality* (7th edition, Routledge, 2018).

Cristina Temenos is an Urban Studies Postdoctoral Research Fellow at the School of Environment, Education and Development, and the Manchester Urban Institute at the University of Manchester. She is an urban geographer studying the relationships between social justice and the mobilization of social, health and drug policies across cities in the Global North and Global South. Her work on urban policy mobilities has been published in *Annals of the Association of American Geographers*, *Environment and Planning A*, *International Journal of Urban and Regional Research* and *The Routledge Handbook of Mobilities*.

David Wachsmuth is the Canada Research Chair in Urban Governance and an Assistant Professor of Urban Planning at McGill University. He is an interdisciplinary urbanist whose research examines urban governance problems which exceed the spatial and conceptual boundaries of the city. His recent publications have examined large-scale local economic development partnerships in the United States, new forms of sustainability thinking in global urban policy, and the impact of globalization on local housing markets. He is also the co-editor of *Whose Streets? The Toronto G20 and the Challenge of Summit Protest* (Between the Lines, 2011).

Kevin Ward is Professor of Human Geography, School of Environment, Education and Development and Director of the Manchester Urban Institute at the University of Manchester. His research focuses on the geographies of urban policy making, state re-organization, and the politics of urban and regional development. Author and editor of numerous journal articles and books, including *Researching the City* (Sage, 2014), *Urban Theory: New Critical Perspectives* (Routledge, 2017) and *Cities Under Austerity: Restructuring the US Metropolis* (SUNY Press, 2018), he is also currently Editor-in-Chief of the journal *Urban Geography*.

Sven Daniel Wolfe is a Doctoral Candidate in Geography at the University of Lausanne. He is an urban and regional geographer interested in policy mobilities, multiplicities, mega-events and Russia. His recent publications have focused on neopatrimonial relationships in the development of the 2018 Russian World Cup, and the partial successes of the 2014 Sochi Olympics in reframing popular perceptions of Russia.

ACKNOWLEDGEMENTS

The Editors and Publisher are grateful for permission to reproduce the following material in this book:

Chapter 6, excerpt from McNeill, D. (2015) 'Global firms and smart technologies: IBM and the reduction of cities', *Transactions of the Institute of British Geographers,* 40(4): 562–74. Republished with permission of John Wiley & Sons Inc and conveyed through Copyright Clearance Center, Inc.

Chapter 8, excerpt from Brenner, N. and Schmid, C. (2014) 'The "urban age" in question', *International Journal of Urban and Regional Research,* 38(3): 731–55. Republished with permission of John Wiley & Sons Inc and conveyed through Copyright Clearance Center, Inc.

Chapter 10, excerpt from Smith, N. (1987) 'Gentrification and the rent gap', *Annals of the Association of American Geographers,* 77(3): 462–65. Reprinted by permission of the publisher (Taylor & Francis Ltd, http://www.tandfonline.com).

Chapter 10, excerpt from Massey, D. (1984) 'Introduction: Geography matters' in D. Massey and J. Allen, with Anderson, J., Cunningham, S., Hamnett, C. and Sarre, P. (eds), *Geography Matters! A Reader* © The Open University 1984, published by Cambridge University Press and reproduced with permission.

Chapter 10, excerpt from Celestina, M. (2016) '"Displacement" before displacement: time, place and the case of rural Urabá', *Journal of Latin American Studies,* 48(2): 367–90. © (2016), with permission from Cambridge University Press.

Chapter 12, some sections overlap with Keil, R. (2018) *Suburban Planet.* Cambridge: Polity Press. Republished with kind permission of Polity Books.

Chapter 16, excerpt reprinted from Taylor, P. J. (1997) 'Hierarchical tendencies amongst world cities: a global research proposal', *Cities,* 14(6): 323–32, © with permission from Elsevier.

1

MAKING SENSE OF THE GLOBAL URBAN

John Harrison and Michael Hoyler

It goes without saying that urban research has become increasingly global in its outlook. Irrespective of whether you are an urban geographer, urban sociologist, urban political scientist, urban historian, urban economist, favouring a qualitative, quantitative or mixed methods approach, the challenge that confronts researchers as they attempt to participate in and engage with our increasingly 'globalized' urban studies remains fundamentally the same – how to make sense of urban complexity.

One quick and easy observation is that the quest to understand our globalizing and urbanizing modern world has seen urban scholars leave no stone unturned in the pursuit of new theory production. From Ananya Roy's (2009) call for new geographies of urban theory to understand the 21st-century metropolis through to the emergence of a new critical urban theory (Brenner, 2009; Marcuse, 2009) and a more internationalized urban theory (Parnell and Oldfield, 2014; Robinson, 2011a) it is impossible to ignore how urban studies has been experiencing its own globalizing tendencies of late.

One reflection of this is how the prefix 'global' has been attached to all manner of different urban ideas, concepts and processes. We can reflect how in the 1990s cities research, which traditionally focused on cities as part of national urban systems, gave way to a new wave of 'global cities' research examining how cities are connected into international circuits of capital accumulation and political decision-making in globalization (Sassen, 1991; Taylor and Derudder, Chapter 3; Neal, Chapter 4; Acuto, Chapter 7). We can see how in the 2000s erstwhile spatial concepts such as the 'city-region' became reimagined and rejuvenated as 'global city-regions' (Scott, 2001), while classic urban processes such as gentrification and suburbanization were recast as global urban processes through the lenses of 'global gentrifications' (Lees et al., 2015; Smith, 2002) and 'global suburbanisms' (Keil, Chapter 12). The transition from 'cities' through 'globalizing cities' to 'globalized urbanization' is today being extended as urbanization is increasingly reframed as a planetary process through notions of 'planetary urbanization' (Brenner, 2014; Katsikis, Chapter 2) and 'planetary gentrification' (Lees et al., 2016; Shin, Chapter 10).

But what, we ask, can be said about the current state of empirical research and the methodological approaches we possess for *doing* global urban research? And what does it actually mean to *do* global urban research?

Now you might be thinking that this is a somewhat peculiar set of questions to ask at this point. If we are all part of the globalization of urban research then intuitively we must know when we are doing it, where we are doing it, how we are doing it, why we are doing it and what it means to be doing it. Surely the current state of urban studies guarantees we are all doing global urban research and, by virtue of this, becoming global urban researchers? We may well be but these are some of the seemingly straightforward questions we are often guilty of overlooking as researchers.

For all of the talk surrounding the move towards more globally oriented urban studies there has been a notable silence regarding the practice of doing global urban research. Attaching the prefix 'global' to established theories and processes is an easy, often neat, conceptual move, yet translating this into the practice of actually doing urban research presents many more challenges. Indeed, if you are reading these words then it is a challenge that you are most likely facing. The problem as we see it is that the practice of doing global urban research is often implied, lurking in the background, or largely hidden from view. This is our point of departure: in this book we aim to put the practice of doing global urban research centre stage.

Our beginnings

How do you research planetary urbanization? This seems to be another one of those simple questions. But as we discovered a few years ago, it can be rather more difficult to answer. Picture this:

- The question 'How do you research planetary urbanization?' comes from a group of final-year undergraduate students, many of whom are also doing their undergraduate research project at the time.
- The students asking the question are in the last week of the two semester-long modules we teach: 'Globalized Urbanization' and 'Regional Worlds'.
- The final part of both modules sees students exposed to current research agendas and new frontiers in urban and regional studies respectively.

At the time 'planetary urbanization' was just emerging to be one of the hottest topics in urban studies. Unbeknown to us, but perhaps not too surprisingly in hindsight, we each changed our lectures that year to talk about the emerging recent trends in urban and regional studies, as they are embodied in concepts such as 'planetary urbanization', 'global suburbanisms' and 'megaregions'. So here were a group of students being taught about the latest big 'global' ideas in urban and regional studies and logically they wanted to know how they could do it. This left us faced with a question which should be relatively straightforward to respond to but in many ways it does not avail an easy answer.

Part of the challenge is that neither of us had done actual research on planetary urbanization – or, for that matter, many of the topics covered in this book. This means we cannot fall back on an answer reflecting our own research experience. Part has to do with the globalization of urban studies and whether it is feasible to do primary research on urban concepts and processes prefixed with the words 'global', 'planetary' or 'mega'. Here is a challenge. Ask yourself the question 'How do you research gentrification?', 'How do you research urbanization?' or 'How do you research regions?'. The answers you come up with will most likely arrive quickly and afford you with a range of options. Now ask yourself the same questions but add the aforementioned prefixes ('How do you research *global* gentrifications?', 'How do you research *planetary* urbanization?', 'How do you research *mega*regions?') to see if you can come up with a similar range of options. We suspect not. The challenge is that new theories and concepts for framing the global urban have developed at a far faster rate than the empirical tools and techniques necessary to provide the evidence. The final part of the challenge is that there is no book or collection of articles on how to do this. While we do not set out to provide you with a manual for doing global urban research, we do aim to provide you – the reader – with insights into the opportunities and challenges, the tools and techniques, the theories and the empirical case studies that can enable you to do global urban research.

Our vantage point

It is not lost on us how our vantage point impacts on how we perceive the field of global urban studies: after all, we think from where we are, are influenced by where we have been and where we are heading, and our thoughts are constantly shaped by the encounters we have along the way. We have already discussed one such encounter with a group of students on the modules we teach, but for us there is more to it than this.

Our vantage point is Loughborough, a relatively small university town (c. 60,000 population) in England, located some 150 kilometres north of London and 75 kilometres east of Birmingham. It is not exactly the global urban, but its prominent place on the global urban studies map is its legacy as the birthplace of the Globalization and World Cities (GaWC) research network (www.lboro.ac.uk/gawc) of which we are both part.

Back in 1998, Peter Taylor together with Jon Beaverstock founded GaWC to contribute to solving the empirical/methodological problem of doing global urban research. His prompt was the dearth of accessible inter-city data to analyse what was being variously conceptualized as a 'global network of cities' (King, 1990), 'transnational urban system' (Sassen, 1994) or, as Castells (1996) famously framed it, a global 'space of flows', with cities as the nodes in the network. In one of the formative GaWC research articles, Taylor notes:

> I doubt whether social scientists as a body of practitioners have fully appreciated the implications of globalization for their research practices. Despite the plethora of recent writings on globalization themes, it is by no means clear that a concomitant proportion of social science research projects address global-level processes. I suspect that this is an important topic where theory has progressed much further than the evidence actually warrants. (Taylor, 1997: 323)

In his own words 'a plea is made for readers to join in the proposed global study' (Taylor, 1997: 323). It was a plea that has been followed by two decades of global urban study.

For Peter Taylor himself, the challenge of creating a set of global data to enable better conceptualizations of the complexity of worldwide inter-city networks resulted in the 'interlocking network model' (Taylor, 2001), which was then applied to 315 cities worldwide and a 'world city network' derived including measures of network connectivity between cities (Taylor, 2004). What is often referred to as the 'GaWC methodology' has since been applied widely in global urban studies and inspired significant critical engagement and debate (Derudder and Parnreiter, 2014).

Following the establishment of a global cities thesis, a growing body of literature has emerged focusing on reviewing existing strategies for comparing cities. Amongst others, Jennifer Robinson's advancement of a postcolonial approach has led her to speculate on what potential 'comparative methodologies' exist for researchers who wish for an urban studies 'conducted "on a world scale"' (Robinson, 2011b: 2; 2016; Parnell, 2016). Allied to this we have seen a focus on ethnography as an approach for doing urban research which is 'global' or 'comparative', such as AbdouMaliq Simone's ethnographies of African and South East Asian cities (Simone, 2001), Colin McFarlane's idea of 'translocal assemblage' developed from ethnographic research into the relations between informality, infrastructure and knowledge in informal settlements in urban India (McFarlane, 2011), or Tim Bunnell's multi-sited collaborative ethnographic research project investigating the remaking of Asian cities (Bunnell, Chapter 13; see also Goh et al., 2015).

Urban geographers have also become increasingly interested in researching the geographies of policy mobility – specifically how knowledge (of complex urban processes, models, concepts) circulates globally and how it crystallizes on the ground in different urban contexts (Ward, 2010; Temenos and Ward, Chapter 5). Central to this urban research is understanding how the increasing interconnectedness of policy regimes between places and across scales vis-à-vis the extant power of state territoriality results in '(im)mobile urbanism' globally and in place (McCann and Ward, 2011). Most useful in reinforcing our aim with this book, Jamie Peck and Nik Theodore observe how:

> If processes of policy mobilization have indeed become increasingly transnational in reach and cross-scalar in constitution, if they are manifest in ever more complex relational combinations, *then there is an inescapable need to confront new methodological challenges*. Spatially demarcated forms of policy evaluation certainly will not do. *New methodological strategies must be developed* to expose and critically interrogate the interconnectedness of policy regimes between places and across scales. (Peck and Theodore, 2010: 171, emphasis added)

Then there is the question of doing urban research on a global scale. This is the challenge currently facing the 'Global Suburbanisms' project team led by Roger Keil at York University in Toronto (Keil, Chapter 12). The first major research project to systematically take stock of worldwide suburban developments, this major collaborative research initiative comprises a team of 50 researchers and 18 partner organizations. Their aim is to systematically understand suburbanization in the Americas, Europe, Africa and Asia, with objectives to (i) 'document and evaluate the diversity of global suburbanisms in their various contexts'; (ii) 'explore the mutual and co-constructive elements of environmental or financial crisis with the production and governance of global suburban space'; and, perhaps most significant in the current context, (iii) 'use [their] wide-ranging empirical data and analysis to intervene in urban theory' (Keil, 2017).

Of course at this point we could go on mentioning many more emergent themes that have given rise to global urban studies research agendas (indeed, many more are covered by the chapters in this book) but the point we are trying to make here is that two decades on from Peter Taylor's plea from Loughborough for a global study, today we have a plethora of global studies responding (directly or indirectly) to his call to appreciate the implications of globalization for their research practices. However, from our vantage point in Loughborough, we are struck by the lack of actual discussion about these research practices. It was this that prompted us to begin the journey towards this book.

Our approach

Our journey began in 2013. This is when we were faced with groups of students asking us how they could go about doing global urban research. It was also a time when we had been having discussions about the nature of global urban studies. One observation was how we were finding ourselves listening to an increasing number of conference presentations, and reading more and more papers, where authors were engaging with theories and concepts relating to the global urban, but in many cases their research did not appear to have a global dimension. This led us to ask of ourselves the question, are we doing global urban research?

For two researchers working in Loughborough as part of the Globalization and World Cities research network you might reasonably expect the answer to be a simple yes. In fact, we found it to be a deeply challenging question. In trying to answer it we found ourselves coming up with a whole series of other questions: What is global urban research? How do we know global urban research when we see it? How can we do global urban research? When and where are people doing global urban research? Is global urban research even possible? The list goes on. We suspected that if we were challenged by this question, many others researching the global urban might be facing a similar challenge. We also came to realize that one problem is that the industry-standard 8000-word journal article or 20-minute conference presentation does not allow researchers the scope to discuss the practice of doing global urban research.

Two years later, in 2015, Loughborough was the destination for a three-day international conference on 'Doing Global Urban Research', supported by the Urban Studies Foundation, that set out to ask these questions, and to try and find answers. Breaking with the traditional conference format we allowed each presenter 40 minutes. Our aim was to bring together researchers working across the diversity of global urban studies, and to allow them time to present their research ideas and findings, but crucially to openly discuss how they do global urban research – what they understand by it, the opportunities and challenges afforded by it, and how they see the practice of it as it links to the new geographies and internationalization of urban theory. In addition to an open call from which we selected 45 presentations, the conference was structured around five keynote presentations from Roger Keil, Susan Parnell, Christian Schmid, Peter Taylor and Kevin Ward about their experience of doing global urban research in relation to global suburbanisms, southern urbanism, planetary urbanization, world cities and policy mobilities respectively.

This context is important because it is out of this conference that this book has emerged. As with any edited collection, the final outcome is necessarily selective. We know the book will not cover all approaches, themes and topics within global urban research. We also know that our book will overlap and fit alongside others within the field of (global) urban studies. It is to these we now turn.

The first group of books are those which aim to mark out the terrain for urban research. Central to each is an attempt to entice readers into the field of urban research by showcasing the dynamism, plurality and explanatory power of urban theory in contemporary urban research (Harding and Blokland,

2014; Jayne and Ward, 2017; Parker, 2015; Short, 2014). They do this by exploring the state-of-the-art thinking to outline the important conceptual advances that identify the field of urban studies, and the process of urban theory making, as offering a critical take on 21st-century urbanism. We can also include in this group a number of books tailored to particular disciplinary approaches: for example, on urban politics (Davidson and Martin, 2013) or urban geography (Jonas et al., 2015). Nevertheless, what is interesting to us is that while all of them are implicitly global given the nature of urban studies today, none are explicitly global (but see McNeill, 2017), nor do they have any sustained engagement with methods or the practicalities of doing urban research.

The second set of books explicitly focuses on the increasingly global nature of urban studies. In these the emphasis once again tends towards presenting readers with state-of-the-art research findings, alongside arguments pertaining to the explanatory power of new conceptual approaches or analytical frameworks (Brenner, 2014; Harrison and Hoyler, 2015; Keil, 2018a; Lees et al., 2015; McCann and Ward, 2011; Pacione, 2009). Once more there is little or no mention of methods or the practicalities of doing this type of globally oriented urban research.

A third set of publications are the various handbooks and surveys produced of late. Consisting of a large number of often shorter entries these books provide a useful starting point if you are looking to gain an initial overview of a particular field or topic. Nevertheless, while there are a series of urban handbooks and surveys which are global in scope (Derudder et al., 2012; Hannigan and Richards, 2017; Taylor et al., 2011), they are not particularly instructive for researchers looking to find their way in understanding how to go about doing global urban research. In part this is due to the all-encompassing nature of these collections. But part is also due to the sheer scale of putting together these volumes. Both are tasks somewhat removed from the more grounded reality of day-to-day urban research.

The fourth and final set of works which have become more prominent in the past two decades are those dedicated to the actual research methods employed by urban scholars. Very clearly aligned to the expansion of the higher education sector, and the increasing numbers of undergraduate and graduate students doing research projects, methods books range from the generic, to the disciplinary, all the way through to the topic based. In the field of urban studies, we can look to Kevin Ward's 2014 book, *Researching the City*, as an exemplar for guiding researchers through the process of designing, executing and writing up urban research. Often missing from these works, however, is the clear connection to theory and concepts.

All have their merits and offer much to advance research and teaching in urban studies, but the focus of this book is squarely on the practice of doing global urban research. This does not mean that urban theory drops out, nor does it see methods relegated from the collection. Likewise it is not a zero-sum argument for theory over methods or methods over theory. We very clearly see this book sitting between theory and practice, or, perhaps more accurately, we position this book as a bridge between them.

We are also conscious that many readers will be in the formative stages of undertaking urban research and, as Ward (2014: 5) notes, both undergraduate and graduate dissertations 'tend to consist of a mix of theory, methods and empirics and both require analytical and management skills'. It is in this spirit that this collection brings together contributions discussing theory, methods and empirics. But it also does something else. From the outset we were keen that contributors reflect on their practice. As well as having a consistent approach across the chapters to allow you to easily compare, it was for these reasons that contributors were asked in their chapters to follow a similar structure.

Each chapter in this collection is written in the author's own style, meaning there are differences between them; however, authors were asked to structure their contributions around five themes. Each chapter begins with an introduction outlining why people research this topic. Section One of each chapter will help you to identify the key theories, ideas and concepts that are shaping this area of urban research, and an overview of the current state of academic debate in this field. Section Two then highlights some of the challenges facing researchers. In some cases these challenges are more theoretical and conceptual, in others they are more practical and empirical. In Section Three, authors focus on some of the techniques available to you if you are interested in doing this type of urban research. Here again – reflecting each author's own unique style – some chapters focus on methodological approaches while others address the actual methods themselves, and, similarly, some highlight the techniques they have used in their own research while others also identify techniques which have been utilized by others working in their field. Section Four provides a case study – or case studies when there are multiple authors – of how the chapter author has done this in their own work, enabling you to see how they have practised the doing of global urban research. Finally – in Section Five – there are some reflections from each author on their experience of doing global urban research. Taken together, the contributions to this book offer encouragement and guidance for a reflexive engagement with the many ways of doing global urban research (Hoyler and Harrison, Chapter 16).

References

Acuto, M. (2018) 'Engaging with global urban governance', in J. Harrison and M. Hoyler (eds), *Doing Global Urban Research*. London: Sage, pp. 96–109.

Brenner, N. (2009) 'What is critical urban theory?', *City*, 13(2–3): 198–207.

Brenner, N. (ed.) (2014) *Implosions/Explosions: Towards a Study of Planetary Urbanization*. Berlin: Jovis.

Bunnell, T. (2018) 'Comparative ethnographic urban research', in J. Harrison and M. Hoyler (eds), *Doing Global Urban Research*. London: Sage, pp. 182–95.

Castells, M. (1996) *The Rise of the Network Society*. Oxford: Blackwell.

Davidson, M. and Martin, D. (eds) (2013) *Urban Politics: Critical Approaches*. London: Sage.

Derudder, B. and Parnreiter, C. (2014) 'Introduction: The interlocking network model for studying urban networks: Outline, potential, critiques, and ways forward', *Tijdschrift voor Economische en Sociale Geografie*, 105(4): 373–86.

Derudder, B., Hoyler, M., Taylor, P.J. and Witlox, F. (eds) (2012) *International Handbook of Globalization and World Cities*. Cheltenham: Edward Elgar.

Goh, D.P.S., Bunnell, T. and van der Veet, P. (2015) 'Introduction: Doing Asian cities', *Ethnography*, 16(3): 287–94.

Hannigan, J. and Richards, G. (eds) (2017) *The SAGE Handbook of New Urban Studies*. London: Sage.

Harding, A. and Blokland, T. (2014) *Urban Theory: A Critical Introduction to Power, Cities and Urbanism in the 21st Century*. London: Sage.

Harrison, J. and Hoyler, M. (eds) (2015) *Megaregions: Globalization's New Urban Form?* Cheltenham: Edward Elgar.

Hoyler, M. and Harrison, J. (2018) 'Advancing global urban research', in J. Harrison and M. Hoyler (eds), *Doing Global Urban Research*. London: Sage, pp. 225–32.

Jayne, M. and Ward, K. (eds) (2017) *Urban Theory: New Critical Perspectives*. London: Routledge.

Jonas, A.E.G., McCann, E. and Thomas, M. (2015) *Urban Geography: A Critical Introduction*. Oxford: Wiley.

Katsikis, N. (2018) 'Visualizing the planetary urban', in J. Harrison and M. Hoyler (eds), *Doing Global Urban Research*. London: Sage, pp. 12–33.

Keil, R. (2017) 'Global suburbanisms: Our objectives'. http://suburbs.info.yorku.ca/about-us/our-objectives (accessed 31 August 2017).

Keil, R. (2018a) *Suburban Planet: Making the World Urban from the Outside In*. Cambridge: Polity.

Keil, R. (2018b) 'Constructing global suburbia, one critical theory at a time', in J. Harrison and M. Hoyler (eds), *Doing Global Urban Research*. London: Sage, pp. 169–81.

King, A. (1990) *Global Cities: Post-imperialism and the Internationalization of London*. London: Routledge.

Lees, L., Shin, H.B. and López-Morales, E. (eds) (2015) *Global Gentrifications: Uneven Development and Displacement*. Bristol: Policy Press.

Lees, L., Shin, H.B. and López-Morales, E. (2016) *Planetary Gentrification*. Cambridge: Polity.

Marcuse, P. (2009) 'From critical urban theory to the right to the city', *City*, 13(2–3): 185–97.

(Continued)

McCann, E. and Ward, K. (eds) (2011) *Mobile Urbanism: Cities and Policymaking in the Global Age*. Minnesota, MN: University of Minnesota Press.

McFarlane, C. (2011) 'The city as assemblage: Dwelling and urban space', *Environment and Planning D*, 29(4): 649–71.

McNeill, D. (2017) *Global Cities and Urban Theory*. London: Sage.

Neal, Z. (2018) 'Analysing cities as networks', in J. Harrison and M. Hoyler (eds), *Doing Global Urban Research*. London: Sage, pp. 52–65.

Pacione, M. (2009) *Urban Geography: A Global Perspective*. London: Routledge.

Parker, S. (2015) *Urban Theory and the Urban Experience: Encountering the City*. London: Routledge.

Parnell, S. (2016) 'Defining a global urban development agenda', *World Development*, 78: 529–40.

Parnell, S. and Oldfield, S. (eds) (2014) *The Routledge Handbook on Cities of the Global South*. London: Routledge.

Peck, J. and Theodore, N. (2010) 'Mobilizing policy: Models, methods, and mutations', *Geoforum*, 41(2): 169–74.

Robinson, J. (2011a) 'The travels of urban neoliberalism: Taking stock of the internationalization of urban theory', *Urban Geography*, 32(8): 1087–1109.

Robinson, J. (2011b) 'Cities in a world of cities: The comparative gesture', *International Journal of Urban and Regional Research*, 35(1): 1–23.

Robinson, J. (2016) 'Thinking cities through elsewhere: Comparative tactics for a more global urban studies', *Progress in Human Geography*, 40(1): 3–29.

Roy, A. (2009) 'The 21st-century metropolis: New geographies of theory', *Regional Studies*, 43(6): 819–30.

Sassen, S. (1991) *The Global City: New York, London, Tokyo*. Princeton, NJ: Princeton University Press.

Sassen, S. (1994) *Cities in the World Economy*. Thousand Oaks, CA: Pine Forge Press.

Scott, A.J., (ed.) (2001) *Global City-Regions: Trends, Theory, Policy*. Oxford: Oxford University Press.

Shin, H.B. (2018) 'Studying global gentrifications', in J. Harrison and M. Hoyler (eds), *Doing Global Urban Research*. London: Sage, pp. 138–52.

Short, J.R. (2014) *Urban Theory: A Critical Assessment* (2nd edition). London: Palgrave Macmillan.

Simone, A.M. (2001) 'On the worlding of African cities', *African Studies Review*, 44(2): 15–41.

Smith, N. (2002) 'New globalism, new urbanism: Gentrification as global urban strategy', *Antipode*, 34(3): 427–50.

Taylor, P.J. (1997) 'Hierarchical tendencies amongst world cities: A global research proposal', *Cities*, 14(6): 323–32.

Taylor, P.J. (2001) 'Specification of the world city network', *Geographical Analysis*, 33(2): 181–94.

Taylor, P.J. (2004) *World City Network: A Global Urban Analysis*. London: Routledge.

Taylor, P.J. and Derudder, B. (2018) 'Exploring the world city network', in J. Harrison and M. Hoyler (eds), *Doing Global Urban Research*. London: Sage, pp. 34-51.

Taylor, P.J., Ni, F., Derudder, B., Hoyler, M., Huang, J. and Witlox, F. (eds) (2011) *Global Urban Analysis: A Survey of Cities in Globalization*. London: Earthscan.

Temenos, C. and Ward, K. (2018) 'Examining global urban policy mobilities', in J. Harrison and M. Hoyler (eds), *Doing Global Urban Research*. London: Sage, pp. 66-80.

Ward, K. (2010) 'Towards a relational comparative approach to the study of cities', *Progress in Human Geography*, 34(4): 471-87.

Ward, K. (ed.) (2014) *Researching the City*. London: Sage.

2

VISUALIZING THE PLANETARY URBAN

Nikos Katsikis

Why visualize the planetary urban?

At the beginning of the 21st century, urbanization is widely recognized as a major factor in the extensive social, economic and environmental transformations that have been reshaping life on the planet (Soja and Kanai, 2007). Within this challenging context, one of the most prominent debates in global urban studies today centres on the emerging paradigm of *planetary urbanization*. Inspired by the writings of Henri Lefebvre (1970 [2003]), in the early 2010s Neil Brenner and Christian Schmid embarked on an intellectual journey to highlight the limitations of the 'urban age thesis' (Brenner and Schmid, 2014) and move beyond this to develop a new epistemology of the urban. The agenda was born and cemented in a series of landmark publications (Brenner and Schmid, 2011, 2015; Brenner, 2013, 2014), supported by groups of researchers working as part of the Urban Theory Lab at the Harvard Graduate School of Design and ETH Zürich, alongside other engaged scholars (most notably Merrifield, 2013; Sevilla-Buitrago, 2014).

The emerging paradigm of planetary urbanization is invested both in the theoretical and the epistemological redefinition of the urban as a condition that transcends the city, as well as in the establishment of conceptual and methodological toolkits that would allow for a systematic investigation of a generalized condition of *urbanization without an outside*. Central to the planetary urban thesis is the stated aim for new urban theory in which, in Brenner's words, 'the conditions and trajectories of agglomerations (cities, city-regions, etc.) must be connected analytically to larger-scale processes of territorial reorganization, circulation (of labour, commodities, raw materials, nutrients, and energy), and resource extraction that ultimately encompass the space of the entire world' (Brenner, 2013: 103–4).

Alongside new theories and concepts, the emerging paradigm of planetary urbanization is also driving forward important developments as we think through how best to do planetary urban research. New methods of cartographic investigation, geospatial analysis and visualization are forming an important part of the work examining the planetary urban. While terms such as the Urbanthropocene (Luke, 2014) try to highlight the expansive reach and complex nature of urbanization processes, continuous technological advancements in remote sensing, data science and Geographic Information Systems promise that their unprecedented dimensions can be thoroughly understood, charted, and eventually adequately managed (Potere and Schneider, 2007; Solecki et al., 2013). As grasping the multi-scalar urbanization processes becomes increasingly important to questions of uneven social and ecological development, the proliferation of new tools and methodologies of visualizing the planetary urban offers exciting new potentials.

However, while technical and quantitative advancements in visualizing the planetary urban are necessary, they are on their own largely insufficient to fully grasp the complexities of urbanization processes, as long as they are limited by a particular conceptualization of the urban: a conceptualization framed around the condition of agglomerations in their various forms (city, metropolis, megalopolis), primarily focusing on their socio-spatial configuration (growth, expansion, economic and demographic performance) and their relationships with each other (networks of cities, polycentric urban regions). This conceptualization has led to a paradoxical condition. While the importance of the relationship of agglomerations to the rest of the planetary terrain is widely recognized, it is poorly understood. Moreover, when it is considered, it is often framed through an unproductive binarism, that of the urban world exercising some sort of influence over its rural surroundings (Seto et al., 2012; Seitzinger et al., 2012). A summary of this understanding is offered by an introductory statement of the UN-Habitat agenda on 'the global context': cities, although covering no more than 2% of the total land area, host the majority of the world population and contribute around 70% of world GDP. At the same time, they absorb over 60% of global energy resources, and generate more than 70% of greenhouse gas emissions and 70% of global waste (UN-Habitat, 2016). In short, the urban world is a small percentage of the earth's surface where the majority of the population is concentrated (Burdett and Sudjic, 2007; UN, 2012), characterized by the ability to contribute economic surpluses (Glaeser, 2011; Florida, 2012), but also ecological deficits, which are sourced and spread upon a great external, rural world of sparsely populated areas of low productivity (Rees and Wackernagel, 1996; Seto et al., 2010).

Subsequently, most attempts to visualize the planetary urban have been reduced to an effort to predominantly chart the dimensions, growth and expansion of dense agglomerations, of how the urban world morphs over a great exterior. Figure 2.1 highlights this dichotomy. The major agglomeration zones on the planet are plotted in black against a light-grey background that delineates the rest of the used part of the earth's surface. These landscapes include agricultural areas, grazing and forestry zones, as well as built-up areas beyond dense settlements, such as infrastructural systems and road and rail transportation networks. According to this visualization, the totality of the used planet covers almost 70% of the earth's land surface, while at the same time agglomeration zones cover no more than 2% of this utilized whole. Visualizing the planetary urban has been a task of visualizing the world's agglomerations, in effect visualizing the world's 2%.

While the transformative agency of urbanization in organizing life on the planet is widely recognized, the majority of the planetary terrain remains a great exterior to the urban, a world apart. Thus, grasping and visualizing the full dimensions of urbanization in the world requires an understanding of urbanization beyond agglomeration, as the planetary urbanization paradigm suggests. This contribution builds upon this paradigm, and especially upon the framework of conceiving urbanization as a dialectical relationship between what has been framed as *concentrated urbanization*, broadly referring to agglomeration zones in their various forms, and *extended urbanization*, including landscapes of agricultural production, resource extraction, circulation and waste disposal (Brenner, 2013).

Following this framework, it is suggested that urbanization should be understood as a condition of geographical organization connected to particular forms of social and spatial division of labour that emerge out of the concentration of population and economic activities in dense settlements, but

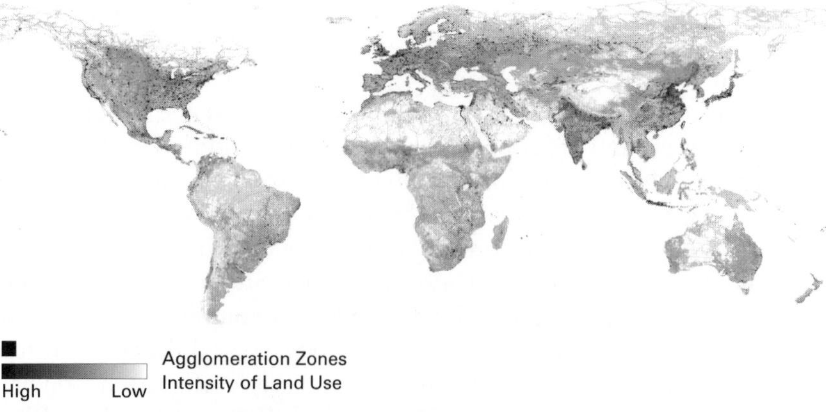

Figure 2.1 Visualizing the planetary urban: Major agglomeration zones and land use intensity

Sources: European Commission Joint Research Centre (2016); Erb et al. (2007); Vector Map Level 0 (VMap0) dataset released by the National Imagery and Mapping Agency (NIMA) (1997); map by Nikos Katsikis

are spread beyond them. What is the essence of urbanization is not the condition of concentration per se, but rather the condition of geographical interdependency that emerges out of it, transforming both the dense agglomeration landscapes (concentrated urbanization) and a multitude of operational landscapes (extended urbanization). While the *urban fabric* has often been limited to chart the former, the black areas in Figure 2.1, the *urbanization fabric* should be extended to include the latter, the grey zones of the map. These landscapes, the other 98% that have traditionally been considered to constitute the hinterlands of cities, have also been undergoing intense transformations under globalized urbanization, which has led to their increased specialization and regional decoupling. And while the relationship between cities in globalization has been a topic of considerable research (Taylor and Derudder, Chapter 3), this aspect of globalized urbanization, the relationship between cities and their increasingly globalized hinterlands, or between agglomeration landscapes and their operational landscapes, has remained quite obscure.

As urbanization becomes generalized and globalized, the condition of geographical interdependence tends to integrate the whole used area of the planet. How can this condition of geographical interdependency be conceptualized and charted? How can we conceive the contours of urbanization beyond agglomeration? The rest of this chapter highlights the major conceptual and methodological challenges of this task in order to outline potential ways forward in planetary urban research.

Challenges of visualizing the planetary urban

Rethinking urbanization not only in terms of the structure of agglomerations, but also in terms of their multiscalar interdependencies with all sorts of operational landscapes, undeniably explodes the scope, but also the challenges of visualizing the planetary urban. At the same time, the unprecedented scale and intensity of human transformation on the planet has been accompanied by unprecedented technological developments in the means and methodologies of monitoring, analysing and modelling it. Since the early 1970s, signalled by the launch of the Landsat mission, advancements in remote sensing and environmental monitoring have been coupled with the continuous development of Geographical Information Systems, leading to the proliferation of georeferenced data and geospatial analysis (Elvidge et al., 2011; Kurgan, 2013). These recent developments are undeniably suggesting a renewed potential for developing alternative visualizations of the urban.

However, this potential of technical and methodological advancements is significantly hindered by the persistence of the problematic conceptualizations of urbanization which reproduce the dichotomy between the urban and the non-urban. Thus the major challenge of visualizing the planetary urban is a *metageographical* one. The concept of metageography has been introduced by historians Martin Lewis and Kären Wigen, in order to highlight the underlying conceptions of sociospatial order that all cartographical representations presuppose (Lewis and Wigen, 1997). Together with Neil Brenner, I have tried to examine how this notion applies to the construction of geospatial knowledge on urbanization (Brenner and Katsikis, 2014). One of our major arguments is that the advent of geospatial approaches to the visualization of urbanization has, to date, done little to contravene such misunderstandings, due to the pervasiveness of what we have defined as the *bounded city metageography*.

The bounded city metageography is based on the conceptual pre-assumption that the urban is something that can and should be delineated spatially. In its most typical expression, it can be seen as an effort to define the boundaries of the urban fabric, corresponding to densely built-up and densely populated areas. The presupposition of the urban as a clearly delineated entity is aligned with, and constitutes part of, the persistent 'urban age' ideology dividing the world's population in urban and non-urban (Brenner and Schmid, 2014). In short, the bounded city metageography is central to an understanding of urbanization as a condition of population concentration in dense agglomerations, and the associated expansion of their boundaries (Angel et al., 2012). With the diffusion of densities, the emerging polycentric structure of cities and the densification of infrastructural systems, the effort to capture the boundaries of emerging forms of agglomerations becomes increasingly elusive. This condition poses not only a growing challenge, but also a rather unnecessary one, one that disorients research from what could be a more productive scope: uncovering how these morphing agglomeration landscapes are actively interrelated with the much greater matrix of operational landscapes produced by urbanization processes.

Thus, transcending the bounded city metageography presents one of the main challenges of visualizing the planetary urban. Overcoming this conceptual challenge could allow for a renegotiation of a critical set of technical and methodological challenges. The most important challenges in this respect concern the establishment of complete, detailed and accurate datasets, the organization and classification of geospatial information in meaningful ways, and finally their comprehensible and accessible representation (Pesaresi et al., 2016). The recent advancements in remote sensing and geospatial analysis have introduced considerable developments in all three stages, the most important of which are briefly overviewed below. However, as will be discussed in the examples unpacked in the next section, the persistence of the bounded city metageography has severely hindered their potential.

The proliferation of remote sensing technologies has led to an explosion in the quality, quantity and resolution of data, with satellites covering the whole surface of the earth, almost on a daily basis. This has constituted a radical shift in relation to traditional forms of data collection through national agencies, which are both limited in their administrative regimes and subdivisions, as well as in their turnover time (Sutton et al., 2001). However, although the state monopoly over statistics, or *stateistics*, has been challenged (Shaw and Miles, 1979), remote sensing data have not replaced, but rather complemented census data, which continue to be much more detailed, including categories that could hardly be monitored from space. As a result, problems related to the nature and distribution of census data continue to pose important challenges. The progress accomplished since the postwar era from international organizations such as the UN has indeed helped in the establishment of global repositories of data. However, these datasets have still been largely dependent on the structure and quality of data reported by contributing state agencies (UN, 2012). As a result, the process of standardization of different indicators and the harmonization of resolutions and scales, both temporal and spatial, continue to pose important challenges.

One of the most important problems in this respect has been the pervasiveness of administrative and statistical subdivisions as data containers. Traditionally, census agencies have been classifying information into census tracts; with nested statistical spatial categories often starting from the individual census block and scaling up to the city, region and the state itself. These data containers are in general far from standardized, and vary greatly in shape and size, within countries and from country to country. Census containers have proved problematic due to the homogenization of data over often very uneven areas, and due to the associated challenges of undertaking comparative analysis. The development of remote sensing and geospatial analysis has offered an alternative way of georeferencing and organizing spatial information with the development of gridded geospatial datasets (Tobler et al., 1995). Contrary to census tracts, gridded datasets are based on the distribution of information over a standardized grid corresponding to pixels assigned with Cartesian coordinates, with every square of the grid corresponding to a square spatial unit on the ground (for example $1km^2$). Although this has offered a standardized, universal framework, gridded datasets have not replaced, but rather complemented (often combined with) traditional census data. In fact, most datasets that will be unpacked in the following sections are combinations of data from various sources, remote sensed or census driven.

Finally, a general challenge in visualizing the planetary urban has been that the proliferation of remote sensing and geospatial analysis has mostly been contributing indirectly to research on urbanization, since the majority of satellite sensors and geospatial modelling have been geared towards environmental purposes. In most cases, aspects connected to urbanization have been monitored as part of the broader influence of humanity on the planetary ecosystem, and thus have only been peripheral to the development of means of measurement and classification. It is quite telling that one of the most influential datasets used to monitor urbanization, the nighttime lights of the world dataset shown in Figure 2.2, was not developed for the particular purpose of monitoring light emissions from human activities, but rather as a meteorological sensor calibrated to monitor cloud coverage (Elvidge et al., 1997). And while in most cases the monitoring of urban phenomena is not accidental, it

Figure 2.2 Visualizing the planetary urban: Nighttime lights of the world

Source: NASA Nighttime Lights of the World dataset; map by Nikos Katsikis

could be argued that the conceptual stagnation in relation to what defines urbanization has severely restricted research towards the development of particular and dedicated measurements, sensors and methodologies.

Multiple approaches and examples for visualizing the planetary urban

As a condition of geographical organization, urbanization can only be visualized indirectly through a series of socio-spatial indicators that are considered to be associated with it. Undeniably, the most common and prominent indicators that have been used to monitor urbanization have been population and land cover, as the urban has been considered a condition of densely populated, densely built-up settlements (Potere and Schneider, 2007). In what follows, I will examine the potentials and limitations of the two approaches and present a series of examples developed under these frameworks and positioned in relation to some cases which significantly depart from them.

Starting with the framework of population, perhaps the most common visualization of urbanization is that of the world made out of cities of varying sizes, such as the one shown in Figure 2.3, representing only cities with a population of over 300 000. Nodes weighted according to population size are positioned at the theoretical geographic centres of cities, allowing for an easy comparison and observation of their distribution, but also obscuring their actual geographic configuration, and detaching them from their surrounding landscapes. Moreover, reducing the actual distribution of population into statistically defined nodes depends upon variable census operations, brought together under this seemingly seamless representation. As agglomeration patterns morph and expand, national statistical agencies still struggle to define the characteristics cities should display in order to be classified as such, based on variables typically including thresholds in population size and density (for example the US census requires a population of more than 2500; the Australian a density of more than 200 persons per square kilometre), but in some cases also including more specific socioeconomic criteria, such as type of employment (ILO, 2010). These largely arbitrary thresholds are often enough to delineate urban areas and populations from the rural that is left outside. The multitude of different thresholds and definitions used by the various agencies reveals not only a methodological uncertainty and a lack of clear definition of what 'the urban' actually is, but questions the whole foundation upon which this framework is built. Indeed, large dense settlements are central to urbanization, but why should the definition of the urban be exhausted around a particular size threshold or at the spatial boundaries of cities?

Undeniably, the continuous densification of population has been one of the major trends in socio-spatial organization. Positioning urbanization within the broader patterns of population redistribution could allow for a fuller understanding of the dynamics between population change and geographical organization. The global map of population densities in the year 2000 in Figure 2.4 offers a general overview of population distribution. This map has been developed from a combination of sources, redistributing and harmonizing statistical information from various census agencies by combining them with inputs from remote sensing data, and in particular from the nighttime lights of the world dataset (Balk et al., 2006). The result has been a gridded

Figure 2.3 Visualizing the planetary urban: Urban population (cities with population >300,000)

Source: UN (2014); map by Nikos Katsikis

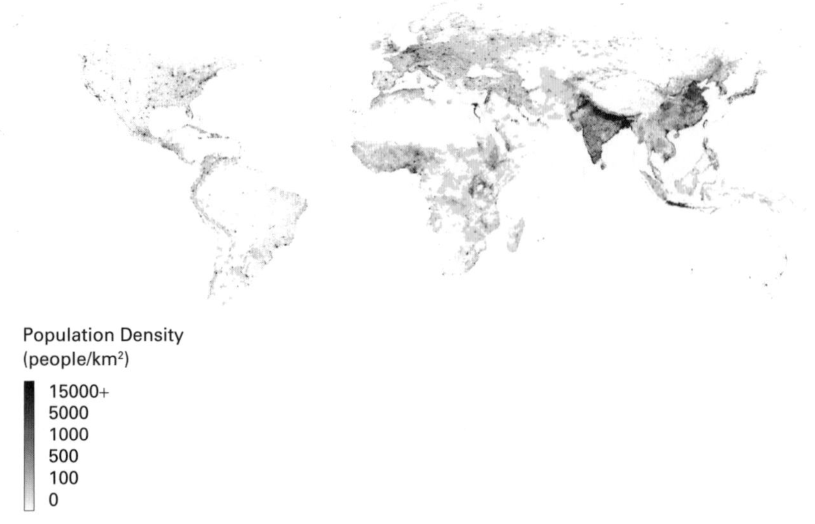

Figure 2.4 Visualizing the planetary urban: Population density gradients (nighttime population)

Source: CIESIN et al. (2011); map by Nikos Katsikis

geospatial dataset that allows a more precise appreciation of the predominantly continuous patterns of population density gradients around the world.

Nevertheless, even this recent effort embodies with it strong aspects of the bounded city metageography: For a complementary dataset developed as part of the same project, researchers felt the need to use these density gradients to delineate what they considered should be the extents of urban areas, extracting them through a combination of particular thresholds developed from census statistics and remote sensing data. In the resulting map of urban extents, shown in Figure 2.5, agglomeration zones are delineated and detached from

Figure 2.5 Visualizing the planetary urban: Urban extents

Source: CIESIN et al. (2011); map by Nikos Katsikis

the empty rural exterior, which is presumably hosting the remaining population of the world (CIESIN et al., 2011). According to this operation, the urban is limited to a total area in the range of 3.5 million square kilometres.

An additional methodological issue that often prohibits census data to capture the dynamism and fluidity of population distributions is the fact that, in most cases, census data register nighttime population, which is where people are residing, and not where their multiple activities are. As a result, important aspects of urbanization related to the daily mobility of populations, from commuting through to travelling to popular areas, such as commercial and recreation locations, are largely obscured. An alternative approach that aims to overcome this problem is offered by the LandScan dataset, which uses a complex probability coefficient to capture the fluid movement of populations over a 24-hour period, based on land use and infrastructure types (Dobson et al., 2000). This averaged population is intended to approximate more closely the actual daily distribution of people in space, as shown in Figure 2.6. Although in this map dense agglomeration zones are clearly highlighted, the database does not impose boundaries upon urban areas, which seem to expand along transportation and commuter routes that criss-cross large territorial zones.

The second seminal methodological framework for visualizing the urban is concerned with elements of land use and land cover that are considered to define it. Here the consensus is that the urban condition can be registered as a physical condition on the earth's surface, connected to densely built-up areas where artificial constructed surfaces are dominant over other types of

Figure 2.6 Visualizing the planetary urban: Population density gradients (averaged population)

Source: Oak Ridge National Laboratory (2012); map by Nikos Katiskis

landscapes. In all major land cover datasets, the urban land use class is always defined in relation to a certain threshold (often more than 50%) of built-up land cover per landscape unit (Potere and Schneider, 2007). It should be noted here, that although land cover datasets have highly benefited from remote sensing technologies, they have been mostly calibrated for monitoring aspects of the natural environment, and not so much human patterns and infrastructures. Among the numerous indicators of different types of vegetation and hydrological features (often more than a dozen), land cover classes that are thought to be associated with urbanization are only one or two, and always connected to densely built-up zones. The implications of this approach for visualizing urban land cover around the world are presented in Figure 2.7, which is derived from the 2010 GlobCover dataset. The bounded city metageography is again predominant, with urbanization ending at the thresholds of densely developed land, and limited to no more than one million square kilometres.

However, as in the case of population, the actual distribution of artificially constructed surfaces extends well beyond dense agglomeration zones, and could be thus much better grasped through a gradient, rather than this binary condition. A recent effort focused predominantly on monitoring the artificially constructed surfaces around the world through the use of very high-resolution satellite imagery. It allows for a classification of their distribution without a threshold along a 0% to 100% density gradient (Pesaresi et al., 2016). Figure 2.8 reveals a thick mosaic of built-up areas threaded unevenly around the world, which does not only correspond to dense agglomeration zones, but also grasps concentrations of other structures and infrastructures such as transport corridors, dams and canals, etc. Nevertheless, as in the previous case, this research project also eventually reveals the pervasiveness of the bounded city metageography: Through a combination of the built-up area dataset with census data on population and administrative boundaries, a complementary dataset is

■ Urban Land Cover

Figure 2.7 Visualizing the planetary urban: Urban land cover

Source: ESA (2012); map by Nikos Katsikis

developed, one highlighting only very dense urban centres and dense urban clusters, extracting them from the remaining surrounding rural cells. This visualization of urban clusters around the world, seen in Figure 2.9, calculates the urban in the range of 2.3 million square kilometres.

The overemphasis on dense population has heavily influenced a series of associated conceptualizations and visualizations of urbanization. Two of the most important ones are what could be broadly framed as the economic and ecological interpretations of urbanization. As already mentioned, over the last two decades cities have been celebrated as economic engines, a development largely connected to the development of a spiky world metageography, one in which dense agglomerations stand out as the sole performance centres of an otherwise empty economic landscape (Florida, 2005). This economic

Figure 2.8 Visualizing the planetary urban: Distribution and density of built-up areas

Source: European Commission Joint Research Centre (2016); map by Nikos Katsikis

Figure 2.9 Visualizing the planetary urban: Urban land cover

Source: European Commission Joint Research Centre (2016); map by Nikos Katsikis

conceptualization of urbanization is presented in Figure 2.10, which maps the world GDP, weighting national GDP according to the distribution of population densities (UNEP, 2012). The mechanics of GDP calculations, combined with the assumption that the population distribution offers a meaningful proxy for its spatial representation, offer a striking view of the world economic landscape, privileging dense agglomeration zones over low-density landscapes.

At the same time, population density is also an important driver for the ecological interpretation of urbanization, although this time offering a contrasting view. As already mentioned, similarly to the emphasis on the economic role of cities, the past decades have also seen a surge of interest in the ecological role of cities. And while economic interpretations have revealed dense agglomeration zones as growth engines of economic value, ecological interpretations have largely revealed cities as entropic black holes, areas of consumption of ecological surplus, in the form of food, energy, etc., and generators of waste. Figures 2.11 and 2.12 aim to grasp the distribution of consumption of this ecological surplus, based on two datasets of the human appropriation of net primary production (HANPP); that is, the biomass produced by plants and vegetation initially through photosynthesis and harvested through extractive activities such as agriculture and forestry (Erb et al., 2009). Figure 2.11 monitors the consumption of biomass, with the areas highlighted corresponding to the areas with the major population concentrations and the highest metabolic needs. Cities and agglomerations are presented as black holes of biomass consumption (Imhoff et al., 2004). On the other hand, the

Figure 2.10 Visualizing the planetary urban: Distribution of global GDP, 2010

Source: UNEP (2012); map by Nikos Katsikis

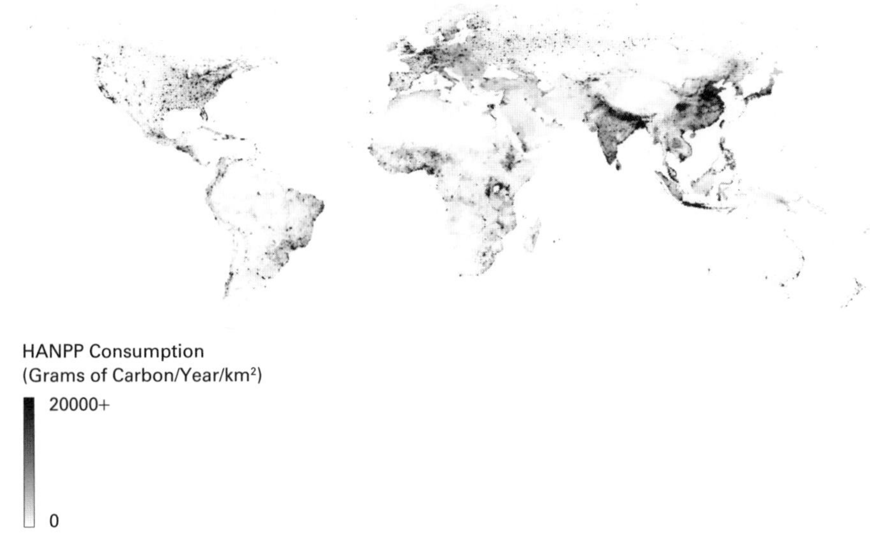

Figure 2.11 Visualizing the planetary urban: Distribution of HANPP consumption

Source: Imhoff et al. (2004); map by Nikos Katsikis

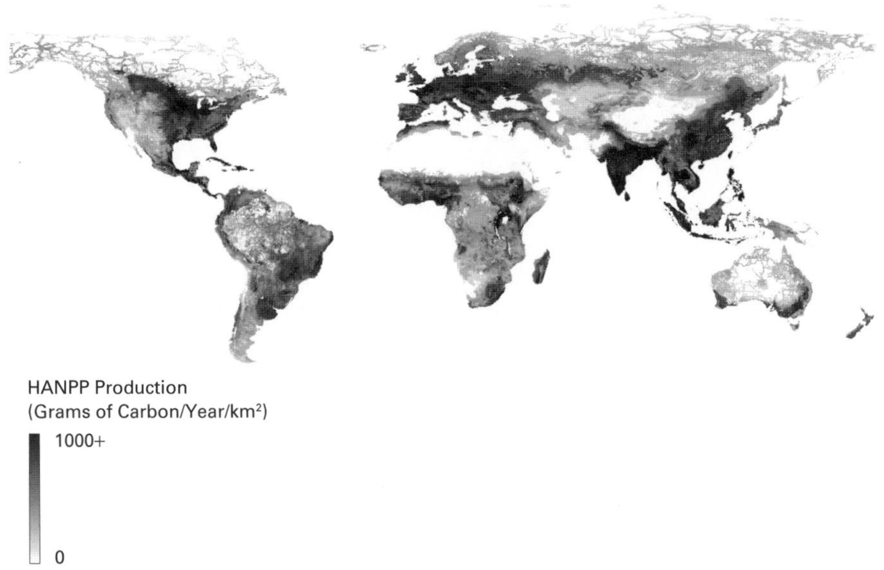

Figure 2.12 Visualizing the planetary urban: Distribution of HANPP production

Source: Haberl et al. (2007); map by Nikos Katsikis

second dataset in Figure 2.12 shows the areas in which biomass is produced and harvested (Erb et al., 2009). Agricultural areas, forestry zones and grazing zones are emphasized as the generators of ecological value and at the same time reveal a stark contradiction highlighting the different economic and ecological interpretations of the relation of cities with their broader productive landscapes: cities are conceived as economic generators, but ecological black holes. Their metabolic hinterlands are presented as ecological engines, but empty of economic production.

This seemingly paradoxical relationship highlights the need to appreciate the full extent of the economic and ecological landscapes of urbanization more thoroughly. As the *urbanization fabric* is not exhausted around the dense urban fabric of agglomeration zones, in the same way *urbanization economies* are not exhausted in the particular social and spatial divisions of labour that urban economies suggest. Urbanization economies include the full spectrum of interdependencies that characterize urbanization and organize a multiplicity of landscapes beyond dense settlements, from infrastructure networks to landscapes of primary production.

The extents of the urbanization fabric can already be observed through the unbounded gradients in Figures 2.4, 2.6, 2.8 and 2.12. A series of additional visualizations aim to further sketch the multiplicity of operational landscapes that constitute it. Figure 2.13 shows the global distribution of agricultural landscapes around the world, covering an area of more than 15 million square kilometres, while Figure 2.14 shows the distribution of grazing zones which utilize more than 45 million square kilometres and Figure 2.15 the extents of forestry areas, potentially affecting more than 35 million square kilometres of

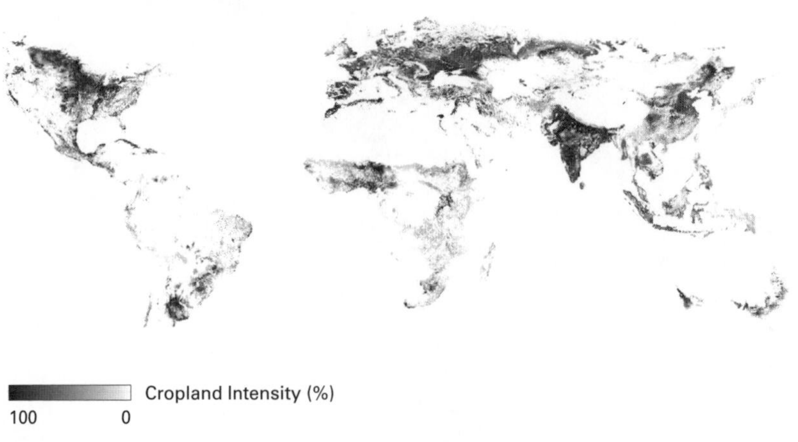

Figure 2.13 Visualizing the planetary urban: Distribution and density of cropland areas

Source: Erb et al. (2007); map by Nikos Katsikis

forests. These operational landscapes of primary production are the ones predominantly composing the ecologically productive areas of Figure 2.12. Compared to the no more than one million square kilometres of built-up surfaces shown in Figure 2.8, it is revealed that the majority of the urbanization fabric is constituted by softscapes. Still the structure and scale of hardscapes, mostly composed of transportation infrastructures, are central for their organization and synthesis into an operational matrix that connects them with each

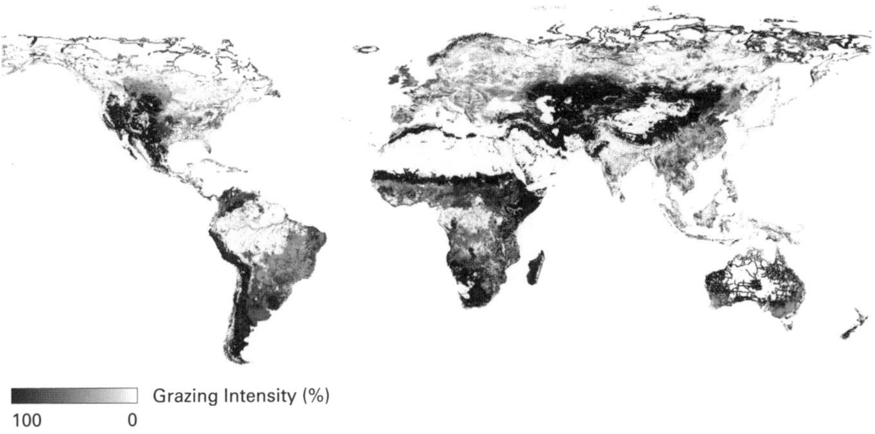

Figure 2.14 Visualizing the planetary urban: Distribution and density of grazing areas

Source: Erb et al. (2007); map by Nikos Katsikis

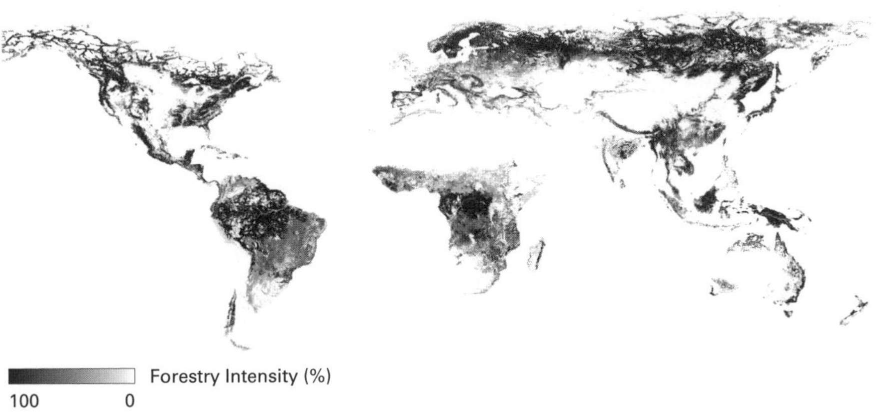

Figure 2.15 Visualizing the planetary urban: Distribution and density of forestry areas

Source: Erb et al. (2007); map by Nikos Katsikis

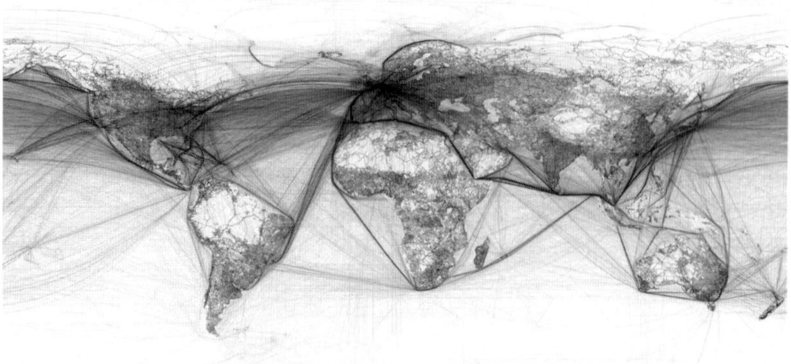

Figure 2.16 Visualizing the planetary urban: Ground, marine and aviation transportation networks

Sources: Road and rail networks are based on the Vector Map Level 0 (VMap0) dataset released by the National Imagery and Mapping Agency (NIMA) in 1997; marine routes are based on the Global Commercial Activity (shipping) dataset compiled by The National Center for Ecological Analysis and Synthesis (NCEAS); aviation networks are based on the Open Flights Airports Database; map by Nikos Katsikis

other, as well as with agglomeration landscapes. The map in Figure 2.16 offers a more elaborate view of the structure of these systems, showing the general distribution of the major road and rail transportation networks, along the patterns of major marine and flight routes around the world. This dense web of transportation suggests an additional layer of operational landscapes of connectivity, crucial to the organization of the geographies of urbanization.

Reflections on visualizing the planetary urban

The introductory map of Figure 2.1 can now be revisited and its composition better comprehended. The grey zone is revealed not as an indifferent exterior background, but as an intensely activated set of production and circulation areas, integral layers of the interdependencies of urbanization. The main challenge, however, remains. As population continues to densify in expanding agglomeration zones, urbanization unfolds as a process of generalized geographical organization, under which for every unit of agglomeration area, more than twenty units of operational landscapes are activated. The persistent and largely elusive efforts to accurately delineate the boundaries of agglomeration landscapes have contributed nothing more than to allow for the framing of this ratio in relation to an unacknowledged exterior. The value of this comparison is not in discretely classifying spatial categories and accurately measuring them. It is not an issue of how much and how many, but rather an issue of interrelationships.

What has been completely unaddressed, as efforts to visualize the urban have focused on its extraction from the rest of the planetary terrain, has been exactly the way this broader terrain is activated as part of the urbanization process. The maps have tried to offer a descriptive first step in decoding the nature and organization of these landscapes. Including uninhabited zones, agricultural production areas, inter-city transport networks, mining and forestry zones, even oceanic and aviation routes, in the study of urbanization, might at first appear as a counterintuitive proposition. But it is rendered as such only if the essence of urbanization is reduced to the condition of population concentration. Recognizing that the essence of urbanization is not the condition of population concentration per se, but rather the broader set of geographical interdependencies that emerge out of it, these landscapes become a necessary part of decoding how urbanization is organizing the surface of the earth, underwriting all major processes of social and ecological development.

While this conceptual (metageographical) shift is a fundamental step towards this goal, what should also be noted is the need for a critical appreciation of the capacities of newly developed techniques and methodologies for geospatial analysis and cartographic representation. It could be argued that under technological advancements, most progress in Geographic Information Systems has been limited to the Information and Systems aspects, with the Geographic*al* aspect, the development of conceptual and methodological frameworks, remaining quite weak. Within this context, the exaggeration of purely technical improvements, especially in regards to the increased abilities to manipulate, model and refine larger and larger datasets, have led to a narrow interpretation of the agency of GIS. Generating more accurate views of the urban world is often reduced to the development of more accurate quantifications of spatial processes. Improved understanding is often directly connected to improved data resolution, a tendency enabled by the advancement of satellites sensors, and the overabundance of georeferenced data, as for example those generated by mobile devices. The overabundance of data is also suggesting a rather problematic proliferation of data-driven research paradigms, with research frameworks often being developed on top of existing data pools, instead of the other way round. In fact, as several of the examples above display, what is often required is not better resolution but, on the contrary, alternative abstractions and conceptualizations of processes, which could in turn lead to the need for the development of completely new, dedicated datasets.

Arguably, these propositions suggest only a first step towards a long process of exploring visualizations of the planetary urban, which will not only be able to chart the various landscapes activated, but also contribute to decoding their often-fluid interrelationships in a meaningful way. It should be highlighted that this does not suggest a shift of focus away from dense agglomeration zones, which indeed still need to be the central aspect of investigation. Rather, these zones need to be interrogated not as standalone entities, but as parts of the greater transformations of the geographical organization of planetary urbanization.

Acknowledgement

This contribution is part of an ongoing research project on the metageographies of planetary urbanization, developed with Neil Brenner in the Urban Theory Lab at the Harvard Graduate School of Design (GSD). The project page can be found under www.urbantheorylab.net.

References

Angel, S., Parent, J., Civco, D.L. and Blei, A.M. (2012) *Atlas of Urban Expansion*. Cambridge, MA: Lincoln Institute of Land Policy.

Balk, D.L., Deichmann, U., Yetman, G., Pozzi, F., Hay, S.I. and Nelson, A. (2006) 'Determining global population distribution: Methods, applications and data', *Advances in Parasitology*, 62: 119–56.

Brenner, N. (2013) 'Theses on urbanization', *Public Culture*, 25(1): 85–114.

Brenner, N. (ed.) (2014) *Implosions/Explosions: Towards a Study of Planetary Urbanization*. Berlin: Jovis.

Brenner, N. and Katsikis, N. (2014) 'Is the Mediterranean urban?', in N. Brenner (ed.), *Implosions/Explosions: Towards a Study of Planetary Urbanization*. Berlin: Jovis, pp. 428–59.

Brenner, N. and Schmid, C. (2011) 'Planetary urbanization', in M. Gandy (ed.), *Urban Constellations*. Berlin: Jovis, pp. 10–13.

Brenner, N. and Schmid, C. (2014) 'The "urban age" in question', *International Journal of Urban and Regional Research*, 38(3): 731–55.

Brenner, N. and Schmid, C. (2015) 'Towards a new epistemology of the urban?', *City*, 19(2–3): 151–82.

Burdett, R. and Sudjic, D. (eds) (2007) *The Endless City*. London: Phaidon Press.

CIESIN (Center for International Earth Science Information Network, Columbia University), IFPRI (International Food Policy Research Institute), The World Bank and CIAT (Centro Internacional de Agricultura Tropical) (2011) Global Rural-Urban Mapping Project, Version 1 (GRUMPv1): *Urban Extents Grid*. Palisades, NY: NASA Socioeconomic Data and Applications Center (SEDAC). http://dx.doi.org/10.7927/H4GH9FVG (accessed 6 September 2017).

Dobson, J.E., Bright, E.A., Coleman, P.R., Durfee, R.C. and Worley, B.A. (2000) 'LandScan: A global population database for estimating populations at risk', *Photogrammetric Engineering & Remote Sensing*, 66(7): 849–57.

Elvidge, C.D., Baugh, K.E., Kihn, E.A., Kroehl, H.W. and Davis, E.R. (1997) 'Mapping city lights with nighttime data from the DMSP Operational Linescan System', *Photogrammetric Engineering & Remote Sensing*, 63(6): 727–34.

Elvidge, C.D., Baugh, K.E., Sutton, P.C., Bhaduri, B., Tuttle, B.T., Ghosh, T., Ziskin, D. and Erwin, E.H. (2011) 'Who's in the dark – satellite based estimates of electrification rates', in X. Yang (ed.), *Urban Remote Sensing: Monitoring, Synthesis and Modeling in the Urban Environment*. Chichester: John Wiley & Sons, pp. 211–24.

Erb, K.H., Gaube, V., Krausmann, F., Plutzar, C., Bondeau, A. and Haberl, H. (2007) 'A comprehensive global 5 min resolution land-use data set for the year 2000 consistent with national census data', *Journal of Land Use Science*, 2(3): 191–224.

Erb, K.H., Krausmann, F., Lucht, W. and Haberl, H. (2009) 'Embodied HANPP: Mapping the spatial disconnect between global biomass production and consumption', *Ecological Economics*, 69(2): 328–34.

ESA (European Space Agency) (2012) CCI Global Land Cover Dataset, 2008–2012. www.esa-landcover-cci.org/ (accessed 6 September 2017).

European Commission Joint Research Centre (2016) Global Human Settlement Layer. http://ghsl.jrc.ec.europa.eu/ (accessed 6 September 2017).

Florida, R. (2005) 'The world is spiky: Globalization has changed the economic playing field, but hasn't leveled it', *Atlantic Monthly*, 296(3): 48–51.

Florida, R. (2012) *The Rise of the Creative Class, Revisited*. New York: Basic Books.

Glaeser, E.L. (2011) *Triumph of the City: How Our Greatest Invention Makes Us Richer, Smarter, Greener, Healthier, and Happier*. New York: Penguin.

Haberl, H., Erb, K.H., Krausmann, F., Gaube, V., Bondeau, A., Plutzar, C., Gingrich, S., Lucht, W. and Fischer-Kowalski, M. (2007) 'Quantifying and mapping the global human appropriation of net primary production in Earth's terrestrial ecosystems', *Proceedings of the National Academy of Sciences*, 104(31), 12942–7.

ILO (International Labour Organization) (2010) Inventory of official national-level statistical definitions for rural/urban areas. http://ilo.org/wcmsp5/groups/public/---dgreports/---stat/documents/genericdocument/wcms_389373.pdf (accessed 6 September 2017).

Imhoff, M.L., Bounoua, L., Ricketts, T., Loucks, C., Harriss, R. and Lawrence, W.T. (2004) 'Global patterns in human consumption of net primary production', *Nature*, 429(6994): 870–3.

Kurgan, L. (2013) *Close Up at a Distance: Mapping, Technology, and Politics*. Cambridge, MA: MIT Press.

Lefebvre, H. (1970 [2003]) *The Urban Revolution*. Trans. R. Bononno. Minneapolis, MN: University of Minnesota Press.

Lewis, M.W. and Wigen, K.E. (1997) *The Myth of Continents: A Critique of Metageography*. Berkeley, CA: University of California Press.

Luke, W.T. (2014) 'Urbanism as cyborganicity: Tracking the materialities of the Anthropocene', in D. Ibañez and N. Katsikis (eds), *New Geographies 06: Grounding Metabolism*. Cambridge, MA: Harvard University Press, pp. 38–51.

(Continued)

Merrifield, A. (2013) 'The urban question under planetary urbanization', *International Journal of Urban and Regional Research*, 37(3), 909–22.

Oak Ridge National Laboratory (2012) LandScan 2012™ High Resolution Global Population Data Set. http://web.ornl.gov/sci/landscan/ (accessed 7 September 2017).

Pesaresi M., Melchiorri, M., Siragusa, A. and Kemper, T. (2016) *Atlas of the Human Planet 2016: Mapping Human Presence on Earth with the Global Human Settlement Layer*. Luxembourg: Publications Office of the European Union. http://publications.jrc.ec.europa.eu/repository/handle/JRC103150 (accessed 6 September 2017).

Potere, D. and Schneider, A. (2007) 'A critical look at representations of urban areas in global maps', *GeoJournal*, 69(1–2): 55–80.

Rees, W. and Wackernagel, M. (1996) 'Urban ecological footprints: why cities cannot be sustainable – and why they are a key to sustainability', *Environmental Impact Assessment Review*, 16(4–6): 223–48.

Seitzinger, S.P., Svedin, U., Crumley, C.L., Steffen, W., Abdullah, S.A., Alfsen, C., Broadgate, W.J., Biermann, F., Bondre, N.R., Dearing, J.A., Deutsch, L., Dhakal, S., Elmqvist, T., Farahbakhshazad, N., Gaffney, O., Haberl, H., Lavorel, S., Mbow, C., McMichael, A.J., deMorais, J.M.F., Olsson, P., Fernanda Pinho, P., Seto, K.C., Sinclair, P., Stafford Smith, M. and Sugar, L. (2012) 'Planetary stewardship in an urbanizing world: Beyond city limits', *Ambio*, 41(8): 787–94.

Seto, K.C., Sánchez-Rodríguez, R. and Fragkias, M. (2010) 'The new geography of contemporary urbanization and the environment', *Annual Review of Environment and Resources*, 35: 167–94.

Seto, K.C., Reenberg, A., Boone, C.G., Fragkias, M., Haase, D., Langanke, T., Marcotullio, P., Munroe, D.K., Olah, B. and Simon, D. (2012) 'Urban land teleconnections and sustainability', *Proceedings of the National Academy of Sciences*, 109(20), 7687–92.

Sevilla-Buitrago, A. (2014) '*Urbs in rure*: Historical enclosure and the extended urbanization of the countryside', in N. Brenner (ed.), *Implosions/Explosions: Towards a Study of Planetary Urbanization*. Berlin: Jovis, pp. 236–60.

Shaw, M. and Miles, I. (1979) 'The social roots of statistical knowledge', in J. Irvine, I. Miles and J. Evans (eds), *Demystifying Social Statistics*. London: Pluto Press, pp. 27–38.

Soja, E. and Kanai, M. 2007 'The urbanization of the world', in R. Burdett and D. Sudjic (eds), *The Endless City*. London: Phaidon Press, pp. 54–69.

Solecki, W., Seto, K.C. and Marcotullio, P.J. (2013) 'It's time for an urbanization science', *Environment: Science and Policy for Sustainable Development*, 55(1): 12–17.

Sutton, P., Roberts, D., Elvidge, C. and Baugh, K. (2001) 'Census from heaven: An estimate of the global human population using night-time satellite imagery', *International Journal of Remote Sensing*, 22(16): 3061–76.

Taylor, P.J. and Derudder, B. (2018) 'Exploring the world city network', in J. Harrison and M. Hoyler (eds), *Doing Global Urban Research*. London: Sage, pp. 34–51.

Tobler, W., Deichmann, U., Gottsegen, J. and Maloy, K. (1995) *The Global Demography Project (95-6)*. UC Santa Barbara: National Center for Geographic Information and Analysis. https://escholarship.org/uc/item/0kt69058 (accessed 6 September 2017).

UN (2012) *World Urbanization Prospects: The 2011 Revision*. New York: United Nations Department of Economic and Social Affairs/Population Division.

UN (2014) *World Urbanization Prospects: The 2014 Revision*. New York: United Nations Department of Economic and Social Affairs/Population Division.

UNEP (United Nations Environment Program) (2012) 'Gross Domestic Product 2010', Global Risk Data Platform. http://preview.grid.unep.ch (accessed 6 September 2017).

UN-Habitat (2016) The New Urban Agenda. www.habitat3.org/the-new-urban-agenda (accessed 6 September 2017).

3

EXPLORING THE WORLD CITY NETWORK

Peter J. Taylor and Ben Derudder

Why do world city network research?

Research on the world city network has been stimulated by two main triggers, one conceptual and the other empirical. The former refers to a critical lacuna emerging in urban studies in the late twentieth century and the latter to a faltering response to this situation in the new global city literature. We deal with each in turn.

Traditionally, most research on cities has focused upon internal relations and structures within cities. This is to treat the city as a distinctive place, which, of course, it is. But it is not the whole story. As Jacobs (1969) observed many years ago, cities do not exist in isolation; rather they always come in groups. Thus there is a second inherent feature of cities to be researched: inter-city relations and structures. The latter research has been intermittent in urban studies. The most coherent and sustained effort came in the decades between the late 1950s and the early 1980s when Anglo-American geographers recognized the importance of Christaller's (1933 [1966]) central place theory to their programme of redefining geography as spatial science (Berry and Pred, 1965; Bunge, 1966; Haggett, 1965). This theory described cities as service centres for their hinterlands arranged in a hierarchical structure of increasing size evenly spread across the landscape. This did produce a large and vibrant research literature (Bourne and Simmons, 1978) but one which largely disappeared with the demise of the idea of an autonomous spatial science of human behaviour. Therefore, while research on intra-city processes blossomed in the last decades of the twentieth century, consideration of inter-city relations all but disappeared: the topic was simply not mentioned in contemporary reviews of urban research (for example Bassett and Short, 1989). This is the lacuna referred to above.

The lacuna emerged at an inopportune time for urban studies. The last decades of the twentieth century witnessed the rise of globalization as an intensely interconnected world in which cities were seen to play an important role. This elicited two inconclusive responses. One was to designate a new type of city – 'global city' – that had particular new internal processes that enabled globalization (Knight and Gappert, 1989; Sassen, 1991). Notice the concept is specified in the singular: this is a continuation of the traditional focus of treating 'the city' as place. The second was a tentative return to central place thinking by up-scaling the old idea of a 'national urban hierarchy' to a new 'world city hierarchy' (Friedmann, 1986; Friedmann and Wolff, 1982). Both approaches had similar outcomes with specific identification of London, New York and Tokyo as the leading cities within globalization; key locales where globalization was being transnationally organized and reproduced. But in the process this new urban studies got embroiled in globalization debates in which the very veracity of the concept was being challenged: what was the evidence for the purported change from an international world to a transnational world (Held and McGrew, 2007; Hirst and Thompson, 1996)? In other words, these innovative conceptual developments were far ahead of the necessary empirical grounding to make them credible.

In urban studies the poverty of empirical evidence was voiced by Short et al. (1996) as 'the dirty little secret of world cities research', by Cox's (1997) reference to 'so-called "world cities"', and through Taylor's (1997, 1999) identification and illustration of a 'data deficiency problem'. The latter showed that the key issue was that the current research was largely based upon attribute data (describing city as place) to the neglect of using relational data (showing links between cities). Furthermore, on occasions where the latter were used, the data were about the infrastructures that facilitated inter-cities relations, notably airline networks (Smith and Timberlake, 2001), rather than the actual urban processes which create globalization. It was this need to produce an operational database for researching inter-city relations at the global scale that stimulated the creation of the Globalization and World Cities (GaWC) virtual research network in 1998 (www.lboro.ac.uk/gawc).

But databases need more than data; they require conceptual/theoretical direction on what information to collect. In creating GaWC it soon became apparent that central place theory based upon provisioning hinterlands was not suitable for our undertaking; we were dealing with the 'hinterworlds' of each city (Taylor, 2001a). Sassen's classic global city concept was deployed by Castells (1996) in his network society treatise, in which he gave it a decisive twist, moving away from global city as place to global cities in a space of flows. His emphasis on network rather than hierarchy has been crucial in subsequent research. Although sometimes difficult to comprehend (Taylor, 2009), in world city researches and despite the dominance of New York, London and, perhaps, Tokyo or Hong Kong, the fundamental inter-city relations are 'horizontal' rather than 'vertical'. Central place theory is concerned solely with the latter, and therefore a different theory is required which is termed 'central flow theory' with the emphasis on the flows rather than the places (Taylor et al., 2010). To reach this position it has been necessary to think of cities as process, continually unfolding relations (internal and external) as argued, from quite different theoretical positions, by Jacobs (1969) and Castells (1996).

Initial research questions have derived from measuring inter-city relations, leading to an extensive research programme. Typical research questions are: Which are the most important cities within the world city network? What is the regional patterning within the world city network? How is this patterning changing – a shift to the 'East'? How does the world city network relate to the inter-state system?

Challenges of doing world city network research

There have been three key challenges in the development of world city network research. First there is the data problem described above – where or how were the data found or collected? Second and again – as alluded to above – what is the specific process to be measured? And third, having created a basic research frame based upon answers to the first two questions, how can the approach be extended and improved? Answers to the first two questions are closely entwined and we deal with them together before turning to issues of sustainability and development in answering the third question, in which we focus on the challenge of world city network-informed urban policies.

The starting point was to provide a precise specification of the world city network (Taylor, 2001b). Using Sassen's (1991) recognition of producer service firms as the major agents of global city formation, we identified their office networks across cities as the constituents of the world city network. Advanced producer service firms provide the financial, professional and creative means of servicing transnational corporations in their global pursuits. These activities range from resourcing capital, to navigating multiple jurisdictions, to developing generic marketing strategies. These are largely accomplished through face-to-face meetings requiring work to be carried out in offices across all cities where their clients have important interests. The skyscraper cityscapes that epitomize the global city as place are in fact the work centres ('knowledge factories') that make globalization possible through myriad inter-city communications. Thus, to measure world city network formation requires investigation into the offices of producer service firms across leading cities.

But these global service firms are private companies and their intra-firm communications are obviously subject to commercial confidentiality. In any situation where it is not possible to carry out a direct measurement, the alternative is to devise an indirect measure of that process. This uses information that is available, which is inputted into a model of the process to provide credible measurement estimates. In this case information is readily available on firms' websites. It is here that a firm describes its office network to both impress potential clients and attract potential employees (these firms trade knowledge and therefore recruitment is a key activity). From this information on offices in different cities, a data matrix can be created arraying firms (the agents) against cities (where the agents do their work). In effect this shows the global strategies of each firm, variations in their work across multiple cities. It is from this matrix that estimates of knowledge flows (advice, direction, plans, strategies, etc.) can be generated. An interlocking network model is deployed for this purpose and is described in the next section. The outcome is a credible description of the inter-city flows of financial, professional and creative knowledges that comprise the world city network.

This conceptually sound solution to the critical data problem in world city network research required a large customized data collection exercise that has been carried out on five occasions between 2000 and 2016. These have provided the basic research frame to produce rankings of cities in terms of levels of inter-city connectivity and world-regional patterns and changes thereof. This leads to potential for new developments that represent challenges to pushing the research agenda. Some of the challenges are technical in nature and focus on measuring (Neal, 2014) or visualizing (Hennemann et al., 2015) the inter-city flows between cities. A different set of challenges stems from the 'use' of our work in other contexts, most notably by policymakers. We focus on the latter, not in the least because others have warned for baleful policy outcomes – no matter how unintended – associated with world city network research (see the final section).

The question about how world city network research might be useful to urban practitioners and policymakers may seem a straightforward ask but turns out to be anything but that: put simply, urban practitioners find our research interesting but do not know what to do with it! Social science research is expected to contribute to evidence-based policy making for holders of power or authority in given geographical areas: governments or administrations operating at different political levels (or challenges thereto). One key difficulty for translating our research into policy is because of the formal territorial basis of power and authority in modernity: in Castells' (1996) terms policy is devised in spaces of places and our research informs spaces of flows.

Thus the question we are addressing here is very difficult to answer since it requires a leap of imagination beyond modern spatial representation. And 'leaps of imagination' are not generally considered to be a basis for policy making. Based on our dealing with policymakers in a variety of urban settings, three challenges stand out. First, city representatives think competitively – typically they want their city to be a 'global city' or as near as possible – which does not fit well with our network emphasis and what our research is about more generally: a world of multiple 'mini-Londons' or 'little New Yorks' just does not make urban sense! Second, their authority and power is formally limited to the area they have jurisdiction over and therefore our concern for external relations is seen as not directly policy relevant. Third, coming from a Jacobs position on the inherent complexity of cities has led to misunderstandings about what policies are possible. The most stark example of the latter was a seminar presentation we gave at HM Treasury as part of its consultation process about whether the UK should join the euro currency (HM Treasury, 2003). Immediately after our presentation we were asked 'where are your levers?' But cities are not machines: our answer 'we don't have any levers' effectively finished the session!

Techniques for doing world city network research

Techniques for doing world city network research are based on (i) the precise specification discussed in the previous section (the interlocking network model) and (ii) subsequent extensions and modifications of this specification (models that subscribe to the basic premises of this approach, but provide different ways of answering how/when cities are connected). We first deal with the basic data used in world city network analyses, followed by a discussion of the interlocking network model and some of the subsequent extensions and modifications.

World city network research starts from a universe of service firms located in cities (Taylor, 2001b). The elemental measure is a service value v_{ij} with information on the importance of the presence of firm j in city i. These observations can be arrayed as a service value matrix V. Most of the data gatherings use a six-point service value scale, ranging from 0 (no presence) to 5 (for the city that houses a firm's headquarters). The basic strategy of allocation for values 1 through 4 is that all cities with a non-HQ presence of a firm score 2, and this is only altered for specific reasons. For instance, a city where contact with a firm's office is referred elsewhere will be allocated a service value score reduced to 1, while exceptionally large offices with many practitioners will lead to a city scoring 3 and location of regional headquarters will lead to a city scoring 4.

In world city network research, offices are treated as commercial assets of a city that are important because of *flows* of information, knowledge, instruction, ideas, innovations, personnel, etc. between their offices. This implies that V, which simply takes stock of the assets within a given city, needs to be converted so that it gives us insight into the interaction between cities through firms' geographical distribution of offices. In network analysis, V is commonly termed a two-mode network. In contrast to one-mode networks, where actors are directly interlinked (cities x cities), a two-mode network is characterized by connections between two separate sets of nodes (cities x firms). It is, however, possible to infer one-mode networks from a two-mode dataset by applying a 'bipartite projection function'. The interlocking network model is essentially such a function, as it entails specifying how city/firm-interactions contained within V can inform our understanding of city/city-interactions.

The crux of the interlocking network model as a bipartite projection function is the definition of city-dyad connectivity CDC_{a-b} between cities a and b:

$$CDC_{a-b} = \Sigma_j v_{aj}.v_{bj} \qquad a \neq b$$

Equation 3.1 City-dyad connectivity (CDC)

Bipartite projection functions come with specific sets of assumptions. In the interlocking network model, the double conjecture behind conceiving $C\,DC_{a-b}$ as a measure for flows between cities is that (i) the presence of a firm in a pair of cities opens up the potential for interaction, while (ii) the strength of this interaction depends on the size/importance of the presences – the more important the offices, the stronger the connection will be. A city's overall connectivity – which we term 'global network connectivity' GNC_a – can then simply be calculated by aggregating all possible connections:

$$GNC_a = \Sigma_b\, CDC_{a-b} = \Sigma_{bj} v_{aj}.v_{bj} \qquad a \neq b$$

Equation 3.2 Global network connectivity (GNC)

These measures are hard to interpret on their own terms, as they depend on the size of V: the number of firms and cities in the data. To facilitate comparison between analyses of different datasets, we therefore commonly report measures as proportions of the maximum value to provide a common range from 0–100%.

A range of other relational measures can be derived from our universe of m service firms located in n cities. These alternatives consist of either tailored extensions to the interlocking network model (for example Hennemann and Derudder, 2014; Taylor and Derudder, 2016: chapter 6) or modifications by using other bipartite projection functions (for example Neal, 2013, 2014, 2017). The latter implies devising a different answer to how the information contained in V leads to city-pairs being connected. For example,

Neal (2014) reviews three additional bipartite projection-based measures (Pearson, Bonacich and Sorting) to consider which conception of the 'world city network' each can validly measure. The sorting approach, for example, does not focus on the number of co-located firms between pairs of cities as in Equation 3.1. Instead, it seeks to identify pairs of cities whose particular firm populations likely developed through non-random processes (historical, spatial, strategic). This adds a relative dimension to city-dyad connectivity, as rather than being defined as a measure of the absolute importance of co-location in a pair of cities (interlocking), city-dyad connectivity is specified as a measure of the relative importance of co-location given the collection of firms in both cities (sorting). More specifically, this implies that city-dyad connectivity is framed as a question about probabilities, and subsequently placed in a traditional statistical significance-testing framework: a probability function assesses whether the observed number of firms co-located in cities i and j is greater than would be expected based on a random sorting process. Applying this approach to the GaWC data reveals that, from this perspective, connections between New York and London are indeed 'strong': there is statistical evidence that firms present in one of these cities tend to specifically seek out the other city as well (Taylor and Derudder, 2016: chapter 6).

This range of new specifications obviously begs the question of which empirical road to follow in world city network analysis. However, we agree with Neal that this should not be framed as a simple matter of preference or choice:

> Instead, they provide different and potentially complementary understandings of how cities might come to participate in the network and of how the network is structured. Viewing these two perspectives, and the networks they imply, in relation to one another can serve to draw on the strengths of each. (Neal, 2013: 1286)

For example, combining the interlocking network model with the sorting approach would lead to the following set of complementary insights: New York–London are strongly connected in absolute and relative terms; Shanghai–Chicago are strongly connected in absolute terms but not in relative terms; Bucharest–Budapest are strongly connected in relative terms but not in absolute terms; and Rotterdam–Chennai are not strongly connected in either absolute or relative terms.

Case study of doing world city network research

Techniques developed in world city network research are now applied for a wide range of other actors beyond service firms (such as institutes of higher education as in Chow and Loo, 2015; media conglomerates as in Hoyler and Watson, 2013) and in studies focusing on other scales of urban network formation (for example Burger et al., 2014; Hall and Pain, 2006). Meanwhile, world city network research as conceptualized here is part of a much broader suite of quantitative studies of global inter-city relations (for example Alderson et al., 2010; Krätke, 2014a; Rozenblat et al., 2017; Smith and Timberlake, 2001; Wall and Van der Knaap, 2011), while in the previous section we also discussed some of the modifications to the model(s) commonly used in world city network research. However, in our case study we will focus on the analytical core: we present some of the most basic results by applying the interlocking network model to our most recent dataset.

In our latest data gathering, carried out in the summer of 2016, we garnered information on the size and extra-locational information of the offices of 175 service firms across 707 cities (for operational details, see Taylor and Derudder, 2016: chapter 4). Applying equations (3.1) and (3.2) produces measures of global network connectivity (GNC). These are shown in Figure 3.1 on a cartogram illustrating the most connected cities (GNC >20%) to solve the problem of illustrating a very uneven distribution of cities across the world. In the cartogram, each city is given its own equal space in approximately its correct relative position, with darker shades reflecting stronger connectivities. Cities are indicated by two-letter codes, for example 'NY' for New York and 'JB' for Johannesburg.

The figure shows a global archipelago of world cities (Bassens and Van Meeteren, 2015), and the first geographical result is that there is indeed a worldwide pattern of interconnected global service centres, albeit clearly an uneven one. At its simplest, the cartogram reproduces the old 'North–South' divide: higher connected cities in the world city network tend to be in the 'North' and lower connected cities in the 'South', with the Western Pacific Rim firmly bucking this trend. But the geography is, of course, much more complicated: this simple, not to say simplistic, interpretation is only a trend with many lower connectivity cities in the 'North' and some higher connectivity cities in the 'South'. Moving from 'North–South' terminology to world-systems language, Figure 3.1 illustrates clearly the three leading zones of the core of the world economy: Northern America, Western Europe and parts of Pacific Asia. However, this is not a homogeneous core: the three zones have very different histories associated with their trajectories to core status.

The oldest, indeed original, core zone is Western Europe and this is reflected in two features. First, this region has more world cities than the other regions. And second, there is a wide variety of levels of

(Continued)

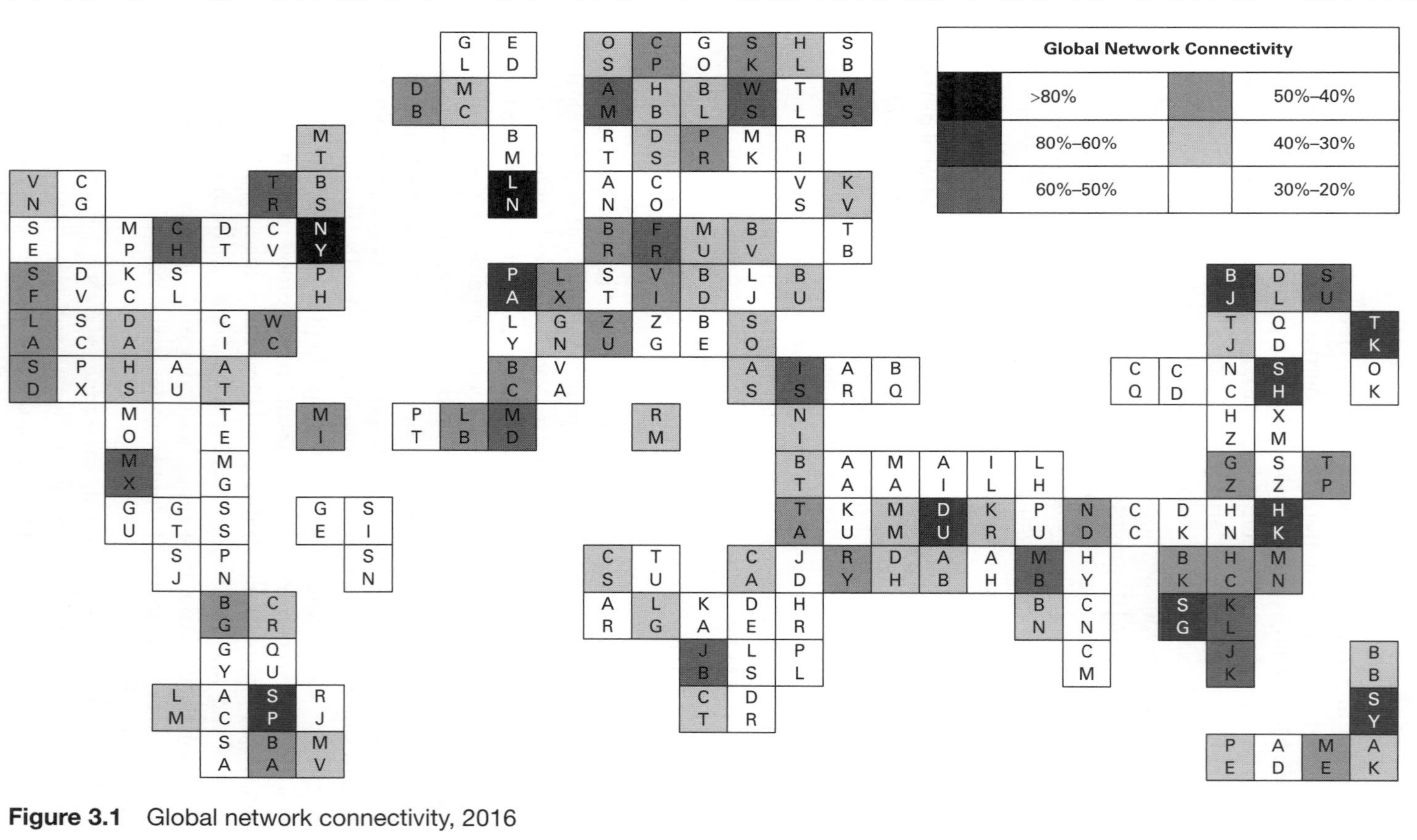

Figure 3.1 Global network connectivity, 2016

City codes: AA Amman; AB Abu Dhabi; AC Asuncion; AD Adelaide; AH Ahmedabad; AI Al-Mawsil; AK Auckland; AM Amsterdam; AN Antwerp; AR Accra; AR Ankara; AS Athens; AT Atlanta; AU Austin; BA Buenos Aires; BB Brisbane; BC Barcelona; BD Budapest; BE Belgrade; BG Bogota; BJ Beijing; BK Bangkok; BL Berlin; BM Birmingham; BN Bangalore; BQ Baku; BR Brussels; BS Boston; BT Beirut; BU Bucharest; BV Bratislava; CA Cairo; CC Calcutta; CD Chengdu; CG Calgary; CH Chicago; CI Cincinnatti; CM Colombo; CN Chennai; CO Cologne; CP Copenhagen; CQ Chongqing; CR Caracas; CS Casablanca; CT Cape Town; CV Cleveland; DA Dallas; DB Dublin; DE Dar Es Salaam; DH Doha; DK Dhaka; DL Dalian; DR Durban; DS Düsseldorf; DT Detroit; DU Dubai; DV Denver; ED Edinburgh; FR Frankfurt; GE Georgetown (Cayman); GL Glasgow; GN Geneva; GO Gothenburg; GT Guatemala City; GU Guadalajara; GY Guayaquil; GZ Guangzhou; HB Hamburg; HC Ho Chi Minh City; HK Hong Kong; HL Helsinki; HN Hanoi; HR Harare; HS Houston; HY Hyderabad; HZ Hangzhou; IL Islamabad; IS Istanbul; JB Johannesburg; JD Jeddah; JK Jakarta; KA Kampala; KC Kansas City; KL Kuala Lumpur; KR Karachi; KU Kuwait City; KV Kiev; LA Los Angeles; LB Lisbon; LG Lagos; LH Lahore; LJ Ljubljana; LM Lima; LN London; LS Lusaka; LX Luxembourg City; LY Lyon; MA Muscat; MB Mumbai; MC Manchester; MD Madrid; ME Melbourne; MG Managua; MI Miami; MK Minsk; ML Milan; MM Manama; MN Manila; MO Monterrey; MP Minneapolis; MS Moscow; MT Montreal; MU Munich; MV Montevideo; MX Mexico City; NC Nanchang; ND New Delhi; NI Nicosia; NY New York; OK Osaka; OS Oslo; PA Paris; PE Perth; PH Philadelphia; PL Port Louis; PN Panama City; PR Prague; PT Porto; PU Pune; PX Phoenix; QD Qingdao; QU Quito; RI Riga; RJ Rio de Janeiro; RM Rome; RT Rotterdam; RY Riyadh; SA Santiago; SB St Petersburg; SC San Jose; SD San Diego; SE Seattle; SF San Francisco; SG Singapore; SH Shanghai; SI Santo Domingo; SJ San Jose; SK Stockholm; SL St Louis; SN San Juan; SO Sofia; SP São Paulo; SS San Salvador; ST Stuttgart; SU Seoul; SY Sydney; SZ Shenzen; TA Tel Aviv; TB Tbilisi; TE Tegucigalpa; TJ Tianjin; TK Tokyo; TL Tallinn; TP Taipei; TR Toronto; TU Tunis; VA Valencia; VI Vienna; VN Vancouver; VS Vilnius; WC Washington, DC; WS Warsaw; XM Xiamen; ZG Zagreb; ZU Zürich

(Continued)

connectedness amongst the region's cities, ranging from the likes of London and Paris to the likes of Lyon and Rotterdam. In other words, in this region, there is a mixture of cities of varying importance all linking into the world city network. This is the opposite of Pacific Asia in which the connectivity levels of the cities is generally top heavy. In spite of booming and now widespread urbanization – the United Nations estimates that today there are almost 200 cities in Asia that have more than 1 million inhabitants, about 100 of which are located in China – few of these cities in the most recently developed core zones are strongly connected. Thus this region has far fewer world cities than Western Europe, although the number increases if we add Australasian cities and Auckland to create a Western Pacific Rim region. The third core zone, Northern America (USA and Canada), is in between the other two in numbers of world cities identified. However, in this case the range of levels of connectedness is very similar to Western Europe with numerous less important cities such as Austin and Cleveland joining the world city network. But there is a regional difference in that in Northern America the more connected cities tend to be in the east and west of the region, leaving the centre bereft of well-connected cities apart from the major exception of Chicago.

Beyond the core there are no regions with concentrations of highly connected cities. In Eastern Europe (the former Communist states), the most common pattern is for capital cities to take on the world city role: apart from St Petersburg, the only cities that feature are capital cities. Having lost its political and economic distinctiveness, this region has become an appendage to the Western European core, albeit one that, unlike Western Europe, has only one well connected city (Moscow) and which shows much greater concentration with generally one (capital) city per state. The same can be said for the contrast between Latin America and Northern America, where again capital cities dominate although in this case São Paulo, despite being neither former nor current Brazilian capital city, has become a highly connected world city in its own right. Together with Mexico City, this city stands out in Latin America. This pattern is also found in South Asia and the large North African/West Asian region, where Mumbai and Dubai as non-capital cities have become highly connected world cities. Sub-Saharan Africa has few cities on this particular map, but it does sport a clear regional leading city in terms of connectivity: Johannesburg.

China presents a very specific pattern, with Shanghai and Beijing – combined with the 'special administrative region' Hong Kong – dwarfing the rest of the 100-or-so cities with more than 1 million inhabitants in a 'tri-primate' pattern of global network connectivity. This is the combined result of the sheer size of the national market, making it difficult to operate from a single city; its historical and ongoing political divisions, with Hong Kong still operating as a quasi-autonomous area in financial and economic terms; boosterist visions of severe inter-city competition among some of China's urban elites, which have led to the active pursuit of world city status in Shanghai; and functional divisions of labour as the Chinese political system imposes a context where producer services need to be near the centre of political decision-making in Beijing irrespective of commercial opportunities in Shanghai or Hong Kong (Lai, 2012).

Reflections on doing world city network research

World city network research has certainly received a fair share of attention within global urban studies. Accounts of urban studies in the late 1990s and early 2000s (Peck, 2015) ascribe a marked importance to then-emerging literature on world city networks. In some quarters, this has led to identifying world city network research at large, typically jointly with Friedmann's (1986) 'world city hierarchy' and Sassen's (1991) 'global cities', as a potentially hegemonic discourse within 'global urban studies' that would stifle alternative approaches, visions and epistemologies. This position may have had some appeal at the time when it was first formulated (Robinson, 2002). However, it can be noted that, over the years, claims about the alleged 'dominance' of world city network research within global urban studies have gradually morphed into a truism that is problematic for at least two reasons (Van Meeteren and Bassens, 2016). First, by continuing to casually refer to the initial triumvirate of Friedmann/Sassen/Taylor, critiques often disregard the ongoing diversity and developments within world city network research. Second, some misguided critiques have become self-asserting, in particular those that equate the world city network research with one of its most conspicuous outcomes: simple rankings of cities. However, doing so implies that some of the crucial contextual information related with the 'why' of doing world city network research is lost, after which the mechanism of simplification by reiteration leads to increasingly hyperbolic critiques. To help re-situating the world city network in the context of doing global urban studies, we therefore conclude with a reflection on the conceptual and empirical remit of two of the major critiques levelled against word city network: the influential postcolonial critique of Robinson (2002, 2005) and an indictment for missing out the state by Therborn (2011).

The first line of critique came in two papers by Jennifer Robinson (2002, 2005). One of the core elements of her critique is a concern for the selectivity in identification of processes/cities so that other processes/cities are, as she famously put it, left 'off the map'. This is a case of a theory developed in and for Western cities being imposed on cities elsewhere and thereby finding them wanting. This critique has recently been reignited by Roy's (2009) claim that the world city network-like research represents a body of 'authoritative knowledge', from the North, '[mapping] a hierarchy of city-regions', which translates into a 'Darwinian ecology of cities: the survival of the fittest in the keen competition of network capitalism' Roy (2009: 820–21). In a reference to the title of Robinson's (2002) paper, Roy observes that in the worldwide rankings that can be gleaned from world city network research '"mega-cities" are usually off the map, seen as big but powerless entities' (2009: 821). Although citation analyses suggest that Robinson's (2002) and Roy's (2009) research is now probably more 'authoritative' within global urban studies than world city network research ever was, it is indeed the case that results in Figure 3.1 show a definite bias towards Western cities. However, the key issue here is to understand what this uneven geography represents in conceptual and empirical terms.

Conceptually, it is important to reiterate how our analysis should be interpreted. We are finding out the degree to which different cities are enabling the reproduction of globalized capitalism. Thus our contribution is an urban-economic geography one, a description of the latest phase of uneven development in the capitalist world economy in which producer services firms play an instrumental role (Bassens and Van Meeteren, 2015). Given the history of uneven development in the capitalist world economy, it is inevitable that such research will generate a Western 'bias' in its results (Parnreiter, 2014). Furthermore, we see our focus on the urban networking processes of producer service firms as part of a broader research agenda that tries to empirically understand 'cities in contemporary capitalism' (Krätke, 2014b). There are other processes that also contribute to this understanding, as well as further processes that reproduce other aspects of contemporary cities. Obviously urban research is and should be conducted on these other processes as well.

Empirically, it can be noted that although uneven globalization continues to spawn an uneven world city distribution, it is most certainly not a simple one. In spite of Roy's (2009) suggestions, we find an increasingly large number of cities from the Global South on the map (see Figure 3.1). The world city network is now less of an exclusionary club of the world's major cities than it was a decade ago, and increasingly has numerous linkages into regions beyond major world cities (Derudder and Taylor, 2016). Furthermore, in addition to the rising numbers of cities from erstwhile less-connected regions as such, there are now also more highly connected cities in these regions. In 2016, Shanghai and Dubai possessed a global network connectivity comparable to that of Chicago and Tokyo.

The second line of critique has been developed by Therborn (2011), who claims that world city network research underestimates the importance of states. He rightly points out that states are directly implicated in the production of globalization, and they are changing as they adapt to new economic circumstances. But the question is to what degree a city-centred analysis of contemporary globalization suppresses this changing and important role of the state (Brenner, 2004; Musil, 2014). Before detailing this response it is necessary to understand that our position on the relationship between cities and states emanates from a more general critique of social science for being state-centric, for treating states as unexamined spatial containers of social, economic and political processes. This argument does not claim that states are not important, but merely that the relevance of states should be justified and empirically shown.

The first point to make is that our analysis of how service firms use cities is circumscribed by the state. For the various financial services there are regulations whose level of control varies by country. For law, states constitute legal jurisdictions that have to be coped with in any transnational commercial project (Beaverstock et al., 2000). States also legitimate professional gatekeepers: who can and who cannot practise law, and other professions, in their territory. For advertising and management consultancy states are less intrusive but here other national effects become important. These are cultural effects on how products will be received. Global advertising not only has to deal with consumers who speak different languages in different countries, they may also have very different reactions to similar translated language or visual signals (Faulconbridge et al., 2011). Global management consultancy has to cope with different business mores and cultures; paternalistic companies where management merely means 'direction' provide a common challenge. The point of all these examples is to reinforce the idea that even in the city-centred world of producer services state spaces are deemed crucial.

The second point is that our empirical results, as already hinted at in the previous section, clearly show the effect of states. In addition to regional patterns there are also 'national market' effects on cities as service centres. The observation that with exception of St Petersburg all cities from former Communist states in Figure 3.1 are capital cities is quite telling in this respect. In terms of the world market of producer services, states are anything but irrelevant to world cities and their connectivities. Hill and Fujita (1995) have referred to 'Osaka's Tokyo problem' but it is clearly much more than a Japanese phenomenon. As well as the Japanese market being largely serviced through Tokyo, the Austrian market tends to be served through Vienna, the Norwegian market through Oslo, the UK market through London, and so on. Thus the leading city in the 'national urban system' often becomes the 'national world city', a national gateway into and out of the world market for services. Note that, in spite of the Eastern European example where capital cities and world cities tend to be synonymous, this leading city does not need to be the capital city – the examples of Mumbai, New York, São Paulo, Sydney, Toronto, Istanbul, Johannesburg and Lagos are clear in this respect. But the point here is that the geography of the world city archipelago shown in Figure 3.1 is also shaped by national differences. The inter-state system thus enters world city network research in its framing of the agents' work and is directly reflected in the empirical outcomes. In fact research on city/state relations has become an important topic of further enquiry (Taylor, 2013).

References

Alderson, A.S., Beckfield, J. and Sprague-Jones, J. (2010) 'Intercity relations and globalisation: The evolution of the global urban hierarchy, 1981–2007', *Urban Studies*, 47(9): 1899–1923.

Bassens, D. and Van Meeteren, M. (2015) 'World cities under conditions of financialized globalization', *Progress in Human Geography*, 39(6): 752–75.

Bassett, K. and Short, J. (1989) 'Development and diversity in urban geography', in D. Gregory and R. Walford (eds), *Horizons in Human Geography*. Basingstoke: Macmillan, pp. 175–93.

Beaverstock, J.V., Smith, R.G., Taylor, P.J., Walker, D.R.F. and Lorimer, H. (2000) 'Globalization and world cities: Some measurement methodologies', *Applied Geography*, 20(1): 43–63.

Berry, B.J.L. and Pred, A. (1965) *Central Place Studies: A Bibliography of Theory and Applications*. Philadelphia, PA: Regional Science Research Institute.

Bourne, L.S. and Simmons, J.W. (1978) *Systems of Cities: Readings on Structure, Growth, and Policy*. New York: Oxford University Press.

Brenner, N. (2004) *New State Spaces: Urban Governance and the Rescaling of Statehood*. New York: Oxford University Press.

Bunge, W. (1966) *Theoretical Geography*. Lund: Royal University of Lund, Department of Geography; Gleerup.

Burger, M.J., Van der Knaap, B. and Wall, R.S. (2014) 'Polycentricity and the multiplexity of urban networks', *European Planning Studies*, 22(4): 816–40.

Castells, M. (1996) *The Rise of the Network Society*. Oxford: Blackwell.

Chow, A.S. and Loo, B.P. (2015) 'Applying a world-city network approach to globalizing higher education: Conceptualization, data collection and the lists of world cities', *Higher Education Policy*, 28(1), 107–26.

Christaller, W. (1933 [1966]) *Central Places in Southern Germany*. Trans. C.W. Baskin. Englewood Cliffs, NJ: Prentice Hall.

Cox, K.R. (1997) *Spaces of Globalization: Reasserting the Power of the Local*. New York: Guilford.

Derudder, B. and Taylor, P.J. (2016) 'Change in the world city network, 2000–2012', *The Professional Geographer*, 68(4): 624–37.

Faulconbridge, J.R., Beaverstock, J.V., Nativel, C. and Taylor, P.J. (2011) *The Globalization of Advertising: Agencies, Cities and Spaces of Creativity*. London: Routledge.

Friedmann, J. (1986) 'The world city hypothesis', *Development and Change*, 17(1): 69–83.

Friedmann, J. and Wolff, G. (1982) 'World city formation: An agenda for research and action', *International Journal of Urban and Regional Research*, 6(3): 309–44.

Haggett, P. (1965) 'Scale components in geographical problems', in R.J. Chorley and P. Haggett (eds), *Frontiers in Geographical Teaching*. London: Methuen, pp. 164–85.

Hall, P. and Pain, K. (eds) (2006) *The Polycentric Metropolis: Learning from Mega-City Regions in Europe*. London: Earthscan.

Held, D. and McGrew, A. (2007) *Globalization/Anti-Globalization: Beyond the Great Divide*. Cambridge: Polity.

Hennemann, S. and Derudder, B. (2014) 'An alternative approach to the calculation and analysis of connectivity in the world city network', *Environment and Planning B*, 41(3): 392–412.

Hennemann, S., Derudder, B. and Taylor, P.J. (2015) 'Cutting the Gordian knot of visualizing dense spatial networks: The case of the world city network, 2013', *Environment and Planning A*, 47(6): 1332–40.

Hill, R.C. and Fujita, K. (1995) 'Osaka's Tokyo problem', *International Journal of Urban and Regional Research*, 19(2): 181–93.

Hirst, P. and Thompson, G. (1996) *Globalization in Question: The International Economy and the Possibilities of Governance*. Cambridge: Polity.

HM Treasury (2003) *The Location of Financial Activity and the Euro: EMU Study*. London: HMSO.

Hoyler, M. and Watson, A. (2013) 'Global media cities in transnational media networks', *Tijdschrift voor Economische en Sociale Geografie*, 104(1): 90–108.

Jacobs, J. (1969) *The Economy of Cities*. New York: Vintage.

Knight, R.V. and Gappert, G. (eds) (1989) *Cities in a Global Society*. Newbury Park, CA: Sage.

Krätke, S. (2014a) 'How manufacturing industries connect cities across the world: Extending research on "multiple globalizations"', *Global Networks*, 14(2): 121–47.

Krätke, S. (2014b) 'Cities in contemporary capitalism', *International Journal of Urban and Regional Research*, 38(5): 1660–77.

Lai, K. (2012) 'Differentiated markets: Shanghai, Beijing and Hong Kong in China's financial centre network', *Urban Studies*, 49(6): 1275–96.

Musil, R. (2014) 'European global cities in the recent economic crisis', *Tijdschrift voor Economische en Sociale Geografie*, 105(4): 492–503.

Neal, Z. (2013) 'Brute force and sorting processes: Two perspectives on world city network formation', *Urban Studies*, 50(6): 1277–91.

Neal, Z. (2014) 'Validity in world city network measurements', *Tijdschrift voor Economische en Sociale Geografie*, 105(4): 427–43.

(Continued)

Neal, Z. (2017) 'Well connected compared to what? Rethinking frames of reference in world city network research', *Environment and Planning A*, 49(12): 2859–77.

Parnreiter, C. (2014) 'Network or hierarchical relations? A plea for redirecting attention to the control functions of global cities', *Tijdschrift voor Economische en Sociale Geografie*, 105(4): 398–411.

Peck, J. (2015) 'Cities beyond compare?', *Regional Studies*, 49(1): 160–82.

Robinson, J. (2002) 'Global and world cities: A view from off the map', *International Journal of Urban and Regional Research*, 26(3): 531–54.

Robinson, J. (2005) 'Urban geography: World cities, or a world of cities', *Progress in Human Geography*, 29(6): 757–65.

Roy, A. (2009) 'The 21st-century metropolis: New geographies of theory', *Regional Studies*, 43(6): 819–30.

Rozenblat, C., Zaidi, F. and Bellwald, A. (2017) 'The multipolar regionalization of cities in multinational firms' networks', *Global Networks*, 17(2): 171–94.

Sassen, S. (1991) *The Global City: New York, London, Tokyo*. Princeton, NJ: Princeton University Press.

Short, J.R., Kim, Y., Kuus, M. and Wells, H. (1996) 'The dirty little secret of world cities research: Data problems in comparative analysis', *International Journal of Urban and Regional Research*, 20(4): 697–717.

Smith, D.A. and Timberlake, M.F. (2001) 'World city networks and hierarchies, 1977–1997: An empirical analysis of global air travel links', *American Behavioral Scientist*, 44(10): 1656–78.

Taylor, P.J. (1997) 'Hierarchical tendencies amongst world cities: A global research proposal', *Cities*, 14(6): 323–32.

Taylor, P.J. (1999) 'So-called "world cities": The evidential structure within a literature', *Environment and Planning A*, 31(11): 1901–4.

Taylor, P.J. (2001a) 'Urban hinterworlds: Geographies of corporate service provision under conditions of contemporary globalisation', *Geography*, 86(1): 51–60.

Taylor, P.J. (2001b) 'Specification of the world city network', *Geographical Analysis*, 33(2): 181–94.

Taylor, P.J. (2009) 'Urban economics in thrall to Christaller: A misguided search for city hierarchies in external urban relations', *Environment and Planning A*, 41(11): 2550–5.

Taylor, P.J. (2013) *Extraordinary Cities: Millennia of Moral Syndromes, World-Systems and City/State Relations*. Cheltenham: Edward Elgar.

Taylor, P.J. and Derudder, B. (2016) *World City Network: A Global Urban Analysis* (2nd edition). London: Routledge.

Taylor, P.J., Hoyler, M. and Verbruggen, R. (2010) 'External urban relational process: Introducing central flow theory to complement central place theory', *Urban Studies*, 47(13): 2803–18.

Therborn, G. (2011) 'End of a paradigm: The current crisis and the idea of stateless cities', *Environment and Planning A*, 43(2): 272–85.

Van Meeteren, M. and Bassens, D. (2016) 'World cities and the uneven geographies of financialization: Unveiling stratification and hierarchy in the world city archipelago', *International Journal of Urban and Regional Research*, 40(1): 62–81.

Wall, R.S. and Van der Knaap, G. (2011) 'Sectoral differentiation and network structure within contemporary worldwide corporate networks', *Economic Geography*, 87(3): 267-308.

4

ANALYSING CITIES AS NETWORKS

Zachary P. Neal

Why do research on cities as networks?

In the 1964 case of *Jacobellis v. Ohio*, US Supreme Court Justice Potter Stewart famously remarked that pornography is impossible to define, but that 'I know it when I see it'. A city is similarly hard to define, although we usually know when we are in one. In a formal legal sense, a US city is a political entity, created by a charter or articles of incorporation, and given certain powers including holding local elections, collecting taxes, and passing laws. However, this conception of a city is quite narrow and often not particularly useful for understanding the complex metropolitan areas that people and businesses actually occupy. In a demographic sense, a city might be defined in terms of its population and density, as an area with enough people living close enough together. However, this conception of a city leads to more questions about how much is 'enough' and thus is not really helpful as a definition.

These examples suggest that cities are not simply legal or spatial phenomena, and instead point us towards a functional definition that aims to define a city in terms of what happens in a city. Nearly a century ago, sociologist Roderick McKenzie argued that

> [T]he city is more than an aggregation of people or an agglomeration of buildings. It is an organization of activities, an economic and social organism. The metropolitan region thus [. . .] is primarily a functional entity. Generalizing, it may be said that the economic [and social] unity of the metropolitan region is based on a pattern of economic [and social] relations. (McKenzie, 1933: 69–70)

Researching cities as networks is important because it provides us with a formal way of defining and understanding cities as functional entities built from the relationships among people and organizations. Moreover, just as a network perspective can help us define cities, it can also be helpful for defining the newer but still fuzzy concepts of 'world city' (Hall, 1966) and 'global city' (Sassen, 1991).

But what exactly does it mean to view a city as a network? It helps to go back to basics for an answer. A city cannot exist without people and organizations, so these might be viewed as the building blocks or essential ingredients of a city. However, a random assortment of people and organizations does not make a city; they need to be organized and related to one another in particular ways. Figure 4.1 offers a simple hypothetical example: a set of people and organizations linked to one another by friendship, trade, and shopping relations. A sophisticated analysis is not necessary to see that this network of relationships contains two clusters, or in network terminology 'communities', within which there are many relationships and between which there are relatively few. This notion of a network community closely corresponds to a functional conception of a city: a set of people and organizations that interact mostly with one another, but that occasionally interact with other people and organizations. Importantly, this approach to thinking about cities does not make reference to legal boundaries, or geographic location, or demographic size. Thinking of cities as networks allows us to think of cities in terms of what they do and how they work, rather than where they are or how large they are, and this comes closer to the way that people and organizations actually experience cities.

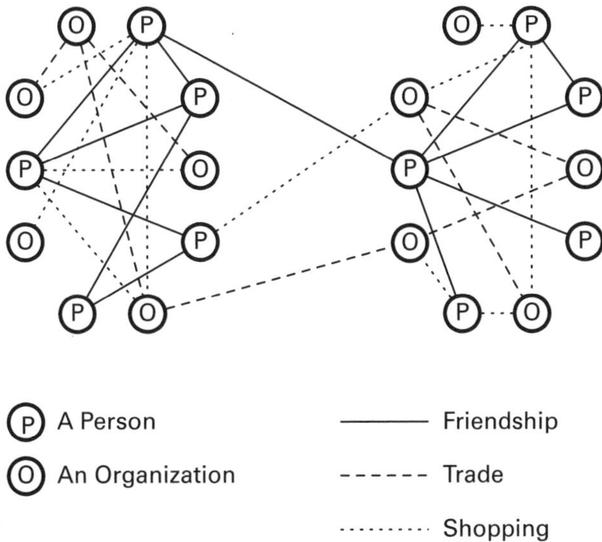

Figure 4.1 Cities as networks

Adopting this network approach to thinking about cities is also important because it allows us to understand the multiple levels of cities. Geographer Brian Berry (1964) once wrote, perhaps somewhat confusingly, about 'cities as systems within systems of cities'. What could he possibly have meant? I think he had in mind that some urban scholars study things that happen inside cities such as land use or local politics, while other urban scholars study things that happen between cities such as migration or investment, and that these are related. Because what happens *in* cities and what happens *between* cities affect each other, we need to think of these two kinds of urban phenomena together, rather than in neatly compartmentalized boxes organized around academic disciplines. Thinking about networks offers a way to do this and an answer to the question: what kind of 'system' did Berry have in mind?

Elsewhere, I have suggested that we can research cities as networks at three different levels: micro, meso, and macro (Neal, 2013). The micro-level focuses on the kinds of networks that might be observed inside a city, including for example the networks of influence that exist among elected officials or the networks of friendship that exist among neighbours (Hipp and Perrin, 2009). The meso-level views the city itself as a kind of network, and might examine how networks of organizational coordination ensure that the trash gets collected or how networks of streets make it possible for people to get around (Strano et al., 2012). Finally, the macro-level considers how entire cities are linked to other cities at the regional, national, and global scales, perhaps through exchanges of people (on immigration, see Tranos et al., 2015), money (on foreign direct investment and interbank transfers, see Cohen-Cole et al., 2015), or information (for example, via the internet; see Ducruet and Beauguitte, 2014). Each level looks at distinctive types of networks, composed of different types of nodes (such as people, organizations, cities) linked by different types of edges (for example, friendship, coordination, exchange). But this framework also allows us to make Berry's call for multi-level thinking a bit more concrete, by considering how networks at one level might impact networks at another level. For example, how does the structure and membership of a city's local political network impact where new roads get built, or how does the density of the friendship network in a city's ethnic enclaves affect the city's position in the global network of transnational immigration?

Challenges of doing research on cities as networks

As important as researching cities as networks might be, it can also come with a unique set of challenges.

Thinking about relationships, not attributes. Nearly all social scientific research is focused around measuring the attributes of each member of a sample or population. For example, urban demographic research involves collecting information on attributes such as race and income from a sample of people, while urban economic research involves collecting information on attributes such as tax revenue or employment from a sample of cities. This approach to research is deeply embedded in the way research methodology is taught, and even in the software used to analyse data, which typically requires that data be organized as a series of cases (in rows) by variables (in columns). Network research simply does not work like this, because its primary focus is on the relationships between the cases, rather than the attributes of the cases. A network-based approach focuses on the patterns of relationships among people (for example, communication, friendship) or among cities (trade would be an example) rather than those people's or cities' attributes. This focus on relationships rather than attributes can be challenging both because it requires rethinking and reframing research questions in relational terms, and because it requires organizing data in ways that capture the structure of relationships (such as in a matrix).

Defining the boundary. Challenges of boundary definition are common throughout geography, and in particular in urban geography where it can be especially difficult to define the areal boundaries of cities and urban areas. When studying, for example, New York City, the researcher must decide whether this case includes only Manhattan, all the boroughs of the city proper, one of the aggregations defined by the US Census Bureau (examples include metropolitan division, metropolitan statistical area, combined statistical area), or something else. Network research encounters a similar boundary definition challenge: which nodes should be included in the network. When studying micro-urban networks inside cities, this might involve deciding which people participate in the network, while studying macro-urban networks between cities involves deciding which cities participate in the network. Such decisions are more influential than simply deciding to study a larger or smaller sample because in network research, which nodes are included (or excluded) can radically alter the structure of the network. Consider, for example, a study about the level of integration of the global urban economy by looking at the economic network among global cities. What counts as a 'global city' and thus gets included in the network matters. Clearly New York and London should be included in the network, but what about Cleveland or Newcastle, or even Lusaka (Robinson, 2002)? These cities likely have fewer connections in the global urban economy, so excluding them may yield a denser network and lead us to conclude that the global urban economy is highly integrated, while including them may lead to the opposite conclusion. In such cases, there is no 'right' answer. The boundaries used when researching cities as networks must be guided by theory and the research question.

Getting, and knowing, the data. Data collection is always challenging, but collecting network data presents a few unique challenges. First, unlike more traditional forms of analysis, network analysis has a very low tolerance for missing data. A good rule of thumb is that network analysis requires less than 20% missing data, and some more sophisticated techniques require even less missingness. This can be difficult to achieve when studying micro-urban networks of people or organizations in cities, especially when the population of people or organizations in the network is large. Second, surveys designed to collect network data can sometimes be fairly long because they must collect information about the relationship between the respondent and every other node in the network. These challenges have led many who research cities as networks to look for archival and existing data sources, rather than to collect data themselves. Indeed, relying on existing data sources is essential when studying macro-urban networks between cities because cities cannot speak or take surveys.

Although use of archival and existing data sources has facilitated researching cities as networks, it also presents its own challenge: knowing the data. When using data collected by someone else, often for another purpose, it is important to really understand how the data was collected and what it represents so that it can be analysed and interpreted correctly. The interlocking world city networks studied by the Globalization and World Cities (GaWC) group offer a good example (Taylor and Derudder, 2016; see also Chapter 3). Their network data contain details about the strength of linkages between a population of 525 world cities, and have been made publicly available for others to analyse. However, analysing these data requires taking a step back and asking: what does a 'linkage' mean in these data (Neal, 2014a), does it measure what my particular research question needs it to measure, and how does it relate to alternative ways of measuring linkages between global cities (Derudder and Witlox, 2008)?

Analysing, not just visualizing, the data. Researching cities as networks readily lends itself to data visualization. Whether the networks capture people interacting in an urban neighbourhood, or cities interacting on the global stage, visualizing the pattern of interactions in a network graph can be very helpful. Indeed, Friedmann's (1986) 'world city hypothesis' triggered the contemporary wave of world city network research with a simple visualization of what the world city network might look like. However, although visualization can be helpful, it is not always helpful or even necessary when researching cities as networks. In many cases, the network is simply too large or too dense for a visualization of the network to be interpretable. In these cases, the network often looks more like a pile of spaghetti than an informative display of urban phenomena. Thus, although network visualizations can be attractive, and although readers of research about cities as networks might be expecting to see network visualizations, it is important to consider whether the visualization is really helpful. It is equally important to resist thinking of network visualizations as a substitute for analysis. In the same way that a scatterplot is not a substitute for a regression model, a network graph is not a substitute for a formal network analysis. Instead, visualizations can serve as complements to, and effective ways of communicating the results of, formal analyses.

There are many different quantitative techniques for analysing networks in cities, or networks of cities (see Neal, 2013). In many ways these techniques closely resemble more traditional quantitative techniques. For example, one might use a network variable such as centrality in a linear regression. However, analysis of network data does present one unique challenge: statistical inference. Many conventional approaches to testing for statistical significance (such as standard errors and p-values) require that the researcher assume the units of observation (for example, people or cities) are independent. However, the whole point of researching cities as networks is that we know these units are not independent. Because the units of analysis in a network, whether people linked by friendship or cities linked by trade, are not independent, testing for statistical significance when using network data and network variables requires special approaches that take into account their interdependence.

Techniques for doing research on cities as networks

Techniques for data collection. There are a number of different techniques for obtaining data to research cities as networks, and each technique has advantages and disadvantages. First, a researcher might collect data directly from respondents. Direct collection of network data often relies on a survey, which begins with a 'name generator' question. The goal of a name generator question is to ask the respondent to identify the others with whom the respondent engages in a specific type of interaction. For example, in a study of community cohesion in an urban neighbourhood, the researcher might ask each neighbourhood resident: 'Can you tell me who in this neighbourhood you talk to on a weekly basis?'. A single survey might include multiple name generator questions that ask about different types of interactions, and each name generator question may be followed by additional questions that ask about specific features of the interaction (for example, how long, how intense). This approach to data collection is most common for micro-urban networks where the nodes are the people or (people serving as representatives of) organizations in the city. Because it requires surveying every person or organization within the boundaries of the network, it is most feasible when the network is relatively small.

Second, a researcher might turn to archival or existing data sources. This approach is common for macro-urban networks where the nodes are entire cities. A key challenge in relying on archival data for researching cities as networks is that major organizations and government entities that typically collect and archive large-scale urban data rarely collect information about cities' interactions with one another. As a result, researchers relying on archival data often have to be creative, using existing data in ways that it was not originally intended. For example, the websites for multinational corporations typically list the location of their global headquarters, as well as of their smaller regional offices and subsidiaries. One might assume that instructions are transmitted from the headquarters to the subsidiary, and use these website data to build a network of global corporate power (Alderson and Beckfield, 2004).

Third, a researcher may use a unique network technique called projection to infer a network from non-network data. In some cases, direct collection of network data from people may be infeasible (for example, there are too many of them), or archival sources of data about a specific type of interaction may not exist (such as data on capacity for economic exchange). In these cases, projection offers a promising alternative. In a network projection, the nodes are linked to the extent that they share some common characteristic. For example, a researcher seeking to measure the social network among people in a large urban neighbourhood might start with data about the events those people have attended, and infer that pairs of people who attend many of the same events likely know each other (Breiger, 1974). Similarly, a researcher seeking to measure the capacity for economic exchanges between cities might start with data about which firms are located in which cities, and infer that pairs of cities that contain the same firms have more capacity for economic exchange (Taylor, 2001). The projection technique begins with data that is often easy to obtain (for example, event attendance, firm locations), but can generate networks within or between cities that would have been difficult to collect directly. However, it is important to remember that the networks generated using this technique are inferred; that is, they are not measured directly but rather rest on crucial assumptions that must be theoretically justified (Nordlund, 2004). The type of networks generated using this approach can also require special care when conducting analysis of them (Neal, 2012, 2014b, 2017).

Techniques for data analysis. Whether the data on networks within or between cities is collected directly, obtained from archival sources, or inferred using projection, there are multiple techniques for analysing it. Different techniques focus on different levels of the data and allow the researcher to ask different types of research questions. At the highest level of aggregation, some analytic techniques focus on the network as a whole. In some cases, these analyses seek to evaluate how well connected the network is, through measures such as density (are there a lot of interactions?), centralization (are they all focused on a single node?), and robustness (does the network hold together if certain nodes or links are removed?). In other cases, they aim to characterize how the network is organized into groups or 'communities' such as the two visible in Figure 4.1 (Derudder and Taylor, 2005; Guimera et al., 2005). Importantly, what these measures and indices mean depends on what the data mean. A dense social network among residents of an urban neighbourhood might be interpreted as evidence of social cohesion and a strong sense of community, while a dense financial exchange network among world cities might be viewed as a precarious arrangement where small problems in one place can affect the whole economic system.

At a middle level of aggregation, other analytic techniques focus on the nodes in the network. Analysis at the node level often uses measures of centrality to identify the most important or influential nodes in the network. Again, precisely what this means depends on the data and its urban context. In addition, because there are multiple conceptions of centrality, what this means depends on the specific measure used. For example, in a social network among residents of an urban community, degree centrality helps identify people with a lot of friends, while betweenness centrality helps identify people who are important for the spreading (or preventing the spread of) information through the neighbourhood. Likewise, in a trade network among cities, degree centrality helps identify cities' trade volume, betweenness centrality helps to identify cities with key trade locations, and closeness centrality helps to identify cities that are likely Christallerian central places (Irwin and Hughes, 1992).

Finally, at the lowest level of aggregation, still other analytic techniques focus on the edges or links in the network. Analysis at the edge level is most often concerned with understanding the forces and processes that lead some pairs of nodes to be linked, and others to not be linked. Different processes might be relevant in different kinds of research on cities as networks. For example, the concept of homophily suggests that similar nodes are more likely to be linked than dissimilar nodes, and may help to understand social network patterns in diverse urban neighbourhoods. The concept of transitivity suggests that two nodes are more likely to be linked if they are each already linked to a common third node, and may help to understand why trading directly between New York and Tokyo is more likely if New York and Tokyo both already trade with London. Identifying the role that such processes play in generating a network, whether among people (Robins et al., 2007) or cities (Liu et al., 2013), is often the task of exponential random graph models (ERGM) and stochastic actor-oriented models (SAOM).

Case study of doing research on cities as networks

For the past several years, I have been interested in urban transportation networks, and in particular in thinking about how airline transportation links cities into a network at the national and global scales. Researching transportation networks, especially in urban settings, is nothing new, but it is full of nuances. The goal of one recent study was to explore some of those nuances (Neal, 2014c), and thus illustrates some of the challenges and opportunities offered by researching cities as networks.

(Continued)

First, thinking about urban transportation from a network perspective requires thinking in terms of *relations, not attributes*. Often cities' national and global statuses are evaluated based on their attributes. For example, the MasterCard Global Destinations Index ranks cities by their number of overnight international visitors, and city boosters routinely note the importance of Atlanta by pointing to the fact that its Hartsfield-Jackson airport (ATL) is the busiest in the world, or of London by pointing to the fact that Heathrow (LHR) offers direct service to many places (C. R., 2015). However, a focus on attributes misses much of the story. Even if ATL is a very busy airport, or if LHR offers excellent service, the passengers using those airports are merely passing through the cities but not actually engaging with the cities. Such a position in a transportation network might make for a profitable airport, but not necessarily for a competitive city. Thus, this study aimed to look not merely at where the big airports are (an attribute), or where airports offer service (a feature of industrial organization), but rather where passengers are actually flying to and from (relations).

Next, studying cities as networks requires *defining the boundary* of the network. In the case of urban air transportation, there are many possibilities for deciding which cities to include and which cities to exclude from the network. Some aspects of the boundary decision are easy: cities that have no airports can be excluded because they cannot participate in air transport relations with other cities. But, what about cities with only small civil airfields, or cities that operate only irregular charter air service? Similarly, should the network include all cities around the world, or only those in a specific region? In this study, the network boundary included metropolitan areas in the continental United States that contain what the Federal Aviation Administration defines as a 'primary hub' airport. This boundary decision has important implications for what the network means. The focus on only primary hub airports means that the network includes the movements of the vast majority of airline passengers, while the focus on only cities in the continental United States means that the network includes most cities between which alternate transportation (such as car or rail) is an option. Perhaps a more important question is, what is missing, and how does it matter? This network leaves out the movements of passengers on small charter flights; because these are rare, this has little influence. It also leaves out passengers travelling to or from any city outside the continental United States, which matters quite a bit. Looking only at domestic passengers might make Atlanta seem critical, and New York's JFK airport seem tiny, while looking at international passengers would tell a different story. The lesson is that all networks must be bounded, and it is important to consider how the boundary impacts on what the network means.

Another challenge for researching cities as networks is getting the data. It would surely have been impractical to survey individual passengers, asking them about their origins and destinations. Many of the common data sets used for urban research, such as the US Census, focus on attributes rather than relations, and so are not particularly helpful. And, although travel websites including Expedia.com or Orbitz.com might be rich sources of data, they tell us more about airline operations (for example, where aircraft are scheduled to go) than about the people actually travelling between cities. In this example, as in many cases of researching cities as networks, getting the data required a bit of creativity. The US Bureau of Transportation Statistics maintains a database called the Airline Origin and Destination Survey, which is typically used by the airline industry to monitor trends in airline fares and aircraft routing. However, it contains the actual movements of a 10% random sample of all domestic US passengers, making it an ideal source of information for studying the network of transportation between cities, despite these data not being created or maintained for that purpose.

Simply obtaining suitable data to research cities as networks is only part of the challenge; the researcher also needs to *know the data*. This is particularly important when using archival or secondary data, which is common in urban network research, because someone other than the researcher collected the data. In this example, knowing the data took some effort because the documentation was filled with airline industry jargon such as 'coupon', 'market', and 'ticket'. Each of these terms refers to a specific way of breaking down the pieces of a single passenger's trip. A 'coupon' is a movement from one airport to another (a single take-off and landing), while a 'market' is the whole movement from an initial origin airport to a final destination airport and might have involved multiple coupons if the passenger had a layover or connecting flight. Understanding these concepts was essential for understanding the network because a city network built from coupons would look very different from a city network built from markets. The former highlights the importance of hub airports as places where people catch connecting flights, while the latter highlights the importance of major population centres as common origins and destinations.

Finally, learning something from researching cities as networks requires the researcher to *analyse, not just visualize, the data*. This study did present a series of visualizations of the network, which were helpful because they illustrate how the transportation network linking US cities to one another is geographically distributed. However, these visualizations supplement a more formal analysis of the networks, which were conducted at

(Continued)

two different levels. At the network level, the analysis focused on exploring whether different ways of conceptualizing an urban transportation network impacts the overall structure of the network. Interestingly, it doesn't. Across seven different ways of measuring and defining the network, the structure consistently exhibited closely connected cities (small world), regional clusters (communities), a few key cities that served as hubs (scale-free). At the node level, the analysis explored what these big-picture structural concepts mean for individual cities (the nodes in the network). For example, although every network features a few hubs, precisely what it meant to be a 'hub' varied depending on what the network meant. In a network based on coupons, being a hub means offering a lot of connecting flights, while in a network based on markets, being a hub means being a popular destination. At an even finer-grained level, in a network based on markets, perhaps not surprisingly, the hubs are warm places in the winter, but they are cool places in the summer. Thus, although the big-picture structural concepts looked similar when looking at entire networks, as the paper argues, the 'devil is in the details' and important differences start to appear when we take a closer look at specific cities.

This study focused on a network of cities at the national, rather than global scale. But, what can it tell us about global urban phenomena? First, it offers a detailed portrait of the US air traffic network, which can be compared to the air traffic networks of other sub-global regions, including Europe (Han et al., 2009), China (Li and Cai, 2004), and India (Bagler, 2008). Such comparisons allow us to explore whether the structural features that appear in national and regional travel patterns can be generalized globally. Second, it offers a starting point to consider how these individual national and regional networks are actually pieces of a multi-level global network of transportation. For example, when a passenger arrives in a destination city, he or she transitions out of the national air traffic network and into the local road or rail network. Likewise, if a passenger is engaged in international travel, he or she transitions between a long-haul international air traffic network to cross oceans and a regional air traffic network to arrive at a final destination. Each of these networks – local roads, regional rail and air, and global air – can be studied on their own, but also connect to one another and can be studied as a complex, multi-level whole (Balcan et al., 2009).

Reflections on doing research on cities as networks

Because researching cities as networks lets us think about how cities work in new ways, it allows us to find better answers to our questions about cities. The case of Chicago and St Louis offers a dramatic example. Today, Chicago is a world city, home to the headquarters of multinational firms, multiple large airports, and significant cultural institutions, while St Louis is a regional metropolis of about one-third the size . . . nice place, but not a world city. But, consider the situation in 1840: Chicago was a tiny frontier village of less than 5000 people, while St Louis was the gateway to the growing American Midwest, home to 17,000 and rapidly expanding. What happened?

From the 1770s and throughout the first half of the nineteenth century, St Louis was America's premier western city. Its role as a major commercial centre was driven by its central location on a natural transportation network formed by the Mississippi, Missouri, and Illinois rivers. The Mississippi river facilitated trade with New Orleans, and because New Orleans was a major ocean port, with the rest of the world, while the Missouri and Illinois rivers facilitated trade with the rapidly expanding frontier. As a result, nearly all the goods flowing in and out of the new American interior passed through St Louis. However, this all changed in 1848 with the opening of the Illinois-Michigan Canal, which connected the river network with another natural transportation network – the Great Lakes – near the small town of Chicago. This small addition (it was less than 100 miles long) to the national network was significant for Chicago for two reasons. First, by providing farmers and pioneers an alternative point of access, Chicago could compete with St Louis for trade along the Mississippi river. Second, by creating a way to move goods from northern manufacturing cities along the Great Lakes to southern agricultural cities along the Mississippi river, Chicago became a key location along a new trade route. With its newfound central position in the national transportation and trade network, Chicago's population and economy grew rapidly, eclipsing the formerly dominant St Louis to become America's 'second city'. The rest, as they say, is history.

By researching cities as networks, we can understand Chicago's status relative to St Louis' as a product of changing network structure, rather than a product of either city's own attributes. That is, the network perspective gives us a more complete answer to the question: why is Chicago bigger? Although this is a backward-looking historical question about a curiosity in the development of the US urban system, it illustrates that adopting a network perspective when researching cities can offer a way to find new answers and to uncover mechanisms. On the global scale, it can help make sense of financial disasters, disease spreading, and nation-building in ways that more traditional analytic approaches cannot. And on the local scale it can help us understand the interplay between social interaction and spatial organization, including, for example, how spatial distances impact on relationship formation (Hipp and Perrin, 2009), or why spatially integrated neighbourhoods tend to be less socially cohesive (Neal and Neal, 2014). It is this flexibility – in terms of both scale of analysis and scope of research question – that makes researching cities as networks so promising.

References

Alderson, A.S. and Beckfield, J. (2004) 'Power and position in the world city system', *American Journal of Sociology*, 109(4): 811–51.

Bagler, G. (2008) 'Analysis of the airport network of India as a complex weighted network', *Physica A: Statistical Mechanics and its Applications*, 387(12): 2972–80.

Balcan, D., Colizza, V., Gonçalves, B., Hu, H., Ramasco, J.J. and Vespignani, A. (2009) 'Multiscale mobility networks and the spatial spreading of infectious diseases', *Proceedings of the National Academy of Sciences*, 106(51): 21484–89.

Berry, B.J.L. (1964) 'Cities as systems within systems of cities', *Papers of the Regional Science Association*, 13(1): 147–63.

Breiger, R.L. (1974) 'The duality of persons and groups', *Social Forces*, 53(2): 181–90.

Cohen-Cole, E., Patacchini, E. and Zenou, Y. (2015) 'Static and dynamic networks in interbank markets', *Network Science*, 3(1): 98–123.

C. R. (2015) 'Do hub airports boost growth?', *The Economist*, December 1. www.economist.com/blogs/gulliver/2015/12/economics-aviation-capacity (accessed 15 September 2017).

Derudder, B. and Taylor, P.J. (2005) 'The cliquishness of world cities', *Global Networks*, 5(1): 71–91.

Derudder, B. and Witlox, F. (2008) 'Mapping world city networks through airline flows: Context, relevance, and problems', *Journal of Transport Geography*, 16(5): 305–12.

Ducruet, C. and Beauguitte, L. (2014) 'Spatial science and network science: Review and outcomes of a complex relationship', *Network and Spatial Economics*, 14(3): 297–316.

Friedmann, J. (1986) 'The world city hypothesis', *Development and Change*, 17(1): 69–83.

Guimera, R., Mossa, S., Turtsch, A. and Amaral, L.A.N. (2005) 'The worldwide air transportation network: Anomalous centrality, community structure, and cities' global roles', *Proceedings of the National Academy of Sciences*, 102(22): 7794–99.

Hall, P. (1966) *The World Cities*. London: Weidenfeld & Nicolson.

Han, D.-D., Qian, J.-H. and Liu, J.-G. (2009) 'Network topology and correlation features affiliated with European airline companies', *Physica A: Statistical Mechanics and its Applications*, 388(1): 71–81.

Hipp, J.R. and Perrin, A.J. (2009) 'The simultaneous effect of social distance and physical distance on the formation of neighborhood ties', *City and Community*, 8(1): 5–25.

Irwin, M.D. and Hughes, H.L. (1992) 'Centrality and the structure of urban interaction: Measures, concepts, and applications', *Social Forces*, 71(1): 17–51.

Li, W. and Cai, X. (2004) 'Statistical analysis of airport network of China', *Physical Review E*, 69, 046106.

Liu, X., Derudder, B., Liu, Y., Witlox, F. and Shen, W. (2013) 'A stochastic actor-based modelling of the evolution of an intercity corporate network', *Environment and Planning A*, 45(4): 947–66.

McKenzie, R.D. (1933) *The Metropolitan Community*. New York: Russell & Russell.

Neal, Z.P. (2012) 'Structural determinism in the interlocking world city network', *Geographical Analysis*, 44(2): 162–70.

Neal, Z.P. (2013) *The Connected City: How Networks are Shaping the Modern Metropolis*. New York: Routledge.

Neal, Z.P. (2014a) 'Validity in world city network measurements', *Tijdschrift voor Economische en Sociale Geografie*, 105(4): 427–43.

Neal, Z.P. (2014b) 'The backbone of bipartite projections: Inferring relationships from co-authorship, co-sponsorship, co-attendance and other co-behaviors', *Social Networks*, 39, 84–97.

Neal, Z.P. (2014c) 'The devil is in the details: Differences in air traffic networks by scale, species, and season', *Social Networks*, 38, 63–73.

Neal, Z.P. (2017) 'Well connected compared to what? Rethinking frames of reference in world city network research', *Environment and Planning A*, 49(12): 2859–77.

Neal, Z.P. and Neal, J.W. (2014) 'The (in)compatibility of diversity and sense of community', *American Journal of Community Psychology*, 53(1): 1–12.

Nordlund, C. (2004) 'A critical comment on the Taylor approach for measuring world city interlock linkages', *Geographical Analysis*, 36(3): 290–96.

Robins, G., Pattison, P., Kalish, Y. and Lusher, D. (2007) 'An introduction to exponential random graph (p*) models for social networks', *Social Networks*, 29(2): 173–91.

Robinson, J. (2002) 'Global and world cities: A view from off the map', *International Journal of Urban and Regional Research*, 26(3): 531–54.

Sassen, S. (1991) *The Global City: New York, London, Tokyo*. Princeton, NJ: Princeton University Press.

Strano, E., Nicosia, V., Latore, V., Porta, S. and Barthélemy, M. (2012) 'Elementary processes governing the evolution of road networks', *Scientific Reports* 2, Article 296. doi:10.1038/srep00296.

Taylor, P.J. (2001) 'Specification of the world city network', *Geographical Analysis*, 33(2): 181–94.

Taylor, P.J. and Derudder, B. (2016) *World City Network: A Global Urban Analysis* (2nd edition). New York: Routledge.

Taylor, P.J. and Derudder, B. (2018) 'Exploring the world city network', in J. Harrison and M. Hoyler (eds), *Doing Global Urban Research*. London: Sage, pp. 34–51.

Tranos, E., Gheasi, M. and Nijkamp, P. (2015) 'International migration: A global complex network', *Environment and Planning B*, 42(1): 4–22.

5

EXAMINING GLOBAL URBAN POLICY MOBILITIES

Cristina Temenos and Kevin Ward

> We have not only looked within the UK, we have looked beyond as well. We have tried to secure access to the best examples and I think the overall judgment that we have come to is that while there are lots of very, very good examples, they have tended to be in particular places around particular programmes and that what we have to do is develop our capability to do this at scale along the lines of our five programmes. Quite frankly, it did dawn on us, it has to be said – towards the end of last year in particular – there are no real examples where this has been done at this scale, certainly in this country and if not in other places in Europe. (Sir Howard Bernstein, Chief Executive of Manchester City Council, House of Commons Health Committee, 2016: Q237)

Why study global urban policy mobilities?

Why, indeed? Well, let us start this chapter with an example. We are writing from Manchester in the North West of England. Since 2014 a lot has been written about the city and the wider city region, Greater Manchester, and their locations as sites of experimentation in the redesign and delivery of government reform. This centres on the devolution of budgets and responsibilities from central government to a combined authority consisting of representatives from the ten local authorities of Greater Manchester.[1] In the areas of health and social care, housing, planning, skills, and transport the Greater Manchester

Combined Authority (GMCA) has taken control over budgets totalling billions of pounds, while also being responsible for the delivery of services in these areas. With no clear blueprint, those involved have looked to elsewhere. As the quote at the beginning of this chapter from the Chief Executive of Manchester City Council, Sir Howard Bernstein, details, those arriving at the Manchester model of devolution sought to learn from the experiences of other cities. Subsequently other English combined authorities have made 'deals' with central government, each a variation on Greater Manchester's, as those developing them have looked to learn from the city region. At the same time, Greater Manchester has hosted a number of visitors from cities elsewhere in the world, whose leaders want to know more about the genealogy of the Manchester model and how its impacts will be measured in the immediate and in the longer term (Haughton et al., 2016).

It is not the first time the city has figured in the wider imagination of policymakers from other cities. During the mid-1990s the city's apparently successful formation of urban redevelopment public–private partnerships in a number of neighbourhoods across the city was widely lauded. The post-1996 IRA bomb regeneration of the urban core and the hosting of the 2002 Commonwealth Games to the east of Manchester were just two of a number of developments that drew in policymakers from cities elsewhere in the world, eager to learn from those involved, examples of the policy tourism that characterizes much of contemporary urban policy and politics (Cook and Ward, 2011; González, 2011; Montero, 2017). Of course Manchester is not alone in this regard. A number of cities have become known for a particular aspect of their policymaking. You might be familiar with some of them. You might even be reading this chapter from one! Think of Barcelona and brownfield regeneration, Chicago and finance, Copenhagen and cycling, Freiburg and sustainability or Porto Alegre and participatory budgeting. Wherever in the world 'local' urban policy is made, there are often elements that draw upon relations with elsewhere (McCann and Ward, 2011).

This increasingly global-urban arriving at and making up of policy has seen a new interdisciplinary field of study emerge since the mid-2000s, referred to as 'urban policy mobilities' (Jacobs, 2012; McCann, 2008; McCann and Ward, 2011; Peck and Theodore, 2010; Temenos and McCann, 2013). At its core are two interrelated and overlapping agendas. One is focused on the mobility of policy and associated expertise and knowledge; the second is focused on the actors and practices through which policy is rendered mobile and travels (Roy, 2012). Working across these two agendas, the field draws upon a number of intellectual antecedents from anthropology, history, human geography, planning, political science and sociology. For example, political scientists have had a long-standing interest in policy diffusion and replication, with an emphasis on movement between countries and with modelling policy transfer (Dolowitz and Marsh, 2000; Benson and Jordan, 2011). More recently in anthropology, the study of how policies move has been given a more global approach directed towards uncovering 'policy worlds', where the emphasis is on the social lives of policy (Shore et al., 2011). In human geography this interest in the development, movement, and implementation of policy focuses on inter-urban policy movements and on the mobilization of policies between governance scales and jurisdictions (McCann, 2011; McCann and Ward, 2011). Finally, within history there is a tradition of work on engineers and planners who moved from one city to another, putting into practice what they learnt along the way, and the organizations who represented these professions and who organized study trips in cities around the world (Healey and Upton, 2010; Cook et al., 2015).

The emergence of urban policy mobilities thus both draws upon what has gone before while critiquing particular aspects of it. In particular, its intellectual impetus is a dissatisfaction with earlier policy transfer literatures and their aspatial, hierarchical, and positivist nature (McCann, 2011; McCann and Ward, 2012; Peck, 2011). It seeks to present an alternative way of thinking about how policy is arrived at in places such as Manchester, and the ways in which policies move and mutate (or don't) between different locations.

A global urban policy mobilities approach has four defining features. The first is a commitment to understanding the production of urban space through global-relational connections, or put it another way, to understand the city in the world and the world in the city; the second emphasizes the political economic structures and trajectories which, in a path-dependent sort of way, both produce and reify the generation of replicable policies; the third is a concern with uncovering socio-material assemblages that make up the day-to-day processes and political arrangements that mediate and translate policy mobilization; and the fourth, and final, feature is an attention to what happens to policies while they are 'in motion', with an understanding that the paths travelled and the things that happen to policies are as important as the policies themselves, their place of origin, and the places they affect (McCann and Ward, 2011; Temenos and McCann, 2013).

Challenges of researching global urban policy mobilities

There are a number of challenges to researching urban policy mobilities, which we group under two headings. The first set of challenges relate to how to conceive, identify and name something as 'the field' into which you will step to do your research. The second set of challenges relate to devising a methodological strategy to accompany a relational understanding of space. In this section we examine each set of challenges in turn.

The first set of challenges are those associated with what Jacobs (2012) believes constitutes a relational turn in urban geography. That is, a turn away from privileging the immediate and the surrounding combined with an awareness of the potential geographically distant but socially proximate sites which appear in the arriving at and making up of urban policy. According to

Robinson (2006: 121), we should approach the city as 'both a place (a site or territory) and as a series of unbounded, relatively disconnected and dispersed, perhaps sprawling and differentiated activities, made in and through many different kinds of networks stretching far beyond [its] physical extent'. In this intellectual vein, those working on urban policy mobility studies have been working across three conceptual provocations.

The first provocation centres on an awareness of how policy is arrived at and made up in one place, but in ways that brings together bits from a range of other places. Of course, this is a highly structured 'market' of ideas, experiences, knowledge and policies, in which some of what has been done in some cities – think Baltimore and its waterfront or Freiburg and its retro-fitted buildings – is more likely to be picked up and moved (Peck, 2011). So, this approach understands cities as 'multiplexes', in the words of Amin and Thrift (1997: 417), in which they are the 'co-presence of multiple spaces, multiple times and multiple webs of relations, tying local sites, subjects and fragments into globalizing networks'.

The second provocation draws attention to the work done by those whose everyday labour involves arriving at and making up urban policy. This means they pay attention to practice while not underestimating the different contexts in which practices occur. Here the focus is not just on so-called 'elites'. Rather it includes a more diverse set of people, such as activists, labour unions and lower-ranking public officials – the middling technocrats which Larner and Laurie (2010) write about. Under pressure to 'deliver' successfully, quickly, and at low cost, such as in the case of the devolution of health and social care across Greater Manchester, actors look elsewhere. To learn more about policies that are represented as having worked, they develop relationships with the places with which they are associated. This is done directly through examples of 'policy tourism' in which actors visit locations, speaking to those involved, take photographs and experience up close policies and their effects (González, 2011). Or it can take place through different types of mediation, such as consultants who offer knowledge in easily consumable, legible, and movable packages or technologies such as webinars in which policies are explained, discussed, and translated (Rapoport, 2015a).

The third provocation draws attention to the role played by comparison in urban policymaking. While its ideological and political uses are not entirely new, a challenge has been to understand how a range of more recent technologies, such as benchmarks, indicators, and rankings, have increased the capacity to perform city-to-city comparisons (Ward, 2006; McCann, 2008). Here the notion of 'comparison' is put to work to locate one city against another. This can be done to either disempower or empower policymakers in a particular city, as their work is constructed as having been a relative 'success' or 'failure'. Further, such comparisons can obscure the often ad hoc relationships which form the basis for establishing the comparisons in the first place (Cohen, 2015).

We now turn to a second set of challenges. These are those associated with methodology (Cochrane and Ward, 2012). In short, how do we create a doable research project? The intellectual developments within global urban policy mobilities research question the privileging of a form of methodological territorialism, the focus on a singular place, that has tended to characterize much of the work on global urban policy and politics. Embracing a more topological approach raises the question of how to organize a research project given what we now know about global urban policy mobilities. Research is never straightforwardly rendered knowable. If we know the outcome, then what would be the point of embarking on the study? Furthermore, some of the more predictable and secure aspects to doing any empirical research project are offset by the ephemeral, fleeting, and harder to know elements of policy travel (Temenos, 2016). So, you might know your point of departure, whether it is a city or a particular policy. However, less might be known about the relations themselves and the geographical reach they may have, which might be uncovered through your fieldwork. To generate a strategy over where and when you will do fieldwork and your choice of methods might have additional complications. Whether you are interested in how policy is arrived at and made up in a particular city or in uncovering the work that goes into moving the policy between locational examples of 'repeated instances' (Jacobs, 2012), it is unlikely to be possible to know all the potential research sites in advance.

What counts as data and how they can be generated is a third and final methodological challenge. What sorts of media articles, meeting minutes, and policy documents exist? Which will you examine? Where are these materials stored? Are they publically accessible? Will you need to request access? And will you need to pay for it? Will you speak to people? If so, who? How do you know with whom to speak? Can you find their contact information? What will you ask them and what do you hope to find out? Will you conduct interviews, observations, surveys or a combination? How will you speak with them; in person, on the phone, email or videoconference? Will they speak to you? This list of questions can be the tip of the iceberg in considering the 'how' of researching global urban policy mobilities. It brings up two considerations which may prove significantly challenging, that of access and resources. Sometimes the two are related, other times they are not. In the next section we consider some of the techniques for addressing the very practical questions associated with what you will study and how, as well as ways in which challenges might need to be overcome.

Techniques for researching global urban policy mobilities

Okay, so now we know what urban policy mobilities are and, given the conceptual and methodological challenges we have just outlined, the chapter turns to address the question, 'how do you do it?', so to speak. In part this is due to the field's multi-disciplinary origins. Each of these has its own particular methodological history, for example, anthropologists immersing themselves in the policymaking field, historians drawing upon archives and human geographers interviewing various types of decision-making actors, from activists to elites. Bring them together and there is a rich portfolio of methods from which to choose. Considering that as scholars of global urban studies you will likely come from a similarly diverse set of disciplines, it is beneficial that global urban policy mobilities is not prescriptive in its methods and, instead, values methodological openness and innovation (Cochrane and Ward, 2012). As the field has developed, there have also emerged several foci and techniques. It is to these that we now turn.

The first question to ask ourselves is, what exactly do we study when studying urban policy mobilities? There are four distinct, yet related, elements of policy which are generally addressed in these studies: knowledge, people, materials, and politics (Temenos et al., forthcoming). Studying global urban policy mobilities is often about studying the mobilization of knowledge. What are the forms and functions policy ideas take on, and where do they travel? As Jennifer Robinson (2015) points out, policies can be drawn from multiple locations and so the routes through which policy ideas travel must be mapped. These are places where mobilized policy knowledge must have an effect somewhere to gain both momentum and moorings. This can be in a city where a policy is created or implemented, but also in extra-local places, for example at conferences, where encounters with specific ideas have the potential to set agendas and provide direction and impetus for policy circulation (Adey, 2006; Temenos, 2016). In this sense, the social relation examined is that between the idea and its associations with various places.

Second, policy mobilities researchers are attentive to people with an interest in mobilizing and adopting policies because they are important figures in whether and how policy gets mobilized. People move policy ideas and, in a sense, 'embody expertise' (Prince, 2010). To different degrees, all policy actors are mobile at one point or another, whether it is an activist marching across a city, a bureaucrat travelling to a conference, or a hyper-mobile star-architect flying across the globe on a speaking tour. It is important to understand who is travelling, and where they go. The mobility of materials is the third element which scholars of urban policy mobilities examine. Their mobility, both virtually and physically can work to prepare the field for policy implementation elsewhere. Materials such as images, policy frameworks, reports, and spreadsheets are mobilized through various spaces on the internet, at conferences, on study tours, etc. (McCann, 2008, 2011; Rapoport, 2015b). Such materials are important data when researching how polices move, though it is important to remember that different artefacts serve different purposes. A report may be about presenting data collected, but the images which accompany it are meant to convey normative atmospheres, in turn influencing how individual policies are perceived. The fourth element of mobile policy that researchers examine is politics, the ideological struggles over how to govern. Urban policy mobilities scholars are attentive to the local contestations over how to manage urban space at the same time that such conversations are structured by more globalized political-economic ideologies. This concern with the relationship between policy and politics then is an overall concern with the ways in which power is understood, exercised, negotiated, and performed.

Keeping these elements in mind, there are three techniques that appear most regularly in studies of global urban policy mobilities. The first is content/discourse analysis. Although not exactly the same, their differences can be suppressed for the sake of discussion. Whether using the archives of city government minutes or the local newspaper, the grey literature of consultancy reports or central government documents, analysing words and their wider meanings remains a significantly used method for studying global urban policy mobilities. This is often where a policy mobility study will begin, with documents, which can form a distinct data set on which to draw out aims, emphasis, intentions, and themes. There are a number of ways in which content can be analysed, but most often, and we are speaking in broad terms here, it is through coding for specific themes, both pre-identified and emergent, which are related to the research questions (Bacchi, 2009).

Technique number two is the semi-structured interview. This usually involves one-on-one interactions between the researcher and someone who has been identified as having something to say on the matter in hand. In some cases content analysis of one document or another can help to identify interview subjects. Semi-structured interviews are formed around a set of questions based on the overall research objectives. The initial questions generally consist of a subset of questions which are the same for each interviewee, and a subset of questions which are tailored to the specific individual and their role in the policy process. These data are usually analysed as they are collected and often used to inform questions for subsequent interviews. It is an iterative learning process. Semi-structured interviews are rarely the only research technique in a study; they are usually accompanied by documentary analysis and can be combined with a number of different methods for studying mobile policy. A mixed-qualitative approach is important when using interviews because it helps to overcome subject bias and triangulation can corroborate findings or raise contradictions between narratives (Cochrane, 2013).

Technique number three is ethnography. A number of disciplines have used ethnography, although none as much as anthropology. There is an attention to being in the field for a significant period of time, even if there is no agreement about when the length of time in the field becomes 'significant', or indeed what constitutes the field! On the one hand this might mean fieldwork in multiple locations, geographically distant but socially proximate through their presence in policymaking networks. A sort of global ethnography as envisaged by Burawoy et al. (2000; see also Bunnell, Chapter 13)! So, for Larner and Laurie (2010: 220) the focus must be on 'longer term immersion in a field where professional and personal networks can be followed over time'. Jacobs (2012) regards the use of ethnographic methods as important to reveal the dynamics and processes through which policy is made, holding open the possibility that the making of policy might fail. On the other hand, in her work on millennial development, Roy (2012: 35) argues against the ontological presence and immersion that has traditionally defined ethnographic studies. Instead she argues for a switch in focus, from locations to circulations, and an attention to 'how socio-spatial scales, from the global to the local, are actively produced'.

Case study of researching global urban policy mobilities

Considering we have addressed the reasons why we study urban policy mobilities, what the challenges are, and how to do it, we now turn to an example of how one of us, Cristina Temenos, conducted the research for her PhD dissertation. The goal of the project was to examine the role of transnational advocacy networks in mobilizing an alternative policy model in cities across the Caribbean, Europe, and North America. The relationship between globally connected and operating social movements, policy change, and local implementation was the main focus of this project. At the time we are writing this chapter, the project remains unique in its focus on activism and on public health and drug policies, rather than the economic development models that much policy mobilities research explores (Temenos, 2015, but see McCann, 2008). The alternative policy that Cristina examined was harm reduction drug policy. The movement for harm reduction is a particular subset of the wider drug policy reform movement. Harm reduction seeks to minimize the physical, psychological, and social harms associated with illicit drug use for both the drug user and society (HRI, 2016). It is a public health approach that serves as an alternative to the dominant criminalization model commonly invoked in discussions of drug use and addictions. Harm reduction is also a global social movement addressing the use of illegal drugs, issues of equality, marginalization, social justice, and human rights.

To examine the relationship between a global social movement and local policy change, the project was designed following Burawoy's (1998) extended case method, which is similar to a multi-sited ethnography, and focused on studying the networks, people, places, and politics surrounding the advocacy for harm reduction drug policy. In response to critiques that much policy transfer literature has a narrow focus on state actors involved in policy making, to the exclusion of others, Cristina examined the wider transnational advocacy network engaged in activism for policy reform and the places where it 'touches down' as a policy and is enacted in practice in eight cities in as many countries (McCann and Ward, 2012). Fieldwork also consisted of research in eight

(Continued)

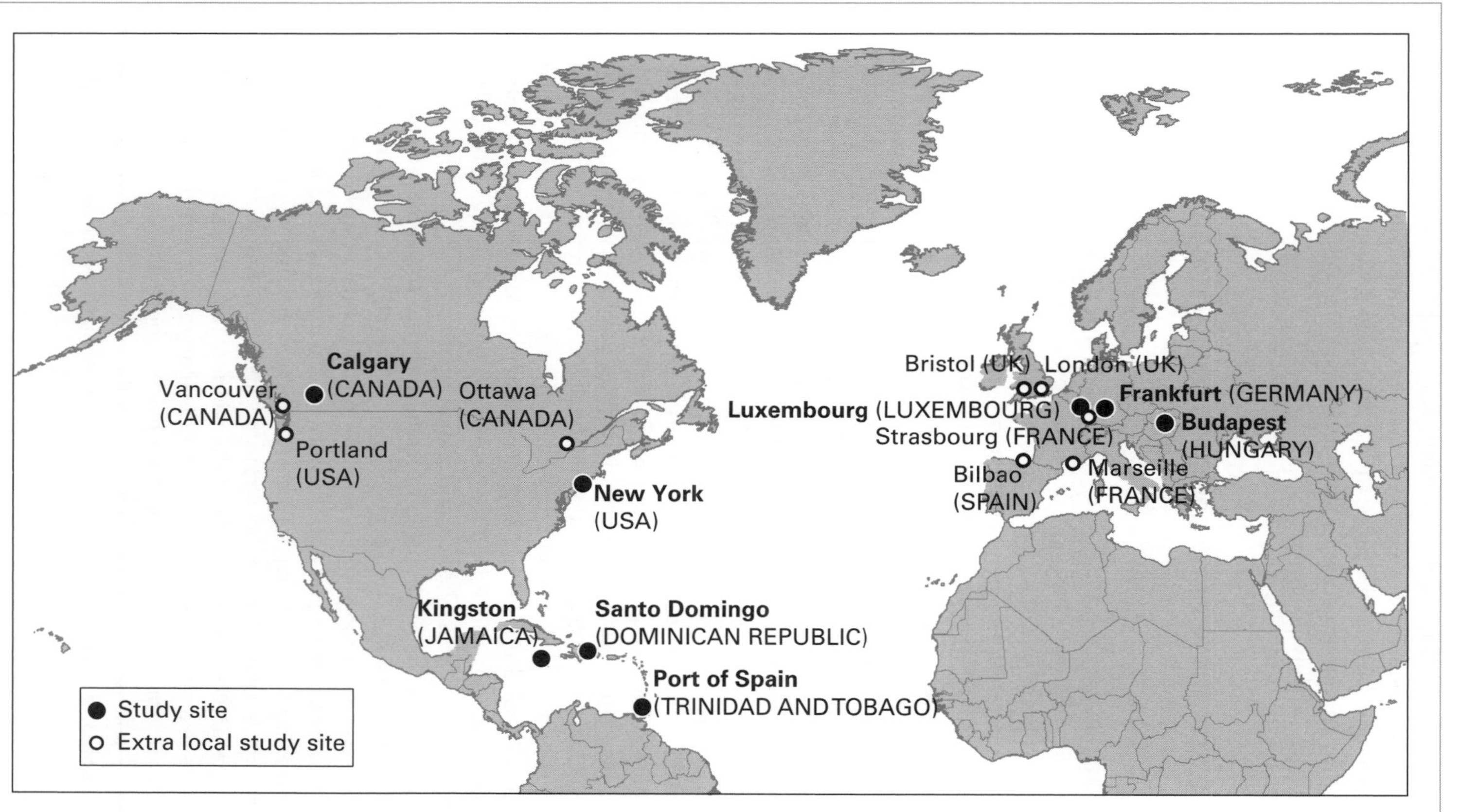

Figure 5.1 Field research sites for drug policy activism study

'extra-local' sites of policymaking and activism such as harm reduction conferences, think-tank headquarters, and government institutions, totalling sixteen cities across eleven countries (see Figure 5.1). These extra-local sites contributed to understanding the overall advocacy network for drug policy reform and drug policy production.

From the beginning of the project design, there were two challenges present. Such a large project, ranging across so many places, requires significant resources: time and money. Time is relatively easy to address; as a student in a programme, there is an advised timeline for fieldwork, though it is rarely firm. In this case, two years was advised. In reality, Cristina began thinking about this project a year before writing the proposal, and the time spent in the field stretched to three years. It is important to design a project with a timeline in mind, and to have a clear idea of how much data you want and how you will get it. Setting these goals before going into the field will help to stay as close as possible to the set timeline. The second resource, money, also shapes your project. When fieldwork beyond your immediate surroundings is required, funding is usually the deciding factor when determining research design and feasibility. In this particular case, funding came from a variety of sources including initial PhD research funding and internal and external research fellowships. A strict budget was planned and followed in order to be able to fit in all of the field sites that were important to incorporate. Therefore, in terms of 'lessons learned' from doing a multi-sited PhD project, thinking through a very basic, practical thing like finding funding is fundamental to answering conceptual research questions.

In order to answer the research questions, the extended case study drew on three main qualitative research methods which were discussed in the previous section: document analysis, ethnographic observation, and semi-structured interviews with informants. The research was conducted in three phases. Phase I was the scoping project. This stage of the research entailed policy and media scans and analysis done in order to gain a comprehensive perspective of drug policy as it relates to harm reduction in the Caribbean, Europe, and North America. Phase I also identified initial contacts in the regions. It was an in-depth scoping project intended to gain a comprehensive regional understanding of harm reduction drug policy. First a jurisdictional scan was conducted focusing on policy documents relating to drug policy in each region, harm reduction policy in each region, and regional, national, and municipal low-threshold[2] public health services aimed at drug users. Several non-governmental organizations were key resources for helping to identify gaps and ensure other stakeholders and documents were not overlooked (Crang, 2002; Imrie, 2000; Schoenberger, 1991).

(Continued)

Phase II was fieldwork data collection and it entailed conducting 72 semi-structured interviews with key actors identified through preliminary research interviews, online activity, and through document and media scans and previous research trips. Particular attention was paid to political leaders, drug policy reform activists and civil society NGOs, and harm reduction service providers. The purpose of the interviews was to collect qualitative data that focused on the processes, meanings, and experiences of policy advocacy, policy production, and policy implementation. Phase II also included direct observation of 22 harm reduction services in several cities, policy meetings, conferences, training sessions, community information meetings, and other places in which drug policy information is disseminated or discussed. This was done to gain an understanding of individual actors' and institutions' practices and understandings of the operation of harm reduction services and their relationship to global policy networks. Observation was concurrent with the interviews and entailed the collection of ethnographic field notes that focused on: the types of policies and practices discussed; the manner of persuasion and argumentation being employed; the materials and techniques used to persuade actors about harm reduction drug policy; and the types of people with whom the communication occurred.

The introduction of international fieldwork presented another important consideration: positionality. Positionality focuses on how the researcher is perceived in the research setting, how the researcher presents themselves and the power relationships in the research setting, as well as changes depending on the place (Rose, 1997; Sultana, 2007; Sundberg, 2004). For McDowell (1992: 402), positionality is a recognition of and way to 'account for our own position, as well as that of our research participants'. For example, in one organization, being a researcher from a North American university meant that Cristina was perceived as already being an expert and welcomed into the organization; in another organization, being a young white woman from another country meant she was perceived as being an outsider and so was met with distrust. The challenge this presents for the researcher is not only an interpersonal one of building trust with research participants and gaining and maintaining access, but it is also an intellectual one of having to ensure they can be confident that the data they are collecting are valid. And, with a multi-sited project, maintaining contact, and therefore trust, with organizations after the researcher has left is an important consideration. In this case, the dual focus on transnational networks and policy implementation meant that involvement in online communities allowed such relationships to be maintained, and are in fact ongoing.

Phase III began while Phase II was still under way. The transcription and analysis of some interviews was undertaken as other interviews were still being conducted. This allowed a degree of learning and reflection over the course of the interviewing process. Overall, Phase III consisted of the transcription of all interviews, and the analysis and write-up of data. Although fieldwork officially ended about one year before the PhD was completed, Cristina remained in contact with the research participants, and document and media analysis was ongoing as new policies and media emerged. When studying an active process or network, decisions and outcomes can change suddenly. Therefore during the write-up, facts, outcomes, and policy processes had to be continually confirmed and updated, both through individual research as well as through email and phone contact with people involved in the research.

Reflections on researching global urban policy mobilities

From our perspective, the relatively recent emergence of global urban policy mobilities has been one of the most exciting intellectual developments in contemporary studies. We would say that, wouldn't we! Nevertheless, in taking aim at the myriad ways in which cities envisage their futures through arriving at and making up policy, the field makes an important contribution to the wider study of the contemporary global urban condition. It highlights the ways in which the global is built up as knowable.

Of course, global urban policy mobilities is part of a larger conversation on how contemporary policy of all types is arrived at and made up. Cities have emerged as important policy-making sites in which the work that is done, whether around climate change or infrastructure, policing or transport is increasingly influential (Acuto, Chapter 7). Yet their growing influence does not mean nation states do not continue to hold very significant power. As we noted in the introduction, Manchester is being used as a model for how other UK cities might interact with the national government and manage new local governance processes and subsequently devolved budget controls, in particular regarding health and social care. This kind of global urban experimentation involves places and actors from across the UK and internationally, and in particular it highlights the importance of examining the relationship between the national government and the local one. In this case, inter-city learning is building on relationships within a national context, rather than a global one. To engage with the concept of the global through a policy mobilities lens is to undertake a global-relational approach, which does not focus on geographical location or distance so much as it focuses on the social relationships – the meanings behind policy-making processes – that make up cities and their place in the world.

Notes

1. These are Bolton, Bury, Manchester, Oldham, Rochdale, Salford, Stockport, Tameside, Trafford, and Wigan.
2. 'Low-threshold' refers to services that attempt to reduce barriers to entry for traditionally marginalized populations, specifically by not requiring that abstinence from illegal drug use is a precondition for access.

References

Acuto, M. (2018) 'Engaging with global urban governance', in J. Harrison and M. Hoyler (eds), *Doing Global Urban Research*. London: Sage, pp. 96–109.

Adey, P. (2006) 'If mobility is everything then it is nothing: Towards a relational politics of (im)mobilities', *Mobilities*, 1(1): 75–94.

Amin, A. and Thrift, N. (1997) 'The ordinary city', *Transactions of the Institute of British Geographers*, 22(4): 411–30.

Bacchi, C. (2009) *Analysing Policy*. Melbourne: Pearson Higher Education.

Benson, D. and Jordan A. (2011) 'What have we learned from policy transfer research? Dolowitz and Marsh revisited', *Political Studies Review*, 9(3): 366–78.

Bunnell, T. (2018) 'Comparative ethnographic urban research', in J. Harrison and M. Hoyler (eds), *Doing Global Urban Research*. London: Sage, pp. 182–95.

Burawoy, M. (1998) 'The extended case method', *Sociological Theory*, 16(1): 4–33.

Burawoy, M., Blum, J.A., George, S., Gille, Z., Gowan, T., Haney, L., Klawitter, M., Lopez, S.H., Ó Riain, S. and Thayer, M. (2000) *Global Ethnography: Forces, Connections, and Imaginations in a Postmodern World*. Berkeley, CA: University of California Press.

Cochrane, A. (2013) 'Interviews', in K. Ward (ed.), *Researching the City*. London: Sage, pp. 38–53.

Cochrane, A. and Ward, K. (2012) 'Guest editorial: Researching the geographies of policy mobility: Confronting the methodological challenges', *Environment and Planning A*, 44(1): 5–12.

Cohen, D. (2015) 'Grounding mobile policies: Ad hoc networks and the creative city in Bandung, Indonesia', *Singapore Journal of Tropical Geography*, 36(1): 23–37.

Cook, I.R. and Ward, K. (2011) 'Trans-national networks of learning, mega-events and policy tourism: The case of Manchester's Commonwealth and Olympic Games projects', *Urban Studies*, 48(12): 2519–35.

Cook, I.R., Ward, S.V. and Ward, K. (2015) 'Post-war planning and policy tourism: The international study tours of the Town and Country Planning Association 1947–1961', *Planning Theory & Practice*, 16(2): 184–205.

Crang, M. (2002) 'Qualitative methods: The new orthodoxy?', *Progress in Human Geography*, 26(5): 647-55.
Dolowitz, D.P. and Marsh, D. (2000) 'Learning from abroad: The role of policy transfer in contemporary policy-making', *Governance*, 13(1): 5-23.
González, S. (2011) 'Bilbao and Barcelona "in motion". How urban regeneration "models" travel and mutate in the global flows of policy tourism', *Urban Studies*, 48(7): 1397-418.
Haughton, G., Deas, I., Hincks, S. and Ward, K. (2016) 'Mythic Manchester: Devo Manc, the Northern Powerhouse and rebalancing the English economy', *Cambridge Journal of Regions, Economy and Society*, 9(2): 355-70.
Healey, P. and Upton, R. (eds) (2010) *Crossing Borders: International Exchange and Planning Practices*. London: Routledge.
House of Commons Health Committee (2016) 'Oral Evidence: Impact of the Comprehensive Spending Review on Health and Social Care, HC 678'. *Hansard*, 21 March http://data.parliament.uk/writtenevidence/committeeevidence.svc/evidencedocument/health-committee/impact-of-the-comprehensive-spending-review-on-health-and-social-care/oral/31040.html (accessed 17 September 2017).
HRI (Harm Reduction International) (2016) 'What is Harm Reduction?'. https://www.hri.global/what-is-harm-reduction (accessed 17 September 2017).
Imrie, R. (2000) 'Disabling environments and the geography of access policies and practices', *Disability & Society*, 15(1): 5-24.
Jacobs, J.M. (2012) 'Urban geographies I: Still thinking cities relationally', *Progress in Human Geography*, 36(3): 412-22.
Larner, W. and Laurie, N. (2010) 'Travelling technocrats, embodied knowledges: Globalising privatisation in telecoms and water', *Geoforum*, 41(2): 218-26.
McCann, E. (2008) 'Expertise, truth, and urban policy mobilities: Global circuits of knowledge in the development of Vancouver, Canada's "four pillar" drug strategy', *Environment and Planning A*, 40(4): 885-904.
McCann, E. (2011) 'Global urban policy mobilities and global circuits of knowledge: Toward a research agenda', *Annals of the Association of American Geographers*, 101(1): 107-30.
McCann, E. and Ward, K. (eds) (2011) *Mobile Urbanism: Cities and Policymaking in the Global Age*. Minnesota, MN: University of Minnesota Press.
McCann, E. and Ward, K. (2012) 'Policy assemblages, mobilities and mutations: Toward a multidisciplinary conversation', *Political Studies Review*, 10(3): 325-32.
McDowell, L. (1992) 'Doing gender: Feminism, feminists and research methods in human geography', *Transactions of the Institute of British Geographers*, 17(4): 399-416.
Montero, S. (2017) 'Study tours and inter-city policy learning: Mobilizing Bogotá's transportation policies in Guadalajara', *Environment and Planning A*, 49(2): 332-50.

(Continued)

Peck, J. (2011) 'Geographies of policy: From transfer-diffusion to mobility-mutation', *Progress in Human Geography*, 35(6): 773–97.

Peck, J. and Theodore, N. (2010) 'Mobilizing policy: Models, methods, and mutations', *Geoforum*, 41(2): 169–74.

Prince, R. (2010) 'Policy transfer as policy assemblage: Making policy for the creative industries in New Zealand', *Environment and Planning A*, 42(1): 169–86.

Rapoport, E. (2015a) 'Globalising sustainable global urbanism: The role of international masterplanners', *Area*, 47(2): 110–15.

Rapoport, E. (2015b). 'Sustainable global urbanism in the age of Photoshop: Images, experiences and the role of learning through inhabiting the international travels of a planning model', *Global Networks*, 15(3): 307–24.

Robinson, J. (2006) *Ordinary Cities: Between Modernity and Development*. London: Routledge.

Robinson, J. (2015) '"Arriving at" global urban policies: The topological spaces of global urban policy mobility', *International Journal of Urban and Regional Research*, 39(4): 831–4.

Rose, G. (1997) 'Situating knowledges: Positionality, reflexivities and other tactics', *Progress in Human Geography*, 21(3): 305–20.

Roy, A. (2012) 'Ethnographic circulations: Space-time relations in the world of poverty management', *Environment and Planning A*, 44(1): 31–41.

Schoenberger, E. (1991) 'The corporate interview as a research method in economic geography', *The Professional Geographer*, 43(2): 180–9.

Shore, C., Wright, S. and Però, D. (eds) (2011) *Policy Worlds: Anthropology and the Analysis of Contemporary Power*. Oxford: Berghahn Books.

Sultana, F. (2007) 'Reflexivity, positionality and participatory ethics: Negotiating fieldwork dilemmas in international research', *ACME: An International E-Journal for Critical Geographies*, 6(3): 374–85.

Sundberg, J. (2004) 'Identities in the making: Conservation, gender and race in the Maya Biosphere Reserve, Guatemala', *Gender, Place & Culture*, 11(1): 43–66.

Temenos, C. (2015) 'Differential policy mobilities: Transnational advocacy and harm reduction drug policy'. PhD dissertation, Simon Fraser University.

Temenos, C. (2016) 'Mobilizing drug policy activism: Conferences, convergence spaces and ephemeral fixtures in social movement mobilization', *Space and Polity*, 20(1): 124–41.

Temenos, C., Baker, T. and Cook, I.R. (forthcoming) 'Inside mobile urbanism', in T. Schwanen and R. van Kempen (eds), *Handbook of Urban Geography*. Cheltenham: Edward Elgar.

Temenos, C. and McCann, E. (2013) 'Geographies of policy mobilities', *Geography Compass*, 7(5): 344–57.

Ward, K. (2006) '"Policies in motion", urban management and state restructuring: the trans-local expansion of business improvement districts', *International Journal of Urban and Regional Research*, 30(1): 54-75.

6

TRACKING THE GLOBAL URBANISTS

Donald McNeill and Andrea Pollio

Why track global urbanists?

In this chapter we consider the approaches and techniques that global cities researchers use to research the often secretive, heavily capitalized interventions in urban space by global 'urban' firms. By focusing on 'global urbanists', our aim is to take a purposely wider view than is sometimes the case in the urban policy literature. Notwithstanding the importance of urban gurus (Peck, 2016), or the wide range of literature on policy transfer (McCann and Ward, 2011; Temenos and Ward, Chapter 5) we want to focus on the role of global technology firms in shaping cities. This has become increasingly important in the literature on 'smart cities' for example (Kitchin, 2015), but also in the ever more pervasive strategies used by the likes of Amazon, Google and Alibaba to transform the experience of urban consumers. Moreover, global technology firms are increasingly enrolled in the day-to-day governance of large cities, and indeed play a significant role in redefining the nature of how the state identifies and creates problems to be solved through 'flow maintenance' (Luque-Ayala and Marvin, 2016).

In many ways, what we are doing here is following through a classic problem of economic sociology and geography: tackling the apparently monolithic power of the global firm. According to Callon and Latour (1981), social scientists too readily accord them 'Leviathan' status, taking their bigness as pre-given and agentic in its own right. And yet, closer examination may reveal these firms to be insecure in their ontological identity: constantly having to experiment, restructure, innovate to address the imperfect assessments of their executive leadership. To address this requires an understanding of the specificities of corporate organization, global market strategy, and the deployment of business models in the starkly contrasting regulatory and demographic profiles of different world cities. In what follows, we briefly outline our research into two global technology firms which have a major impact on cities: IBM (Donald McNeill) and Uber (Andrea Pollio). We begin by providing a brief overview of how these firms could be considered as urbanists, before describing the differing ways in which we tracked them. We then briefly describe how we tracked the material traces that these firms leave behind in specific cities, and conclude by commenting on spatial ontologies of how we might get behind these 'Leviathan' firms.

Challenges of tracking firms as global urbanists

At first sight, nominating technology firms as 'urbanists' might appear to be counter-intuitive. Typically, this term is applied to those sectors with a direct interest in the production of the built environment of cities: property developers, certainly, and also architects, engineers and urban designers. However, since the 'world city' hypothesis (Friedmann, 1986) gained currency, the locational strategies of international corporations have been considered as a proxy of the degree to which a particular city is integrated within the global economy. Sassen's (1991) advocacy of a close study of advanced producer service firms, such as global accountants and consultants, has been highly influential. Similarly, the corporate strategy of global investment banks such as Goldman Sachs have been extremely influential in shaping cities, both through the creation of elite labour markets, and through their direct role in financializing urban assets, such as marketing CDOs (collateralized debt obligations) which effectively bundled poor quality mortgages into financial products to be sold to cities and municipalities around the world (for an example, see Hendrikse and Sidaway, 2014). Moreover, the recent burst of innovation in digital, mobile and internet technology has seen the arrival of new consumer-oriented firms within cities, as well as long-established corporations that are experimenting with new business models to remain competitive. This is why we choose to focus on global technology firms to illustrate our argument, as it is clear that it is software-driven firms that are the most competitive actors in the contemporary global economy.

There are three challenges involved in tracking these firms. The first problem is to understand what the urban effects of global firms are. They may have a large aggregate effect on local labour markets, bidding up wages, real estate costs, and so on. They may actively lobby city or state governments to improve the regulatory environment for their business, or else their presence in the city might be elusive and difficult to ascertain.

The second problem is to understand the nature of the product or activity that is being produced or distributed in the locality. Global firms may actively reshape the everyday life of urban dwellers, and their arrival may be greeted with enthusiasm by many keen consumers of their products (the queues outside Apple or Ikea stores for new product models or discount sales being visible examples). It is important to note that the supply chains of these firms may be worth following in their own right, as it is the distanciated geographies of production and consumption that in many ways make global cities what they are.

The third problem is to peer inside the organizational structure and culture of the firm and work out what is actually travelling, as sometimes global firms are not as unified as they appear. As Boussebaa et al. point out:

> MNC headquarters and subsidiaries develop ways of doing things that are *appropriate* to the different national contexts in which they are embedded. This then creates one of a number of barriers to the effective implementation of globally shared management practices. That is, headquarters might seek to transfer its practices to subsidiaries in order to achieve a degree of firm-wide consistency but, being under domestic institutional pressures, subsidiaries will not necessarily implement (i.e. internalize) such practices at the local level if perceived to be inappropriate in that context – mere "ceremonial adoption" is more likely. (Boussebaa et al., 2012: 467–8)

And so, just following corporate rhetoric may not reveal the specific nature of knowledge or product transfer. Even in the case of the global consulting firms, such as KPMG or McKinsey, there is not a straightforward story of global diffusion in play. As Boussebaa et al. report:

> Our research revealed that the firms under investigation all recognized the pressure to provide high-quality services for clients in and across diverse national settings, and to operate as "global" organizations more generally. In order to do so, they had developed a system for identifying and moving consultants across countries – the global resourcing system – and a related system for delivering transnational client projects – the global service team. Our research also revealed that the subsidiary actors we examined were in support of such coordination mechanisms and the idea of the "global" firm more broadly. Yet, paradoxically, these actors also observed strong countervailing forces to these mechanisms. In particular, they explained that the firms' various offices (including the UK ones we investigated) tended to hoard or protect their own consultants, especially those seen as "stars", and were reluctant to borrow or fully pay for those based in other offices overseas. Client project teams were then constituted through processes of negotiation where, contrary to managerial rhetoric, the interests of particular subsidiaries typically played a greater role than those of the "global" firm and its clients. Thus, our firms' subsidiaries acted in ways that undermined the very systems of which they claimed they were in support. (Boussebaa et al., 2012: 478)

And so in what follows we work through how we tracked two different technology firms, both with eyes on the city, and tried to gain a better understanding of their impacts as global urbanists.

Techniques for tracking firms as global urbanists

The two firms in our research, IBM and Uber, though very different in their corporate structures and strategies, presented similar challenges of access to their practices as urban players. To address these challenges, we both focused on the socio-technical arrangements that these firms had put in place to create markets for their products in various cities across the globe. This kind of research bears methodological similarities to the study programme for examining 'processes of economization' that Çalışkan and Callon (2010) have outlined as 'marketization': 'efforts aimed at describing, analysing and making intelligible the shape, constitution and dynamics of a market socio-technical arrangement' (2010: 3).

Marketization is a mode of economic performance: markets are informed by knowledge produced about them, both by economists and managers (Callon, 2007), but they are also performed by their heterogeneous constituents, like regulatory, metrological and logistic infrastructures, as well as by the materiality of the things that are valued and exchanged. In our work, we turned to these socio-technical arrangements with a range of different techniques that may constitute a useful toolkit to research how enterprises like IBM and Uber intervene in the urban.

As Çalışkan and Callon point out, the socio-technical making of markets can be addressed from different 'vantage points' (2010: 1). The first of these vantage points is that of the calculative agencies that purposively operate to engineer a certain market for a certain product. Central to the analysis of 'marketizing agencies' is the role of internal knowledge and its 'architectures' (Amin and Cohendet, 2004). In our research, we both looked at the corporate organization to understand how the firms deployed various forms of knowledge to create opportunities for profit, but also, in the case of IBM, to address internal challenges and diversify their offer (McNeill, 2015). To do so, given the difficulty in accessing organization charts and directly observing knowledge practices as insiders, we used what was available among the various outputs that firms produce as internal reports and various forms of external releases. In the case of IBM, public speeches and interviews, job postings and the use of pre-existing business reportage revealed the kind of expertise that was being deployed to produce a viable market for a mix of technological products, maintenance and consulting services. By piecing together such information with financial and quantifiable data, business journalist Chris Roush (2011) shows how firms' strategic moves can be uncovered, even when their strategies are only partially made known to their shareholders. In the case of Uber, which is not a public listed company and therefore produces very little information, let alone on the local urban teams, a way of reconstructing their architecture of expertise was to follow the blog posts and tweets to identify the authors and their role in the organization. However, other sources were again business interviews and talks where managers unveiled some of the strategic knowledge formations of their company: Uber's CEO himself explains, in various interviews, that the company enters a new city, or a cluster of cities, by creating an entirely new division:

> We don't look at things in a country-by-country basis; we look at it city by city. And when you are as distributed as us, right, a city manager basically runs regular day-to-day regulatory, biz dev, local marketing, customer support, social media, supply chain and a whole bunch of other things. They're really running a business. (Fortune, 2013)

In this sense, we both created formal transcripts of interviews that were not conceded to us directly, but available through other media platforms, like the one above.

Among various forms of business expertise, marketing itself was a form of knowledge that was central to our research, and offered another vantage point for looking at the creation of urban markets. We analysed the practices that were mobilized in the process of marketization by observing the strategic alliances through which both IBM and Uber enrolled local partners, and the discursive rationalities of their advertising material. We collected diverse outputs, papers, reports, blog posts, approaching them not only as documents, but as material objects that contribute to the making of urban markets. For IBM, this entailed reading approximately 100 press releases, 6 substantial company reports and white papers, and 2 corporate biographies, and watching and transcribing 10 YouTube videos. For the study of Uber, the data amounted to 96 ethnographic sketches of various lengths, recorded as digital fieldnotes, 7 life-story interviews, and a 138-page collection of coded tweets, along with several other outlets, from video transcripts to blog posts.

The materiality of these artefacts speaks to another way of framing the research on global urbanists starting from 'the things in the market' (Çalışkan and Callon, 2010: 1). Whilst the elaboration, the design, the experimentation, the making and the maintenance of IBM and Uber's goods was not accessible, the final product could be engaged and understood through its material features. In this sense, various scholars have pointed out the possibility of using ethnographic techniques in understanding material infrastructures (Larkin, 2013; Leigh Star, 1999). In the case of Uber, downloading and using the app as a customer produced several annotated screenshots that were used to describe the agency of the software in performing a market of urban mobility, and could also be used to track how its features were adapted to the local context.

A final vantage point found in our research is that of 'market encounters', the moments when different market actors come together for an exchange (Çalışkan and Callon, 2010: 14). Market encounters are crucial to understand both goods and calculative agencies, but they do not always happen above board. Many firms operating as urbanists trade in intangible assets that are difficult to track, and in secretive ways. However, some market encounters are easier to observe, because they involve the lay users of the products of these firms. In this sense, ethnographic vignettes were used to observe Uber's ride-sharing transactions where the researcher was at the same time customer and participant observer. These sketches shed light on the capacity of the software to embed marketizing narratives, but also on the way in which drivers tinker with its features to open other possibilities (Pollio, forthcoming).

Ethnography used to account for the materialities of urban products and market encounters complete our toolkit of techniques that may be used to address global players that look like 'Leviathans' precisely because they strategically choose to do so (Callon and Latour, 1981). The impossibility to access the 'laboratories' of the global firms in our research demanded a diverse set of techniques that addressed global urbanists from various vantage points on their practices of market making.

Case studies of tracking firms as global urbanists

Tracking 'smart city' products: IBM (Donald McNeill)

During 2015 and 2016, I was researching the emergence of smart cities as an important new trend within urban policy. For many city governments, the opportunity to introduce new ways of organizing services to tackle traffic congestion, burst water mains, or allocate police resources was immediately appealing. At the same time, many firms – large and small – were developing new software applications and hardware kit to implement in urban sites. One of the most prominent and vocal of these was IBM, the global technology firm that for several decades dominated office computing services. IBM was having to diversify rapidly, and began to orient itself towards generating new revenues from data analytics that it could run on its large-scale computing infrastructure. It began to target city governments directly, exploring different ways of understanding the daily work of urban administrations, both to provide new ways of visualizing urban problems (via screen dashboards, primarily) and new ways of offering consulting services combined with hardware and software solutions (see McNeill, 2015, 2016).

My research interest was therefore to understand how this apparent Leviathan, a global technology firm, was working experimentally in different localities to try to generate economies of scale in a newly constructed market. This to me was a classic 'global city' research challenge: being able to survey how an apparently global actor 'landed' or territorialized in different places, with different outcomes, while simultaneously reviewing its centralized corporate strategic performances. What was intriguing to me was that IBM was clearly struggling to do this: it was an innovation challenge that, despite its multi-million dollar marketing budgets, was difficult to implement. In one of the papers, I argued that IBM's Smarter Cities strategy was

> in fact a product of a problem of "bigness", where the many "communities" of expertise within the firm are being "remixed" within the boardroom of the firm. Despite the fact that these global corporations have the scale and intention to significantly influence both the nature of technological infrastructure and urban management in coming years, they still rely on the patience of their shareholders to achieve this. As a result, they adopt a strategically narrow set of urbanised service areas for systematised analysis [...] (McNeill, 2015: 563)

So, the challenge was to gain access to information that could generate insights into how the firm was doing this. There were three main data sources that I drew upon. First, there was the need to account for the geographical spread of IBM. I wanted to understand how the Smarter Cities strategy was being tested out in different places at different times. To understand this, I looked closely at corporate press releases. In themselves, they would typically be understood within firms as being one-sided documents, carefully edited prior to release by the firm's corporate communications department. Yet taken together, they constituted a useful evidence base of what the company was doing in different places.

Second, there was the need to step through the fact that corporate strategy is only partially made available to the public, and this usually to allow the share market to get a sense of the future direction of the firm. However, IBM does have quite a strong public outreach, partly because it needs a diverse customer base to buy its products. So the papers drew from a range of outputs either on www.ibm.com or other platforms such as its YouTube Smarter Planet channel.[1] But I also went through a diverse set of outputs such as job recruitment boards (which show the areas in which the firm is recruiting), and relied on the important coverage given by the business press in diverse outlets.

Third, I also drew on transcripts of presentations given by IBM executives and senior managers on various public media outlets, which were often uploaded onto YouTube. Other biographies of IBM and its Chief Executive Officers were also examined (Garr, 1999;

(Continued)

Maney et al., 2011; Palmisano, 2006). Again, the use of corporate biographies and autobiographies in academic research requires a significant degree of critical analysis, yet this can be an important research technique in itself.

Finally, there were some serendipitous government inquiries which threw some light on how the firm organized. Although not directly engaged with Smarter Cities, the Queensland Health Payroll Inquiry Report (2013) provided a detailed, parliament-commissioned investigation of hitherto confidential negotiations and implementation of a major IBM government contract that had gone wrong. Such government inquiries are useful because they allow a degree of scrutiny that corporations otherwise can avoid: senior executives are often summoned to give evidence that provides data on operational and strategic questions that would otherwise remain hidden.

Taken together, my research argued that IBM's Smarter Cities campaign was initiated as an experimental market-testing moment in order to bring together the firm's existing strengths in national markets and hardware provision, with newer skills in data analytics and smart sensing. My argument was that IBM were deliberately 'reducing' the city to a narrow set of technocratic problems in order to achieve spatial economies of scale.

Tracking urban mobility: Uber (Andrea Pollio)

In August 2015, halfway through my PhD field research in Cape Town, I attended the South Africa Innovation Summit, the country's most important networking event on the state of the art of business, government and social innovation. In his introductory keynote, the head of the business school that co-hosted the event concluded the speech by telling the audience – as an example of how South African cities can be territories of innovation – that he had reached the conference venue thanks to Uber. 'Think of that', he said, 'they didn't have a product but just innovated a business model' (personal notes).

At that point, I had been using Uber, conducting interviews with Uber drivers and collecting various documents produced by the San Francisco based ride-sharing company, from tweets to public statements, for at least four months. The idea that Uber did not have a product but just an innovative business model struck me as very naïve. I had witnessed how the software informed the livelihoods of its drivers, but also how e-hailing (the act of calling an Uber driver) begat a product with its own aesthetic, original, material form: a user-friendly, flexible, market-elastic application to be downloaded from the App store or Google Play.

However, it was not only the existence of a tangible product that, in my own experience of Uber, made those remarks inaccurate. Uber did not just have a business model that was disrupting the taxi industry; it was also a global corporation with strategic divisions and local marketing teams, capable of creating the conditions for its e-hailing business model to work in very different cities across the world. In other words, Uber was an urban player that showed incredible market-making capacities for engineering the possibilities of profit in settings as different as San Francisco and Mumbai.

My attempts to research the local market-making strategies of Uber in Cape Town had posed a series of difficult research issues. And yet, this was interesting in itself: a study of the 'marketization' (Çalışkan and Callon, 2010) of e-hailing could shed significant insights on how Uber, as a global urban firm, had entered Cape Town through calculated, organized manoeuvres. The challenges were immediate. First, there was a problem of access to those that had put those manoeuvres in place: although Uber's founders and executives had been featured in various TV interviews and TED Talks, a version of what Erica Schoenberger (2001) analysed as 'corporate autobiographies', managers and strategists were out of reach. Even the local marketing team in Cape Town, despite my e-mails, turned down my meeting requests. A second problem was of materiality: how did these secretive, strategic marketing practices translate into actual, material features of the software? And how did the software, in turn, perform certain economic arrangements? A third and final issue concerned the temporalities associated with ever-changing business models and global firms: by the time I finished my fieldwork, Uber had introduced new software features that rendered some of the transactions that the drivers were using to create alternative forms of gains through e-hailing impossible.

To address these three issues, my response was determined both by the impossibility of 'corporate interviews' (Schoenberger, 1991) and by the possibility of extending ethnography beyond participation (Feldman, 2011; Tsing, 2015), to the software and to the various artefacts that 'marketizing' practices leave behind: ads, YouTube videos, tweets, blog posts. In my research, following these objects disclosed some of the strategies through which firms like Uber become city-shaping agents. For example, Uber's advertising videos in South Africa revealed how the

(Continued)

company used developmental narratives of entrepreneurial empowerment to present e-hailing as a mechanism for fighting unemployment, an alternative narrative to the various controversies in which the company was involved, especially concerning local regulatory frameworks. Uber's urban marketing campaigns, whose traces remain in the local Twitter feed, also showcased a strategic alignment to the 'worlding' practices (Ong, 2011) of Cape Town as a city becoming a global tourist destination (McDonald, 2008). The blog posts showed instead the political machinations of the company on the occasion of a taxi drivers' strike that took to the streets of the city to propose a ban on Uber. As a response, the firm launched a media campaign under the hashtag #CTneedsuber, which involved tweet-bombing the profiles of local authorities and an online petition accessible through various outlets. Collecting these – mainly digital – artefacts was my way of engaging with the strategic, often technically impenetrable, practices of a firm that was significantly changing the urban experience of mobility. Having this kind of pictorial record revealed to be crucial given that, over time, Uber deleted and reorganized some of their social media accounts in relation to regional changes in the managerial structure.

However, whilst posts and tweets were revealing proxies, the software itself had a specific materiality that deserved ethnographic attention. Having used the app, I was struck by how drivers related to the possibilities and the limits of their work, how their livelihoods became entrenched within the affordances of the software, and how diverse were the urban, often informal, economies built on its margins. Though I managed to interview some drivers in a traditional way, sitting at a table with a list of questions, it was through my direct engagement with the software that I gathered a better understanding of that diversity. Just as many drivers used Uber beyond its strict possibilities, I used the app as a tool of ethnographic enactment. My own transactions became a way of moving around the city, a way of recruiting informants, a way of tracking the diverse forms of economic exchange performed through the software, a way of 'revisiting' my findings (Burawoy, 2003), but also a way of navigating the material reach of the company's headquartered programming expertise. Once informed about my research, many drivers generously shared their stories. Others offered to keep driving me around until I had asked everything I wanted to know about Uber in Cape Town – at the price set by Uber itself. The richness of their insights showed me how the software had become a sometimes malleable, sometimes strict, device of their livelihoods, as well as how Uber had transformed urban mobility, while adapting to the local context.

However, the rapid changes of Uber's business strategy also posed challenging issues of temporality. A new software feature or product might render obsolete a year-long research into the ways in which technologies are manipulated at the interface with existing urban economies, as my research shows in the case of Uber (Pollio, forthcoming). Various anthropologists have pointed out this issue more generally: ethnography in unstable, rapidly changing contexts is a difficult business (Maurer, 2003). Whilst there are not easy solutions to the short-lived validity of what can be observed in the interaction of global firm products and local urban markets, tracking a rapidly growing global firm like Uber also illustrated some contours of transition of urban economies of Cape Town towards forms of ephemeral, on-demand labour amidst an already complex landscape of formal and informal markets.

Reflections on tracking global urbanists

In this chapter we have provided accounts of two influential technology firms, Uber and IBM, and their strategic attempts to significantly influence urban policy and markets in cities worldwide. Our approaches contrasted: the IBM study was an attempt to provide an interpretation of the firm-level decisions that steer the product development and market shaping strategies of very large firms. The Uber study was based on an 'on the ground' interpretation of how human subjects responded to the firm's arrival in Cape Town. But in both cases we had to consider different ways of 'figuring' the firm – perhaps as a remote or even vaguely mythical being, as Uber drivers often see their employer, or as a mighty, stodgy organizational machine, such as IBM, with its own internal cultural problems of innovation and product development and marketing. We have argued that a framing of the firm, and what we could call its 'spatial ontology', is thus an important element in explaining why global cities are constituted as they are (McNeill, 2017).

There are several reasons why tracking corporations as global urbanists is an important scholarly project, but here we prioritize two. First, it provides a stronger understanding of how the diverse processes of investment and disinvestment that structure the economic life of cities are being orchestrated. We have lightly suggested that a topological, rather than hierarchical or scalar, framework allows more space for the analysis of the calculative and performative practices that drive capital accumulation at all levels, from household to global firm. This has a very direct material impact on how urban space is configured and engineered (McNeill, 2017). An important element to consider here is how to work with different approaches to conceptualizing distance and size. Global city theories have tended to polarize around actor network approaches which emphasize practices and networks, and scalar approaches which tend to be more interested in hierarchy (McNeill, 2017).

Second, only by close tracking can we detect how firms may change strategies to remain competitive, which in turn will have many implications for spatial economic analysis. As Hendrikse and Sidaway (2014) reflect in their study of the impact of financialization on a German municipality, the once conservative financial practices of the national Deutsche Bank shifted rapidly during the 1990s and 2000s as the firm adopted global parameters for its investment strategies. Or as Muellerleile (2009) demonstrates in his analysis of Boeing's headquarter relocation from Seattle to Chicago in the early 2000s, the corporate culture and organizational capacity of firms is strongly influenced by place. Our case studies also accidentally speak to Saxenian's (1996) famous study of the contrasting cultures of West Coast and East Coast US corporations: the extremely 'lean' Uber, a Silicon Valley company, is an interesting contrast with IBM, headquartered in ostensibly 'conservative' upstate New York. The need to understand the 'firm–territory nexus', a concept developed by Dicken and Malmberg (2001), has arguably become even more important in an age of digital platforms. Standard practices of global firms play out in very different ways in different national and local sites, and over different time horizons. However, even in the context of Uber's decentralized managerial practices, local teams that replicate the executive structure of the core leadership of the organization are still hard to get hold of. Besides, Uber is constantly changing and experimenting with its organizational structure, adding and removing managerial layers at different geographical scales: since the end of the research described in this chapter, the company has entirely reshuffled the executive architecture and reporting lines that connect the global headquarters with its local teams (adding, in the case of Cape Town, a regional operational structure).

What both researches into IBM and Uber suggest is that one way of overcoming the obstacles in understanding the market-making schemes of global firms is to imitate their tentative, distanced and experimental urban tactics, as well as the localized transactions that generate their profits. It is still challenging to show how global firms connect with the everyday products or financial structures of the city: it is usually only through painstaking forensic or ethnographic research that these spatial ontologies can be revealed. However, when this is done, a significant insight into the constitution of the contemporary global urban condition can be gained.

Note

1. www.youtube.com/playlist?list=PL967B46DC541A923A

References

Amin, A. and Cohendet, P. (2004) *Architectures of Knowledge: Firms, Capabilities, and Communities*. Oxford: Oxford University Press.

Boussebaa, M., Morgan, G. and Sturdy, A. (2012) 'Constructing global firms? National, transnational and neocolonial effects in international management consultancies', *Organization Studies*, 33(4): 465–86.

Burawoy, M. (2003) 'Revisits: An outline of a theory of reflexive ethnography', *American Sociological Review*, 68(5): 645–79.

Çalışkan, K. and Callon, M. (2010) 'Economization, part 2: A research programme for the study of markets', *Economy and Society*, 39(1): 1–32.

Callon, M. (2007) 'What does it mean to say that economics is performative?' in D. MacKenzie, F. Muniesa and L. Siu (eds), *Do Economists Make Markets? On the Performativity of Economics*. Princeton, NJ: Princeton University Press, pp. 311–57.

Callon, M. and Latour, B. (1981) 'Unscrewing the big Leviathan: How actors macro-structure reality and how sociologists help them do so', in K. Knorr-Cetina and A.V. Cicourel (eds), *Advances in Social Theory and Methodology: Toward an Integration of Micro- and Macro-Sociologies*. London: Routledge & Kegan Paul, pp. 277–303.

Dicken, P. and Malmberg, A. (2001) 'Firms in territories: A relational perspective' *Economic Geography*, 77(4): 345–63.

Feldman, G. (2011) 'If ethnography is more than participant-observation, then relations are more than connections: The case for nonlocal ethnography in a world of apparatuses', *Anthropological Theory*, 11(4): 375–95.

Fortune (2013) 'Travis Kalanick CEO of Uber Technologies Speaks at Brainstorm Tech 2013'. www.youtube.com/watch?v=vGbuitwkZiM (accessed 18 September 2017).

Friedmann, J. (1986) 'The world city hypothesis', *Development and Change*, 17(1): 69–83.

Garr, D. (1999) *IBM Redux: Lou Gerstner and the Business Turnaround of the Decade*. New York: HarperCollins.

Hendrikse, R.P. and Sidaway, J.D. (2014) 'Financial wizardry and the Golden City: Tracking the financial crisis through Pforzheim, Germany', *Transactions of the Institute of British Geographers*, 39(2): 195–208.

Kitchin, R. (2015) 'Making sense of smart cities: Addressing present shortcomings', *Cambridge Journal of Regions, Economy and Society*, 8(1): 131–6.

Larkin, B. (2013) 'The politics and poetics of infrastructure', *Annual Review of Anthropology*, 42: 327–43.

Leigh Star, S. (1999) 'The ethnography of infrastructure', *American Behavioral Scientist*, 43(3): 377–91.

(Continued)

Luque-Ayala, A. and Marvin, S. (2016) 'The maintenance of urban circulation: An operational logic of infrastructural control', *Environment and Planning D: Society and Space*, 34(2): 191–208.

Maney, K., Hamm, S. and O'Brien, J.M. (2011) *Making the World Work Better: The Ideas That Shaped a Century and a Company*. Upper Saddle River, NJ: IBM Press-Pearson.

Maurer, B. (2003) 'Please destabilize ethnography now: Against anthropological showbiz-as-usual', *Reviews in Anthropology*, 32(2): 159–69.

McCann, E. and Ward, K. (eds) (2011) *Mobile Urbanism: Cities and Policymaking in the Global Age*. Minneapolis, MN: University of Minnesota Press.

McDonald, D.A. (2008) *World City Syndrome: Neoliberalism and Inequality in Cape Town*. New York: Routledge.

McNeill, D. (2015) 'Global firms and smart technologies: IBM and the reduction of cities', *Transactions of the Institute of British Geographers*, 40(4): 562–74.

McNeill, D. (2016) 'IBM and the visual formation of smart cities', in S. Marvin, A. Luque-Ayala and C. McFarlane (eds), *Smart Cities: Utopian Vision or False Dawn?* London: Routledge, pp. 34–51.

McNeill, D. (2017) *Global Cities and Urban Theory*. London: Sage.

Muellerleile, C.M. (2009) 'Financialization takes off at Boeing', *Journal of Economic Geography*, 9(5): 663–77.

Ong, A. (2011) 'Introduction: Worlding cities, or the art of being global', in A. Roy and A. Ong (eds), *Worlding Cities: Asian Experiments and the Art of Being Global*. Chichester: Wiley-Blackwell, pp. 1–26.

Palmisano, S.J. (2006) 'The globally integrated enterprise', *Foreign Affairs*, 85(3): 127–36.

Peck, J. (2016) 'Economic rationality meets celebrity urbanology: Exploring Edward Glaeser's city', *International Journal of Urban and Regional Research*, 40(1): 1–30.

Pollio, A. (forthcoming) 'Forefronts of the sharing economy: Uber in Cape Town', Unpublished manuscript.

Queensland Health Payroll System Commission of Inquiry (2013) Report Published 31 July by The Honourable Richard N. Chesterman. www.healthpayrollinquiry.qld.gov.au (accessed 18 September 2017).

Roush, C. (2011) *Show Me the Money: Writing Business and Economics Stories for Mass Communication* (2nd edition). London: Routledge.

Sassen, S. (1991) *The Global City: New York, London, Tokyo*. Princeton, NJ: Princeton University Press.

Saxenian, A. (1996) *Regional Advantage: Culture and Competition in Silicon Valley and Route 128*. Cambridge, MA: Harvard University Press.

Schoenberger, E. (1991) 'The corporate interview as a research method in economic geography', *The Professional Geographer*, 43(2): 180–9.

Schoenberger, E. (2001) 'Corporate autobiographies: the narrative strategies of corporate strategists', *Journal of Economic Geography*, 1(3): 277–98.

Temenos, C. and Ward, K. (2018) 'Examining global urban policy mobilities', in J. Harrison and M. Hoyler (eds), *Doing Global Urban Research*. London: Sage, pp. 66–80.

Tsing, A.L. (2015) *The Mushroom at the End of the World: On the Possibility of Life in Capitalist Ruins*. Princeton, NJ: Princeton University Press.

7

ENGAGING WITH GLOBAL URBAN GOVERNANCE

Michele Acuto

Why study global urban governance?

Today cities are increasingly on the world stage. On 14 October 2016 over 800 city leaders gathered in Bogotá for the Second World Assembly of Local and Regional Governments[1] to agree three key messages: (i) local democracy, decentralization and a stronger urban governance are key to answer the needs of an increasingly urbanized world; (ii) the United Nation's New Urban Agenda will be instrumental to achieving the 2030 Agenda of the Sustainable Development Goals (SDG), including the COP21 Paris Climate Agreement; and (iii) local and regional governments will need a seat at the global table if a sustainable future guided by the demand of the communities is to be achieved (UCLG, 2016a). Two days later, on 16 October 2016, the United Nations issued its New Urban Agenda (NUA) at the Habitat III Conference in Quito, with recommendations to guide urban development policy across the world for the coming decades (UN-Habitat, 2016). The latter built on an analogous meeting of over 500 mayors at the Habitat II Conference in Istanbul some twenty years before, and mirrors similar efforts to tackle global challenges through urban governance: for example, the global summit of local leaders which was integral to the Paris Climate Agreement achieved in December 2015.

The significance of these meetings and agreements is the increasing importance of urban policymakers on the world stage, something which is reflected in the rise of what we have come to know as global urban governance. The 2016 statement issued in Quito – calling upon the *international* community of multilateral officials and state negotiators to 'embark on a new era of partnership in global governance' which should begin by renewing 'the relationship between local and regional governments and the UN to include the structural consultation of our constituency' (UCLG, 2016b: np) – points towards new forms of *global* urban governance. In this chapter, I argue that events such as those that took place in Quito and Paris are putting cities in the spotlight of global, not just national and local, politics. But what does this mean for *doing* global urban research? More specifically, what opportunities and challenges does it present for taking global urban politics seriously, and for urban scholars interested in researching the sensibility of such approaches?

These are important questions, both intellectually and practically. Jennifer Robinson (2016), among others, has repeatedly called for a more 'global' urban research. 'Global' is interpreted here as inclusive, post divisions such as North/South and cities as globalized/ordinary. But this spirit of inclusiveness could – and as I argue in this chapter *should* – be taken further: global urban research needs a more disciplinarily inclusive scholarship that puts the social and political sciences into ever greater dialogue with the physical and natural sciences; equally, global urban research would benefit from taking the students and practitioners of the 'global' more seriously when it comes to understanding urban governance.

So why should we 'do' global urban governance research? There are twin policy and interdisciplinary reasons for this. On the one hand, we are faced with a mounting number of multilateral processes that are progressively highlighting the centrality of cities. As the UN Sustainable Development Goals now outline, cities are key to harnessing the 'transformative forces of urbanization' (UN-Habitat, 2016: 24-5) for achieving a better global future. Likewise, after the Habitat III Conference in Quito, the UN's New Urban Agenda aims to inspire nations, cities and towns to pursue sustainable urban development. This focus by the UN on cities reinforces recent wider multilateral attention to cities through inter alia the Sendai Framework for Disaster Risk Reduction, the 2030 Agenda of the SDGs, the Addis Ababa Action Agenda on financing sustainable development, and the COP21 Paris Climate Agreement (which included a call for a city emphasis by the Intergovernmental Panel on Climate Change (IPCC)). In short, urban scholars and practitioners need to come to terms with the fact that cities are now deeply intertwined with global policymaking processes, but conversely this also means that cities (and their students) have a unique possibility to link local affairs to cross-boundary multilateral processes.

As we have been arguing elsewhere (Acuto and Parnell, 2016), now is a fundamental moment to effectively 'globalize' urban research: to connect scholarship and practice of urban governance to global sensibilities. Indeed, in the few months prior to the Habitat III Conference scholars of different academic background but of similar global sensibility were challenged to think through the role of science and the academe in the implementation of the UN's New Urban Agenda. These scholars publicly advocated the need to reform global urban research in line with shifting policy agendas and institutional structures 'out there' in the global governance sphere (Acuto, 2016; McPhearson et al., 2016). As we noted then, now is the time to forge effective science–policy collaborations as a backbone of effective efforts towards sustainable urban development. These connections can no longer be postponed or sidelined. The SDGs, Paris Climate Agreement, Addis Ababa Action Agenda on financing sustainable development, and Sendai Framework for Disaster Risk Reduction all contributed to putting cities in the spotlight, but the post-Habitat III landscape will see critical steps where the input of expert urban knowledge will be fundamental to the future of the urban age.

As I write, 2017 is a year of change for the UN system with the election of a new secretary-general (likely to pay a keen eye on disasters and cities), who has also been tasked with reviewing the scope and mandate of UN-Habitat (by September 2017), and deciding on its future a year later (by September 2018). The latter has been undergoing a critical review from its Governing Council (in April 2017) as its executive director is set to be stepping down, just when the world will witness a key High Level Political Forum (HLPF) in New York in July 2017. Looking further ahead, the UN system will take critical stock of the progress of the New Urban Agenda in 2018, starting with the World Urban Forum in Kuala Lumpur (February 2018), an IPCC conference centred on cities and the 1.5° challenge (April 2018) and the first HLPF thematic review of SDG11 (July 2018). All of these – and any future – processes inevitably require expert analyses, in-depth reviews and efforts to take stock of how the world is performing in terms of sustainable urban development. Yet they will also require urban scholars to appreciate the intricacies of the UN, World Bank, EU and other multilateral fora (such as the World Economic Forum or the Sendai Framework for Disaster Risk Reduction), as well as take urban matters as planetary matters – thinking of the wider international implications of doing urban research.

Challenges of researching global urban governance

There is no doubt that the global urban agenda is busy and of critical, *international*, importance. Here a clear sensitivity of the global political forces and logics in play is fundamental to researching global urban governance, but it is equally important to ensuring that urban research remains relevant to the powers and processes at play. For instance, it is critical to acknowledge that the role of states and the boundaries of the Westphalian system (fundamental to international relations (IR) theory but less so urban theory) are still the dominant game in town when it comes to global urban governance. States and international forces (business in primis) are central actors which today's urban research, whether focused on local case studies or wider urban(ization) processes, must account for. Equally, the role of *international* urban policymaking, as with the role of Habitat III and SDG negotiations, is central to understanding more-than-local urban policy initiatives such as city networks like C40 or the World Assembly of Local and Regional Governments.

Urban scholars are rarely conversant with what are often perceived as tedious and trivial politics of international institutions. And herein lies the opportunity and the challenge for urban researchers: the opportunity is recognizing that urban expertise is critical for these international frameworks, but the challenge is that it is equally critical for urban researchers to offer cities research that is conversant with the global nature of these processes. This is because little is generally published in the field of urban studies that (explicitly) addresses the world politics of cities. Moreover, United Nations policymaking, processes and law, as well as discussions of 'international organization' (structures, legal frames and politics of international relations), are rarely discussed in urban studies research or teaching. My argument here is that this is not just a call for more serious attention to global urban policy and politics by urban studies researchers, but that this is a challenge which goes beyond urban studies (narrowly defined) and presents the need to redefine urban studies as an (even-more) interdisciplinary field of research.

In addition, urban research needs to take into account that global urban governance is a realm where urban and policy considerations are inextricably intertwined with more popular and market-driven narratives. A key challenge is the growing market and general public embeddedness of scholarly research and other forms of expert urban knowledge that are now very commonly available to practitioners in cities the world over. We cannot forget the important role played by both civil society non-governmental organizations (NGOs) and, even more critically but widely under-acknowledged, philanthropic organizations in sustaining the global diplomatic efforts of cities. The importance of this can be illustrated most clearly by the two urban philanthropy 'giants' which have become key actors in climate action following the success of the C40 Climate Leadership Group: these are the Clinton Foundation (one of the first core sponsors of C40) and Bloomberg Philanthropies (representing much of the legacy of former New York City mayor and C40 Chair Michael Bloomberg). Alongside the Clinton Foundation and Bloomberg Philanthropies we also see Global North sponsors such as Realdania and the Children's Fund playing important roles in the continuation and effectiveness of the C40 Group.

Philanthropies have also spurred initiatives for city networking and capacity building for climate resilience, for example The Rockefeller Foundation's 100 Resilient Cities initiative. These investments lend further legitimacy to the international diplomatic role of cities. They also testify to the belief of the market and the major neoliberal forces at play in global environmental governance that cities are not a transient fad but a long-term investment worth making.

On this, sociology and science and technology studies have been developing a sound understanding of the impact of philanthropy on tackling global (urban) challenges (McGoey, 2015). Likewise, international relations (IR) has become well attuned to these and other donor politics (Whitfield, 2009). My point here is not to say that IR holds the silver bullet to all the global problems of urban studies (quite the opposite, in fact): a 'global' political sensibility can be found in disciplines other than international studies which points towards my call for more interdisciplinary approaches to *doing* global urban studies.

Perhaps less embedded in steering (and for many, worryingly so) the direction of city diplomacy is the whole genus of civil society NGOs campaigning for a variety of social, environmental and spatial (for example North–South) rebalancing agendas. One such example is the collaboration between the ICLEI Local Government for Sustainability network and international NGO groups such as the Global Planners Network; or the broader collaboration between the Cities Alliance, Habitat for Humanity and Slum/Shack Dwellers International, which has a clear Global South rebalancing agenda.

Nevertheless, it is the commercial and business sector which has the biggest impact on the direction and effectiveness of city networking today. The private sector has been key to the growth of city diplomacy, and the extension of city-to-city cooperation beyond twinning into the realm of experimentation with climate mitigation and adaptation strategies. Indeed, the deep engagement of the private sector, industry, corporations, alongside not-for-profit NGOs, in urban action at a transnational and international scale makes it even more complex to assess the patterns of city actions in environmental politics. Yet the widespread fascination and increasing commitment of large multinational companies, philanthropies and global firms is undeniable evidence of the influence of cities onto the direction of global climate action, and of the fact that, after all, no truly *global* action might be possible without cities.

An additional challenge this presents is the 'depth' of global governance. Once again, we should not discount some pre-existent experiments in globalizing urban governance considerations. Studies of the city, as with Robinson's (2011) call for 'comparative gestures' as much as in McCann and Ward's (2011) well-developed work on 'policy mobilities' (Temenos and Ward, Chapter 5), do have a sense of cross-boundary interactions in theoretical and actual policy terms. Equally, as with Brenner and Schmid's (2015) 'planetary urbanization' discussion, urban studies does have some tested ground on the materiality of transnational urban processes and their 'global' implications (Katsikis, Chapter 2). Lastly, and mostly confined to the environmental domain, there is also a tradition of geographical/geopolitical work that has looked at the multiscalar connections between different layers of governance superimposed on cities, and the possibilities of cities as political actors to connect with each other (for example Bulkeley's (2005) work on city networking).

Techniques for researching global urban governance

If IR theory is principally concerned with the dynamics of power that underpins international (and more broadly 'world') politics, what does the city and the 'urban' have to do with it? A critical risk is to take IR as a study of everything global and big. We must also be wary of the possibility of global urban governance research becoming too 'global'. International theorists and commentators nowadays are quite accustomed to, as Charles Tilly (1989) put it in a landmark text for political science, 'big structures, large processes, huge comparisons'. Yet, attention to the inherent complexity of these large phenomena is often lacking in this 'big picture' mentality. This naivety of large numbers provides comfort for the grand assumptions of state diplomats and for the generalizations of international relations, but frequently become the object of discussions rather than the starting point for more nuanced analyses. So is there a way forward?

A serious IR look at cities can respond to current critiques in IR on the state and relative disarray of global governance research and redress these biases. Thomas G. Weiss and Rorden Wilkinson argued provocatively, 'IR teeters on the edge of an abyss' (Weiss and Wilkinson, 2014: 20) as the field's theoretical and methodological precariousness, along with its sectarian fragmentation, has pushed international theory close to self-absorbed irrelevance. This provocation is ripe for engagement and interdisciplinary (but grounded) encounters – akin to those with the city and its students – to 'rescue' IR.

As I have argued elsewhere with my colleague Max Mayer (Mayer and Acuto, 2015), a field of study that holds much promise as a common ground between IR theory and other forms of theorizing geography, planning or science studies is that of the geopolitics of 'large technical systems' (LTS). Our approach is to offer a new materialist contribution to the study of global governance (Connolly, 2013). In this we mirror much of the current 'turn' that part of IR has undergone by being infused with 'new materialist' sensibilities that have inspired experimentation with methods, ontologies and theoretical assumptions derived from Science and Technology Studies (Acuto and Curtis, 2014). Techniques in the new materialist current are often centred on object-oriented analysis (Salter, 2015) that takes a specific location/material/place to unpack the global complexities of IR, or more traditional ethnographic, and similar qualitative efforts. Equally, numerous efforts have taken an 'assemblage' approach much similar to that of urban studies, which – paying attention to the underlying materiality of politics and taking a more explicit appreciation of the assembled complexity of reality – might offer important touch points with urban research in other disciplines (Acuto and Curtis, 2014; Farías and Bender, 2010). This 'new materialist' angle, mostly preoccupied with recovering the 'missing masses' (Latour, 1992) that constitute the material world in which international relations take place, has to date still struggled with empirical (methodological rather than ontological) development.

Conscious of this turn but also its current methodological limitations, Mayer and I argue that integrating more systematic considerations of LTS at the heart of pressing global governance challenges – whether in the shape of multilateral cooperation, pandemic response, information security or human security – can help revitalize and re-open systemic transition questions to a truly cohesive debate on international stability. LTS can, we suggest, take the debates on the status of the international system 'deeper' into global governance. New materialist studies of IR themes have a proven track record of being able to illustrate the depth and localized dimensions of international processes. For instance, depicting the multi-scalar complexity of conflict networks, Nick Srnicek (2010) argues that actor-network theory (ANT) is capable of avoiding the reduction of conflict down to greed, grievance or ancient hatred; rather he argues that they can be (or need to be) examined in their contingent assemblage of local, material and global actors.

This is a two-way benefit for IR and urban studies. As we discussed, an inquiry into the most urbanized LTS can reinforce the appreciation of the 'everyday' dimension of international politics (Mayer and Acuto, 2015). So whilst the international allows an appreciation of the global dimension of urban governance, the city can conversely ground global governance. There are, for example, immediate physical, legal and political relations between garbage collection in major global cities and the planetary political economy of recycling, which are intertwined in physical systems of maritime transportation, ethereal economic and financial linkages, and global corporate machineries deployed by 'waste giants' such as Veolia and SembCorp (Moore, 2011). The enormous intricacy and fragility of management of global waste assemblages, on which the daily functioning of metropolises and urban areas critically depends, regularly intersects with the grand dynamics and material complexities of international relations processes and international law agreements (such as the 1991 Bamako Convention or the 1989 Basel Convention) which demand a better familiarity with global governance amidst the students of the city. This is a more grounded and materialist approach than most of the (limited) scholarship that has dealt with cities in IR, generally through a discussion of city networks (Betsill and Bulkeley, 2006; Bouteligier, 2013) – something I illustrate more extensively in the case study section below.

Critically, I would argue, an urban perspective on world politics, and vice-versa a global politics sensibility to urban studies, offers a critical connection between global processes and the way they 'hit the ground' in cities worldwide. In this sense, the popularity of mayors should not overshadow how city leaders have an important role in representing local interests in international processes (Amen et al., 2011; Gordon, 2016), with the aim of contributing to responsible global actions that are cognisant of everyday issues and the local impact of global processes. Even more critically, and as my colleague Simon Curtis (2011, 2016a) has also long acknowledged, urban politics and its leaders are a critical medium for the localized realities of cities, and the interconnected processes of global city making, to link into the dynamics and institutions of international politics and global order. If we pay closer attention (materially but also politically) to the intersection of urban politics, global governance and global city connections, as Curtis notes (2016b: 455), we can recognize how cities have taken on new governance roles in 'the gaps left by hamstrung nation-states', and how their contribution to an emerging global governance architecture will be 'a significant feature of the international relations of the 21st century'.

Hence if more popular literature on cities and international affairs (for example Barber, 2013) tends to remain focused on the messianic statements on mayors as global leaders, there might be even more effective work to be done in an honestly international (seriously IR-oriented) but still grounded global urban research. This means relating the discussions of city networking, now well rehearsed in IR (Acuto and Rayner, 2016; Lee, 2013), to urban politics and urban processes more clearly, as well as acknowledging the underlying materiality of these politics, without losing sight of the important 'international' view IR offers on politics even in a time of globalized urbanization. So how could this be done in practice? Drawing from my own experience in the 'autobiographical' spirit of this volume, let me offer one example of IR research already gesturing towards the usefulness of global politics to urban studies, as a case study of current urban studies work navigating in between these two disciplines.

Case study of researching global urban governance

Work on city networking has the potential to go beyond discussions of policy mobility or planetary urbanization; to recognize cities as agents not just as places in the dynamics of global governance. This is partly the objective of a research initiative I have been involved in at the UCL City Leadership Lab. This initiative started as an IR inquiry into the role of cities in global governance (Acuto, 2013) but quickly moved onto an analysis of the urban implications of this participation (Acuto and Rayner, 2016) via a collaboration with the 'field' itself in the shape of a partnership with the World Health Organization (Acuto et al., 2016) and through engagement with key multilateral processes (Acuto, 2016) aimed at shaping the urban agendas of states and the UN. Here the principal aim was to think through what global urban research on 'city diplomacy' might look like in the 21st century.

Our study, perhaps the first non-topical and systematic assessment of the panorama of city networking globally, gathered a comprehensive

(Continued)

database of 200 city networks from all over the world (Acuto et al., 2017). Constructed between 2015 and 2017, the database came to represent the range of formal organizations of cities in national and international affairs. While of course not exhaustive, as the overall number of city networks might be higher, this initial look into the formal structures of city diplomacy tells us much about how cities engage externally.

So what form do city networks take globally? National, state-based organizations (such as the US Conference of Mayors) are still dominant, representing 49% of city networks. Having said that, regional networks (for example Eurocities) and international networks (for example United Cities and Local Governments, UCLG) are on the rise – accounting for 21% and 29% respectively. Despite the success of networks such as the C40 Climate Leadership Group or ICLEI, environment is less than one-third of city diplomacy initiatives globally (29%). Themes such as culture (11%), poverty (16%) and gender (8%) represent important foci too.

Central then is the role of cities in progressively setting (at least part of) the agendas of multilateral politics, and in influencing the ways in which UN-like processes take place today. This, in practice, flags important issues about the impact of city networking on global policy. The continuing predominance of nationally scaled city networks reflects how, even in an age of global governance fragmentation and non-state-centric discussions on world politics, cities still relate substantially to their national peers and central governments. In short, national politics still matter for cities – a greater sensibility for the 'global' in urban research should not forget these fundamental units of the Westphalian international system.

Membership is perhaps the most widely varying characteristic of city networks, and one that invites methodological caution. The size of these organizations, as noted above, ranges from small selected pools of cities (as with the Cisco-sponsored City Protocol on smart cities), to larger international and regional networks – such as the Arab Town Organization (22 countries) or the European Forum on Urban Security (250 European cities) – to even wider national groups reaching up to 20,000 members nationally (as in the United States or India). This variety is clearly institutionalized in urban policy. Over 58% of city networks in our database are between 10 and 30 years old, mapping onto the broader proliferation of transnational initiatives that has taken place within global governance since the late 1970s. When considering the emergence of city networks over the last century, and attempting to identify the 'birth dates' of existing initiatives, a marked growth can be detected over the last two decades: about 60 of the 200 networks under consideration in this study were in place by 1985. This number had nearly doubled by the late 1990s and appears to be growing still. This is because city networking is certainly a meaningful activity beyond branding and advocacy.

The results of all of this city diplomacy do not end with its very visible imagery of mayors, public speeches and international events such as Habitat III. There is a conspicuous 'experimental' activity of joint initiatives, for example to curb greenhouse gas emissions or encourage participatory planning. City networks produce regular reports (in 45% of cases), joint pilots and policies (38%) and information exchanges (37% issuing newsletters, 9% publishing magazines or journals, and 24% maintaining blogs, social media accounts or online noticeboards) linking cities and spreading information. It would be profoundly misleading to represent them, and the broader enterprise of city diplomacy, as expressed solely through the conferences reported in news magazines and blogs.

City networks push beyond local govern*ment* politics into highly complex 'hybrid' (public-private) govern*ance* arrangements, and also into innovative modes of cooperation between cities as subnational actors. Our study revealed that, while just over half (54%) of the networks are still single-tiered, that is centred on a single secretariat leading the whole organization, a substantial proportion (30%) operate in two-tiered (with sub-networks) or even pluralized (16%) forms of networked governance. Besides, while city-led initiatives lay behind the majority (58%), NGO-led efforts, mostly prompted by the private sector, account for a considerable 19% of the total, only just behind efforts led by intergovernmental organizations such as UN agencies (23%). The emergence of city networks of this type highlights the increasing role of private actors in city diplomacy. This inevitably raises questions about private interests, but also about the sustainability of so many networked initiatives in a time of resource-strapped local governments. Moreover, and consequently, it might take us back to the challenge of the global politics of LTS that are increasingly urban and urbanized; thus pushing for the students of city diplomacy to not forget the very tangible and applied nature of cities as material entities. Global does not mean fuzzy and intangible, but rather implies wider, and yet still fundamentally political, sensibilities towards urban policy.

Reflections on researching global urban governance

The Habitat III Conference catalysed the world's attention to cities as the places where a global agenda for sustainable development can start. Cities and the many city networks discussed above, notably C40 Cities and UCLG, were firmly on the front stage, with visible performances, commitments and interventions. This tells us that cities are not just an increasingly critical context for an urbanizing 21st century. They can be effective actors, taking part in the dynamics of global governance. Yet doing global urban governance research means taking the cross-scalar political implications of such governance seriously beyond its face value. These considerations are central because global urban research needs to go beyond the attractiveness of the 'pomp and circumstance', 'lists of accomplishment and promises' of mayoral statements and international city leaders summits 'basking in the spotlight' (Weiss, 2015). Whilst some more sensationalist writing on cities has recently argued for mayors to 'rule the world' (Barber, 2013), there is much more that we can learn from the networked (materially and politically) nature of city diplomacy. We need to step beyond the often simplistic arguments in these 'manifestoes' and push for a global urban research that is solidly rooted in evidence-based statements (beyond mayoral profiles, appreciating global trends and political geographies), whilst not losing sight of the centrality of sound-but-readable academic input into the processes of global politics, from the UN to national foreign policy.

While city summits are now a popular facet of the annual climate action calendar, and mayors are increasingly the go-to keynote speakers at events across the whole global governance agenda (Bloomberg, 2015), the most extensive impacts of city networking – and arguably the most promising ground for interdisciplinary global urban governance research – could come from a number of other effects of 'city diplomacy'.

First, technical cooperation between municipal officers, as much as between cities and industry, is of prime importance in shaping the application and innovation of carbon reduction technologies and climate adaptation schemes. Second, policy coordination and exchange amidst cities participating in these networks is essential to the circulation of innovative models and ideas on how to best cope with or mitigate, global challenges such as human security, disaster preparedness and climate change. Innovation, in this sense, has important structural echoes on the governance of cities around the planet. Third, the possibility for building new models of urban governance (as with the Chief Resiliency Officer program of the Rockefeller 100 Cities) offered by these networks, at relatively low additional costs, could enhance the cosmopolitan character of collective global action by cities and strengthen its collaborative nature. Connecting cities means connecting urban governance structures, policies and possibilities. Fourth, a still widely untapped potential is that of higher education and university research institutions present in cities (Addie, 2017). Universities, not just in the Global North, but increasingly in emerging economies and developing countries, are a phenomenal reservoir of expertise. Here city networks could have an even more pervasive impact by linking both the scientific community engaged in global action as well as the more technical community engaged in civil engineering, planning and architectural responses to environmental depletion, with practical application in urban public policy.

Therefore, the capacity of cities to adapt and shift their policy implementation processes and institutions by virtue of being linked to other cities beyond their own national confines is key, and scholars in urban studies should appreciate this systematically by embracing 'other' sensibilities towards world politics.

Overall, research in global urban governance needs to appreciate the 'glocal' bridges these processes are creating. Luckily this is not a *tabula rasa* scenario. There is now a well-established, and some would argue flourishing, interest in the global politics of cities, with a solid 'new materialist' ground where to develop an IR appreciation of the world politics of planetary urbanization, but also 'hybrid' IR–urban studies research (such as that on city networks above) that already intersects the two sensibilities. Hence, if in international law, studies of cities remain a niche, the fields of politics and international relations have progressively embraced what I would argue is a promising interest in urban issues. This, as I highlighted, is also a question of engaging urban scholars beyond the comfortable realm(s) of social sciences, and more explicitly within so-called STEM (Science, Technology, Engineering and Mathematics) disciplines. Engineers, scientists and built environment professionals might in fact have quite a bit to say, and offer, for the translation of 'big' political questions into practical 'urban' matters. Equally, it is a question of tackling themes that can inform international relations practice, not just theory, providing evidence of the international dimensions of urban policy. This is, then, ultimately, a focus towards an applied global urban (governance) research.

Note

1. The World Assembly is the mechanism through which the local and regional government constituency of UCLG (The Global Network of Cities, Local and Regional Governments) made its official inputs to the New Urban Agenda adopted at the Habitat III Conference in October 2016.

References

Acuto, M. (2013) 'City leadership in global governance', *Global Governance: A Review of Multilateralism and International Organizations*, 19(3): 481–98.

Acuto, M. (2016) 'Give cities a seat at the top table', *Nature*, 537(7622): 611–13.

Acuto, M. and Curtis, S. (2014) 'Assemblage thinking and international relations', in M. Acuto and S. Curtis (eds), *Reassembling International Theory: Assemblage Thinking and International Relations*. Basingstoke: Palgrave Macmillan, pp. 1–15.

Acuto, M. and Parnell, S. (2016) 'Leave no city behind', *Science*, 352(6288): 873.

(Continued)

Acuto, M. and Rayner, S. (2016) 'City networks: Breaking gridlocks or forging (new) lock-ins?', *International Affairs*, 92(5): 1147–66.

Acuto, M., Morissette, M. and Tsouros, A. (2016) 'City diplomacy: Towards more strategic networking? Learning with WHO Healthy Cities', *Global Policy*, 8(1): 14–22.

Acuto, M., Decramer, H., Morissette, M., Doughty, J. and Ying, Y.Y. (2017) *City Networking: New Frontiers for City Leaders*. UCL City Leadership Lab Research Report. London: University College London.

Addie, J.-P.D. (2017) 'From the urban university to universities in urban society', *Regional Studies*, 51(7): 1089–99.

Amen, M., Toly, N.J., McCarney, P.L. and Segbers, K. (2011) *Cities and Global Governance: New Sites for International Relations*. Farnham: Ashgate.

Barber, B.R. (2013) *If Mayors Ruled the World*. New Haven, CT: Yale University Press.

Betsill, M.M. and Bulkeley, H. (2006) 'Cities and the multilevel governance of global climate change', *Global Governance: A Review of Multilateralism and International Organizations*, 12(2): 141–59.

Bloomberg, M. (2015) 'City century: Why municipalities are the key to fighting climate change', *Foreign Affairs*, 94(1): 116–22.

Bouteligier, S. (2013) *Cities, Networks, and Global Environmental Governance*. Abingdon: Routledge.

Brenner, N. and Schmid, C. (2015) 'Towards a new epistemology of the urban?', *City*, 19(2–3): 151–82.

Bulkeley, H. (2005) 'Reconfiguring environmental governance: Towards a politics of scales and networks', *Political Geography*, 24(8): 875–902.

Connolly, W.E. (2013) 'The "new materialism" and the fragility of things', *Millennium: Journal of International Studies*, 41(3): 399–412.

Curtis, S. (2011) 'Global cities and the transformation of the International System', *Review of International Studies*, 37(4): 1923–47.

Curtis, S. (2016a) *Global Cities and Global Order*. Oxford: Oxford University Press.

Curtis, S. (2016b) 'Cities and global governance: State failure or a new global order?', *Millennium: Journal of International Studies*, 44(3): 455–77.

Farías, I. and Bender, T. (eds) (2010) *Urban Assemblages: How Actor-Network Theory Changes Urban Studies*. Abingdon: Routledge.

Gordon, D.J. (2016) 'The politics of accountability in networked urban climate governance', *Global Environmental Politics*, 16(2): 82–100.

Katsikis, N. (2018) 'Visualizing the planetary urban', in J. Harrison and M. Hoyler (eds), *Doing Global Urban Research*. London: Sage, pp. 12–33.

Latour, B. (1992) 'Where are the missing masses? The sociology of a few mundane artifacts', in W.E. Bijker and J. Law (eds), *Shaping Technology/Building Society: Studies in Sociotechnical Change*. Cambridge, MA: MIT Press, pp. 225–58.

Lee, T. (2013) 'Global cities and transnational climate change networks', *Global Environmental Politics*, 13(1): 108–27.

Mayer, M. and Acuto, M. (2015) 'The global governance of large technical systems', *Millennium: Journal of International Studies*, 43(2): 660–83.

McCann, E. and Ward, K. (eds) (2011) *Mobile Urbanism: Cities and Policymaking in the Global Age*. Minneapolis, MN: University of Minnesota Press.

McGoey, L. (2015) *No Such Thing as a Free Gift: The Gates Foundation and the Price of Philanthropy*. London: Verso.

McPhearson, T., Parnell, S., Simon, D., Gaffney, O., Elmqvist, T., Bai, X., Roberts, D. and Revi, A. (2016) 'Scientists must have a say in the future of cities', *Nature*, 538(7624): 165–6.

Moore, S.A. (2011) 'Global garbage: Waste, trash trading, and local garbage politics', in R. Peet, P. Robbins and M.J. Watts (eds), *Global Political Ecology*. London: Routledge, pp. 133–44.

Robinson, J. (2011) 'Cities in a world of cities: The comparative gesture', *International Journal of Urban and Regional Research*, 35(1): 1–23.

Robinson, J. (2016) 'Thinking cities through elsewhere: Comparative tactics for a more global urban studies', *Progress in Human Geography*, 40(1): 3–29.

Salter, M.B. (ed.) (2015) *Making Things International 1: Circuits and Motion*. Minneapolis, MN: University of Minnesota Press.

Srnicek, N. (2010) 'Conflict networks: Collapsing the global into the local', *Journal of Critical Globalisation Studies*, 2(2): 30–64.

Temenos, C. and Ward, K. (2018) 'Examining global urban policy mobilities', in J. Harrison and M. Hoyler (eds), *Doing Global Urban Research*. London: Sage, pp. 66–80.

Tilly, C. (1989) *Big Structures, Large Processes, Huge Comparisons*. New York: Russell Sage Foundation.

UCLG (2016a) 'Second World Assembly of Local and Regional Governments', 19 April. www.bogota2016.uclg.org/en/media/second-world-assembly-local-and-regional-governments (accessed 18 September 2017).

UCLG (2016b) 'Statement of the Second World Assembly of Local and Regional Governments to the Third UN Conference on Housing and Sustainable Urban Development – Habitat III', 16 October. www.uclg.org/sites/default/files/statement_of_2nd_world_assembly_to_habitat_iii.pdf (accessed 18 September 2017).

UN-Habitat (2016) *Urbanization and Development: Emerging Futures. World Cities Report 2016*. Nairobi: United Nations Human Settlements Programme. https://unhabitat.org/wp-content/uploads/2014/03/WCR-%20Full-Report-2016.pdf (accessed 18 September 2017).

Weiss, K. (2015) 'Cities bask in spotlight at Paris climate talks', *Nature News*, 10 Dec 2015, doi:10.1038/nature.2015.19006.

Weiss, T.G. and Wilkinson, R. (2014) 'Global governance to the rescue: Saving international relations?', *Global Governance: A Review of Multilateralism and International Organizations*, 20(1): 19–36.

Whitfield, L. (ed.) (2009) *The Politics of Aid*. Oxford: Oxford University Press.

8

EVALUATING GLOBAL URBAN SUSTAINABILITY

John Lauermann

Why research global urban sustainability?

A growing chorus of commentators suggests that cities, and perhaps only cities, can save the planet from environmental catastrophe: the United Nations, World Bank, and OECD have all adopted 'cities and climate change' strategies, while analysts note the growing role of city governments in climate governance (Acuto, 2013, Chapter 7; Wachsmuth et al., 2016). Global environmental fortunes are said to pass through urbanized spaces in the contemporary 'urban age', as cities wield an outsized and growing ecological footprint in terms of energy use, carbon emissions, and consumption patterns. On an increasingly urbanized planet cities sprawl into vast 'megaregions' (Harrison and Hoyler, 2015). Cities likewise anchor extensive 'operational landscapes' (Brenner, 2014), hinterlands, and infrastructure for importing resources and exporting waste which extend urban environmental impact far beyond traditional city boundaries (Angelo and Wachsmuth, 2015). While such 'planetary urbanization' (Brenner, 2014; Katsikis, Chapter 2) exports urban environmental problems, it also offers potential for a new form of sustainable development based on scaling up the environmental benefits of walkable neighbourhoods, energy efficient built environments, urban ecosystem restoration, and 'smart' urban management technology. In this urban age framework, debates over urban sustainability necessarily become debates over global urban sustainable development. In particular, two conversations in global urban research stand out.

First, cities can act as 'urban laboratories' (Karvonen and van Heur, 2014), spaces for testing technologies and design practices to change urban socio-technical systems (Bulkeley and Castán Broto, 2013). In the 'experimental city' (Evans et al., 2016), urban development projects can be used as 'niches' for innovation that seek 'to transform cities into sites of knowledge production that will make them simultaneously more economically viable, socially robust and environmentally friendly' (Evans and Karvonen, 2014: 413). An experimental ethos is applied to a wide range of urban environmental challenges, such as sustainable building design, green infrastructure, or resilience and ecological security. Climate change is a dominant theme as experiments are used to innovate future visions of a low carbon city, to build urban resilience as a means of climate change adaptation, and to articulate more interventionist roles for state institutions as managers of the sustainability experiments.

Second, these urban laboratories take on multi-scalar significance when city leaders act as change agents in environmental policy. That is, city leaders are able to scale up their environmental policy initiatives, in effect exporting knowledge generated in the abovementioned urban experiments (Acuto, 2013). At the city-region scale, the emergence of regional governing partnerships has been leveraged to support investment in infrastructures which support metropolitan sustainability and negotiate urban environmental politics across territories (Krueger and Savage, 2007). At the transnational scale a number of city-to-city policy networks have emerged to transfer technical knowledge and lobby for transnational sustainability action, on themes such as climate policy (C40 Climate Leadership Group, Covenant of Mayors), urban environmental quality (International Council of Local Environmental Initiatives, United Cities and Local Governments), and planning best practices (City Protocol Society, World Association of Mayors).

There is a deeply engrained scalar logic in urban age sustainability politics. Behind the suggestions that cities can save the planet is the idea that local environmental interventions can scale up to address globally significant problems because cities play increasingly dominant roles in global political economy, and that global environmental problems are experienced most directly and significantly in cities because that is where a growing majority of world population resides. Such logic might be critically interrogated with reference to 'politics of scale', the political economic motives and incentives associated with making leaps between the urban and the global (Swyngedouw and Heynen, 2003). Visions of global urban sustainable cities require both 'scale jumping' ('the ability of certain social groups to move to higher levels of activity') and 'scale bending' ('social groups and individuals challenge and undermine existing arrangements which tie particular social activities to certain scales') (MacKinnon, 2011: 24–5). They allow urban leaders to jump scales by using urban-level projects to intervene in global governance debates and bend scales by renegotiating the terms of global environmental debates to re-centre them around cities.

The potential of these interventions is a locally sensitive yet globally impactful model of sustainable development. Exploring this proposition in his book *If Mayors Ruled the World*, Barber (2013: 12) envisions a world in which 'working voluntarily and cooperatively to pursue sustainability, justice, and democratic equality locally, [cities] can mitigate the depredations of fractious states and temper – even regulate – the global markets that states have been unable or unwilling to control'. This ideal of sustainability in the urban age allows national and international institutions to downscale and test their agendas in urban laboratories, and bend scales by offloading some of the responsibility for sustainable development to local governments. The risk is a dilution of sustainability as concept and policy objective, such that references to urban age problems and solutions have become

> a *de rigueur* framing device or reference point for nearly anyone concerned to justify the importance of cities as sites of research, policy intervention, planning/design practice, investment, or community activism. Much like the notion of modernization in the 1960s and that of globalization in the 1980s and 1990s, the thesis of an urban age appears to have become [. . .] an all-pervasive metanarrative. (Brenner and Schmid, 2014: 734)

These conflicting potentials and risks are increasingly being examined through the lens of 'doing' global urban research. Reviewing these approaches and exploring them with a case study of urban sustainability planning, the discussion that follows highlights opportunities for global urban researchers while exploring some significant empirical and conceptual challenges.

Challenges of researching global urban sustainability

A significant challenge for global urban research has been to critically interrogate 'sustainable city visions' (Harris and Moore, 2015), in particular the techniques for articulating and designing urban age sustainability through exemplars, models, and best practices. These visions are expressed through various future-focused planning artifacts: strategic plans, urban vision statements, technical manuals, architectural renderings, and geospatial models and simulations, to name a few examples. Despite this technical format the content of these visions is often idealistic or even utopian, and questions emerge about their assumptions and feasibility.

A shared goal in much of this research is to evaluate the gap between visions of the sustainable city and 'actually existing sustainabilities' (Krueger and Agyeman, 2005). For instance, critical urban theorists have suggested that sustainable visions are leveraged by city elites as part of a 'sustainability fix' (While et al., 2004) which allows business as usual without challenging underlying models of urban development. For example, Wheeler argues that the promises of urban age forms such as megaregions are belied by 'business-as-usual' forms of urban development:

> The result may well be to facilitate the physical sprawl of urban development between cities, to increase the amount that people travel and associated greenhouse gas emissions, to worsen disparities between different populations and communities, and to strengthen economic globalization trends that undermine local place and global sustainability. (Wheeler, 2015: 97)

The fix has reshaped the growth models most closely associated with entrepreneurial urbanism and urban growth coalitions by incorporating environmental politics – especially around carbon control – into cities' inter-urban competition strategies (Jonas et al., 2011). It has also been described as a political mechanism for scale jumping: as 'eco-state restructuring' (While et al., 2010) that allows state institutions to carve out a more interventionist role for themselves by referencing the urgency of challenges such as climate change, or as city officials import extralocal sustainability knowledge as a way to win debates in local political negotiations (Temenos and McCann, 2012).

In the same way, analysts have deconstructed *global urban* sustainability visions. While there is a broad recognition that the urban age presents a new set of environmental challenges, the methods and motivations of sustainability promoters have been scrutinized. Some have pointed to the empirical inconsistencies of defining and measuring the very definition of 'city' in urban sustainability. They show that legal and statistical definitions of a city (and by extension, of its environmental processes) vary widely across national contexts, complicating comparative global urban research (Angelo and Wachsmuth, 2015). Others have pointed to under-acknowledged ideological motivations which belie claims that global urban sustainability justifies investment and intervention. For example, while the search for an 'ecological urbanism' (Mostafavi and Doherty, 2010) has emphasized replicable sustainability interventions (to be transferred through circulating models, exemplars, and best practices), it has also been critiqued because 'even the most elaborate applications of ecological urbanism remain essentially islands within the wider dynamics of capitalist urbanisation' (Gandy, 2015: 152). Thus for many urban theorists, 'global urban sustainability' joins a litany of vague concepts (creative city, resilient city, sustainable city, green city, eco-city, competitive city, inclusive city) which offer buzzwords in place of substantive policy change (Swyngedouw, 2009).

An additional interpretive challenge emerges because the vision can come to influence the actually existing city, narrowing the gap between the two when the latter starts to imitate the former. The purpose of planning/design is to direct the current city towards some alternative urban future. Yet it is important to remember that envisioning a sustainable city, or a global urban environmental future, is a political practice. Modelling these visions might be thought of as a form of 'persuasive storytelling' (Throgmorton, 1996) about the future. While sustainability models are often presented as scientific and technical fact (for example, rigorously documented through planning protocols, or vividly illustrated with architectural renderings), they are not so much literal blueprints for the future as they are tools in a rhetorical campaign which planners must mount to intervene in urban politics. Modelling these visions can also be strategically vague, allowing sustainability to work as a 'meme' (Davidson and Gleeson, 2014), a 'master signifier' (Gunder and Hillier, 2009: chapter 8), or a 'chain of equivalences' (Davidson, 2010) that can be applied to a variety of urban political agendas. This requires doing global urban research that considers the political motivations, leveraging, and impacts surrounding proposals for sustainable futures.

Techniques for doing global urban sustainability research

Urban sustainable development is a broad interdisciplinary field with a diverse set of epistemological priorities and methodological practices, even when one narrows the field to literature that links urban to global. There is a well-established research tradition assessing the ecological processes of urban environments (Forman, 2014), an emerging 'urbanization science' which seeks to measure and explain global urbanization patterns (Solecki et al., 2013), and practitioner-oriented traditions (such as urban design and urban planning) which have likewise linked their interventions in the city to global environmental problems (Mostafavi and Doherty, 2010). These approaches inform global urban research on sustainability in a general way, but the specific making of global urban theory is based in a different methodological tradition.

Doing global urban research often means interrogating what sustainability entails as a concept, how that concept can be mobilized as a policy agenda, and why it is leveraged within urban political agendas. These theory-building techniques derive from social science traditions such as urban geography, urban sociology, and urban affairs, or from fields including planning theory and critical architecture studies. They are distinct in that 'sustainability' is the object of analysis, rather than the outcome of research. Like other areas of urban theory, these theory-making approaches tend to rely on qualitative and mixed-methods techniques such as interviews and surveys, analysis of archives and policy documents, ethnography, and some statistical techniques commonly used in the social sciences (for example, linear regression, factor and principle component analysis, or qualitative comparative analysis). Three types of analytical strategies stand out.

The first examines sustainability as a political tool, evaluating how the concept is used discursively in (global) urban politics. This technique analyses how the sustainable city ideal is constructed rhetorically by urban political stakeholders, often using a combination of interviews and analysis of written and visual materials. For example, Gunder and Hillier (2009) deconstructed a comparative sample of spatial planning documents to conclude that sustainability functions as a 'master signifier', a discursive tool for overwriting specific planning concepts with a more general set of meanings such that 'the narrative of sustainable development is often deployed simply to further the interests of an entrepreneurially-supportive state and its institutions' (2009: 136). Davidson (2010) used in-depth interviews with urban planners to analyse the way in which they use the sustainability concept to construct a 'chain of equivalences' by which contradictory, marginally related political agendas are brought under its discursive umbrella. And in a similar manner, Angelo and Wachsmuth (2015) turned the deconstructive analytic towards urban scholars, using a review of urban political ecology research to suggest that the idea of the green city is circumscribed by a 'methodological cityism' that artificially separates city and countryside.

A second strategy interrogates the political economy of sustainability policy, asking who constructs and promotes environmental policy and how they benefit from the transaction. This technique often maps out city-to-city circuits and mobilities, exploring how policy is translated across cities and how it transforms while on the move. For example, studies have engaged in global urban theory-making by analysing the policy mobilities of the sustainable city (Harris and Moore, 2015). Faulconbridge (2013) used interviews and a case study of green building designers to examine how global expertise on sustainable design is used to make local green infrastructure; the integration is a form of 'bricolage' by which designers embed knowledge from multiple other sites into the new construction site. Rapoport (2015) used ethnographic techniques to observe a 'global intelligence corps' of North American and European firms, whose consulting and contracting on sustainable urban projects around the world led to a convergence around standardized models of sustainable urbanism. And Müller (2015) examined the mobility and immobility of sustainability expertise across Olympic host cities using participant observation, interviews, and a survey with global experts and local planners, finding that despite extralocal pressure to adopt sustainability best practices 'striving to emulate others produced over-ambitious commitments' (2015: 206) that did not live up to the sustainable ideal.

A third strategy examines the material impacts of sustainable city visions, exploring (dis)continuities between the vision and the result while evaluating the power relationships that unfold when implementing the vision. This technique often uses case studies of construction projects that model sustainability best practices. For example, several analysts have used case studies of master planned communities and other new-build projects to critically interrogate the gap between sustainability in theory and the outcomes of these best practices in actually existing urban communities (Hodson and Marvin, 2010: chapter 3; Rapoport, 2014). Moser et al. (2015) used a study of the new master planned cities industry – based on participant observation at trade conferences and site visits to the cities that the industry builds – to unpack how these investments are realized in practice. They describe how new-build projects in Saudi Arabia are used to experiment with a transition to post-oil economies, but identify numerous challenges to developing sustainable communities in 'corporate-driven new cities'. In contrast, Chang and Sheppard (2013) used archival research and key informant interviews to trace the lineage of master planned 'eco-cities' in China, arguing that both urban sustainability and its critiques developed in a Euro-American context necessitate studies that reinterpret the concept through more locally specific varieties of green capitalism.

These three techniques share a common understanding of the purpose of global urban theory-building. Sustainability has become a dominant policy concept in the urban age, one which gains salience in part through its status as a malleable concept that can be claimed by a wide range of stakeholders. While global urban researchers are of course concerned with the design and implementation of solutions for sustainable development, much urban theory building recognizes that the sustainable city ideal is constructed through urban politics. Thus careful interpretive analysis is a first step in exploring how sustainable policy is developed and why it is scaled up through global urban policy agendas.

Case study: Global urban sustainability at the Olympics

I have explored these latter questions in my work on the politics of planning for mega-events such as the Olympics (Lauermann, 2014, 2016; see also Gaffney et al., Chapter 9). Olympic host cities - and cities bidding to become hosts - regularly use global urban sustainability narratives. Games promoters describe their cities as laboratories for experimental architecture, 'smart' urban management, and a variety of technologies for minimizing the environmental footprint of the Games. These experimental proposals are often linked to attempts at developing *replicable* environmental policy models that can be exported to other cities (Lauermann, 2014) through city-to-city circuits of consulting and 'policy tourism' by planners visiting other planners (Müller, 2015).

Visualization of the future city is a central element of these global urban narratives: to promote a sustainable city vision, one must actually show the audience what it will look like. Using maps, models, and renderings, Olympic planners seek to accomplish two tasks: to convincingly promote design concepts to the city's residents, and to persuade the global sports industry that the city will be an effective steward of the Olympic brand. Such visions of a future sustainable city are inherently speculative; the majority of Olympic planning projects fail (as only one city can host even when there are numerous bidders) although failed Olympic bids are often recycled into other planning projects (Lauermann, 2016). These visualizations nonetheless play an important strategic role in policymaking: seeing a vision of sustainability is a necessary step towards believing it, and eventually towards mobilizing resources to support it. These visualizations also play a significant role in the 'scale jumping' that is so common in urban age sustainability policymaking: designed to be replicable across cities, they can be copied – sometimes actually copied and pasted – to emulate a ready-made vision of the sustainable city.

To assess these practices, I draw on a visual content analysis of Olympic planning proposals. The goal was to understand how sustainable city visions are actually visualized in practice, and how those visualizations are mobilized in urban politics. A stratified sample of images was collected from plans for 'Olympic Villages', the housing complexes that host athletes during the Games. They are usually the largest single land investment and most complex design project in any Olympic plan, with an average size of 69.2 hectares and an average construction budget of $596.2 million. These plans were sampled from all Olympic bids placed over a 22-year period, starting with the first attempts at sustainability planning by organizers of the Sydney 2000 Games and continuing through bids to host the 2022 Games (61 bid proposals, dating 1993 to 2015).[1] The image sample includes city- and neighbourhood-scale maps, site plans and digital renderings, along with some pre-digital visual products such as aerial photography, building drawings, dioramas, and sketches (n=616 images). These images were coded based on what type of sustainability intervention was visualized (for example, design strategies, planning concepts), which visualization techniques were used (map, rendering, etc.), and who supported the vision (attributes on ownership, financing, contracting, and pre- and post-Games land use). A second layer of analytical coding was used to interpret how visualization techniques are paired with political messages and strategies used by the Games planners (identified with content analysis of the bidding documents). The two layers of codes were then compared using cross-tabulation to identify strong and weak correlations. This analysis was, finally, triangulated by drawing on data from 30 in-depth interviews with designers, event planners, and programme officers collected in a broader study of the mega-events planning industry.

Visualizations of future sustainability are linked to Olympic planners' attempts to establish themselves in city-to-city networks of expertise. They are a way of modelling best practice, and showing the viewer how a

(Continued)

sustainable policy can be integrated into the existing environment. Maps, models, and renderings that posit a future sustainable city are a way to persuade, and they can be interpreted to determine the types of ideological commitments inside the visions. For example, there is a good deal of erasure as visualizations leave site histories vague – 35 of the 61 plans do not discuss pre-Games land use at all, while another 10 were sited on post-industrial redevelopment and restoration projects – or completely off the page with no explanation at all. This erasure can be strategic, in the sense that other visualizations are used to fill the void with an alternative, more sustainable proposal. This is often accomplished by merging a map or architectural rendering with an aerial photograph of the existing city, as a way of inserting an alternative vision into the landscape (Figure 8.1).

Geographic visualizations of the future city also play a role as currency in networks of urban policy, as they provide a basic design that can be modelled, exported, and imitated. For mega-event planning, sustainable design focuses on the introduction of alternative urban technologies

Figure 8.1 Architectural model of the Beijing 2008 Olympic Park

Source: Jan Spacir, https://commons.wikimedia.org/wiki/File:Beijing_Olympic_Stadium_Model_detail.JPG. This file is licensed under the Creative Commons Attribution-Share Alike 3.0 Unported license (CC BY-SA 3.0).
Original in colour.

(especially renewable energy sources), minimizing ecological footprints with passive design elements (such as using natural light and heating, or designing for walkability), introducing municipal recycling systems, designing for green space, building with locally sourced or recycled materials, or linking the village development to environmental remediation of the site. Visualizations of the future Olympic city often contain multiple combinations of these elements within the same image, using techniques such as architectural rendering or cartography that combines current and future urban features (Figure 8.2).

This modelling is a way to demonstrate the feasibility or scalability of design elements, in ways that parallel planners' promotion of their cities as experimenters or innovators. It is linked to a form of 'networked entrepreneurialism' (Lauermann, 2014) in which local policy innovations are used by Olympic planners to build global reputations. Planners link their innovations to global urban sustainability debates by proposing replicability: designs, planning best practices, and policy templates that can be reproduced in other Olympic cities. Some examples include design practices for 'an ecological city' (bid from Jaca 2002), planning models for

Figure 8.2 Pop-up installation mapping sustainable design elements in London's Olympic Park

Source: author

(Continued)

'environmentally sustainable development' (Beijing 2008, London 2012) and 'sustainable inner city housing' (Tokyo 2016), or common guidelines to 'promote sustainable tourism' (Annecy 2018).

Collectively, these visualization techniques signal the process by which a sustainable city vision is constructed. Using maps, geospatial models, and architectural renderings, Olympic promoters are able to show how the cities might experiment with design techniques, urban technologies, and environmental remediation strategies. These visual modelling techniques correlate with discursive claims to the replicability of the model. By promoting the replicability of these techniques through various practices of policy mobility (Temenos and McCann, 2012; Lauermann, 2014; Müller, 2015; Temenos and Ward, Chapter 5), these same promoters manage to link these visualizations to claims on global urban sustainability policy. These cities are able to claim that they can save the planet because, with a carefully constructed vision, it looks as if they can.

Reflections on global urban sustainability research

To date, research on global urban sustainability can claim several accomplishments in both the practice of doing research and the process of producing urban theory. These include identifying the changing empirical nature of the global urban question, by devising new methods for tracking urban age phenomena, such as planetary scale 'operational landscapes' (Brenner, 2014), and moving beyond 'methodological cityism' in urban environmental research (Angelo and Wachsmuth, 2015). Along the way there have been theoretical advances which uncover the ideological motivations and political economic drivers that influence visions of global urban sustainability, for instance examining how the concept is leveraged by non-environmental agendas or as part of an urban political 'fix' to maintain existing patterns of capitalist urbanization. And these advances have been scaled up to consider the global urban dimension directly, by tracking the city-to-city mobility of sustainability expertise as a way to explain a gradual convergence of sustainability visions.

There are also promising areas for future research. First, while global urban researchers have developed a refined critical lens for deconstructing global urban sustainability, there has been less engagement with alternative interventions that improve on the subjects of critique. That is, how might global urban theory-making inform policy and planning debates more directly? Can theory be co-produced with proposals for a sustainability policy agenda? Promising themes include the role that city-to-city policy networks might play in sustainability governance (Acuto, 2013, Chapter 7) and the use of critical urban theory to inform and refine the practice of sustainability planning (Faulconbridge and Grubbauer, 2015) or on the politics of urban infrastructure (Addie, 2016; Wachsmuth, 2017).

Second, the field can benefit from more direct engagement with debates in urban environmental science and planning/design practice. It is important to recognize the political economic special interests which mobilize around 'sustainability fixes' (While et al., 2004), but it is also important to build alliances with scientific and planning practitioners as a way to design more politically aware environmental interventions. To do this, a more diverse portfolio of methods is needed to communicate theoretical insight – especially methods that mix qualitative approaches with quantitative and geospatial data. This might include engaging with debates over geospatial and land change science approaches to global urban change in urbanization science (Solecki et al., 2013), with those areas of urban ecology which are concerned with global urban processes such as climate change, or around interdisciplinary sustainability research agendas such as the water–food–energy nexus. More broadly it should involve translating critical urban theory insights into a format that can be more readily used by sustainability scientists and practitioners, a form of 'strategic positivism' (Wyly, 2009) already under way in some urban theory making (for example through critical quantitative urban research, or large-sample qualitative studies such as the case study discussed in this chapter).

Note

1. The sample was collected from archives at the Olympic Studies Centre in Lausanne, the LA84 Foundation in Los Angeles, and by request from bid corporations and municipal archives.

References

Acuto, M. (2013) *Global Cities, Governance and Diplomacy: The Urban Link*. London: Routledge.

Acuto, M. (2018) 'Engaging with global urban governance', in J. Harrison and M. Hoyler (eds), *Doing Global Urban Research*. London: Sage, pp. 96–109.

Addie, J.-P.D. (2016) 'Theorising suburban infrastructure: A framework for critical and comparative analysis', *Transactions of the Institute of British Geographers*, 41(3): 273–85.

(Continued)

Angelo, H and Wachsmuth, D. (2015) 'Urbanizing urban political ecology: A critique of methodological cityism', *International Journal of Urban and Regional Research*, 39(1): 16–27.

Barber, B.R. (2013) *If Mayors Ruled the World: Dysfunctional Nations, Rising Cities*. New Haven, CT: Yale University Press.

Brenner, N. (ed.) (2014) *Implosions/Explosions: Towards a Study of Planetary Urbanization*. Berlin: Jovis.

Brenner, N. and Schmid, C. (2014) 'The "Urban Age" in question', *International Journal of Urban and Regional Research*, 38(3): 731–55.

Bulkeley, H. and Castán Broto, V. (2013) 'Government by experiment? Global cities and the governing of climate change', *Transactions of the Institute of British Geographers*, 38(3): 361–75.

Chang, I.-C.C. and Sheppard, E. (2013) 'China's eco-cities as variegated urban sustainability: Dongtan eco-city and Chongming eco-island', *Journal of Urban Technology*, 20(1): 57–75.

Davidson, K. and Gleeson, B. (2014) 'The sustainability of an entrepreneurial city?', *International Planning Studies*, 19(2): 173–91.

Davidson, M. (2010) 'Sustainability as ideological praxis: The acting out of planning's master-signifier', *City*, 14(4): 390–405.

Evans, J. and Karvonen, A. (2014) '"Give me a laboratory and I will lower your carbon footprint!" – Urban laboratories and the governance of low-carbon futures', *International Journal of Urban and Regional Research*, 38(2): 413–30.

Evans, J., Karvonen, A. and Raven, R. (eds) (2016) *The Experimental City*. London: Routledge.

Faulconbridge, J. (2013) 'Mobile "green" design knowledge: Institutions, bricolage and the relational production of embedded sustainable building designs', *Transactions of the Institute of British Geographers*, 38(2): 339–53.

Faulconbridge, J. and Grubbauer, M. (2015) 'Transnational building practices: Knowledge mobility and the inescapable market', *Global Networks*, 15(3): 275–87.

Forman, R.T.T. (2014) *Urban Ecology: Science of Cities*. Cambridge: Cambridge University Press.

Gaffney, C., Wolfe, S.D. and Müller, M. (2018) 'Scrutinizing global mega-events', in J. Harrison and M. Hoyler (eds), *Doing Global Urban Research*. London: Sage, pp. 125–37.

Gandy, M. (2015) 'From urban ecology to ecological urbanism: An ambiguous trajectory', *Area*, 47(2): 150–4.

Gunder, M. and Hillier, J. (2009) *Planning in Ten Words or Less: A Lacanian Entanglement with Spatial Planning*. London: Routledge.

Harris, A. and Moore, S. (2015) 'Convergence and divergence in conceptualising and planning the sustainable city: An introduction', *Area*, 47(2): 106–9.

Harrison, J. and Hoyler, M. (eds) (2015) *Megaregions: Globalization's New Urban Form?* Cheltenham: Edward Elgar.

Hodson, M. and Marvin, S. (2010) *World Cities and Climate Change: Producing Urban Ecological Security*. New York: McGraw Hill.

Jonas, A.E.G., Gibbs, D. and While, A. (2011) 'The new urban politics as a politics of carbon control', *Urban Studies*, 48(12): 2537–54.

Karvonen, A. and van Heur, B. (2014) 'Urban laboratories: Experiments in reworking cities', *International Journal of Urban and Regional Research*, 38(2): 379–92.

Katsikis, N. (2018) 'Visualizing the planetary urban', in J. Harrison and M. Hoyler (eds), *Doing Global Urban Research*. London: Sage, pp. 12–33.

Krueger, R. and Agyeman, J. (2005) 'Sustainability schizophrenia or "actually existing sustainabilities?" Toward a broader understanding of the politics and promise of local sustainability in the US', *Geoforum*, 36(4): 410–17.

Krueger, R. and Savage, L. (2007) 'City-regions and social reproduction: a "place" for sustainable development?', *International Journal of Urban and Regional Research*, 31(1): 215–23.

Lauermann, J. (2014) 'Competition through interurban policy making: Bidding to host megaevents as entrepreneurial networking', *Environment and Planning A*, 46(11): 2638–53.

Lauermann, J. (2016) 'Temporary projects, durable outcomes: Urban development through failed Olympic bids?', *Urban Studies*, 53(9): 1885–1901.

MacKinnon, D. (2011) 'Reconstructing scale: Towards a new scalar politics', *Progress in Human Geography*, 35(1): 21–36.

Moser, S., Swain, M. and Alkhabbaz, M.H. (2015) 'King Abdullah Economic City: Engineering Saudi Arabia's post-oil future', *Cities*, 45: 71–80.

Mostafavi, M. and Doherty, G. (2010) *Ecological Urbanism*. Zürich: Lars Müller.

Müller, M. (2015) '(Im-)Mobile policies: Why sustainability went wrong in the 2014 Olympics in Sochi', *European Urban and Regional Studies*, 22(2): 191–209.

Rapoport, E. (2014) 'Utopian visions and real estate dreams: The eco-city past, present and future', *Geography Compass*, 8(2): 137–49.

Rapoport, E. (2015) 'Globalising sustainable urbanism: The role of international masterplanners', *Area*, 47(2): 110–15.

Solecki, W., Seto, K.C. and Marcotullio, P.J. (2013) 'It's time for an urbanization science', *Environment: Science and Policy for Sustainable Development*, 55(1): 12–17.

Swyngedouw, E. (2009) 'The antinomies of the postpolitical city: In search of a democratic politics of environmental production', *International Journal of Urban and Regional Research*, 33(3): 601–20.

Swyngedouw, E. and Heynen, N.C. (2003) 'Urban political ecology, justice and the politics of scale', *Antipode*, 35(5): 898–918.

Temenos, C. and McCann, E. (2012) 'The local politics of policy mobility: Learning, persuasion, and the production of a municipal sustainability fix', *Environment and Planning A*, 44(6): 1389–1406.

Temenos, C. and Ward, K. (2018) 'Examining global urban policy mobilities', in J. Harrison and M. Hoyler (eds), *Doing Global Urban Research*. London: Sage, pp. 66–80.

Throgmorton, J.A. (1996) *Planning as Persuasive Storytelling: The Rhetorical Construction of Chicago's Electric Future*. Chicago: University of Chicago Press.

Wachsmuth, D. (2017) 'Infrastructure alliances: Supply-chain expansion and multi-city growth coalitions', *Economic Geography*, 93(1): 44–65.

Wachsmuth, D., Cohen, D.A. and Angelo, H. (2016) 'Expand the frontiers of urban sustainability', *Nature*, 536: 391–3.

Wheeler, S.M. (2015) 'Five reasons why megaregional planning works against sustainability', in J. Harrison and M. Hoyler (eds), *Megaregions: Globalization's New Urban Form?* Cheltenham: Edward Elgar, pp. 97–118.

While, A., Jonas, A.E.G. and Gibbs, D. (2004) 'The environment and the entrepreneurial city: Searching for the urban "sustainability fix" in Manchester and Leeds', *International Journal of Urban and Regional Research*, 28(3): 549–69.

While, A., Jonas, A.E.G. and Gibbs, D. (2010) 'From sustainable development to carbon control: Eco-state restructuring and the politics of urban and regional development', *Transactions of the Institute of British Geographers*, 35(1): 76–93.

Wyly, E. (2009) 'Strategic positivism', *The Professional Geographer*, 61(3): 310–22.

9

SCRUTINIZING GLOBAL MEGA-EVENTS

Christopher Gaffney, Sven Daniel Wolfe and Martin Müller

Why do research on global mega-events?

Over the past 20 years, mega-events – such as the Olympic Games or the football World Cup – have become a global urban force. For many cities, hosting a mega-event propels historically large interventions in urban development, remodelling both urban politics and the built environment in the course of a few years. The Olympic Games and the football World Cup have, in this sense, become urban events more than sporting events.

The capital cost of material interventions into the city – upgrading or building new sports venues, roads, railway lines, airports, communication centres, security systems, and hotels – is now several times the operational cost of putting on the event itself. The Russian city of Sochi spent more than USD 50 billion on infrastructure in preparation for the 2014 Winter Games, compared to less than USD 5 billion of operational expenses (Müller, 2014). Some scholars see the degree of urban transformation as one of the key distinctions between events and mega-events. Hiller (2000: 183), for example, suggests that a mega-event significantly alters the urban fabric and reprioritizes the urban agenda.

It is no exaggeration to claim that, over the past two decades, the urban impacts of mega-events have become global. Whereas cities in North America, Western Europe, and Japan were the traditional hosts of mega-events in the twentieth century, Russia, China, Brazil, and South Africa have not just joined their ranks but become dominant players: in the years between 2013 and 2022, Japan is the only host of the Olympics or the World Cup that is not an emerging economy. The period between 1992 and 2022 has seen or will see the first Olympic Games or football World Cup ever in Africa (football World Cup 2010) and the Middle East (Football World Cup 2022), and the first Olympic Games in South America (Rio de Janeiro 2016).

That mega-events can serve as showcases of and catalysts for larger dynamics in urban development makes them relevant as a research topic. Mega-events introduce idiosyncratic urban development dynamics and rationales into specific cities, creating stark differences between event-driven and quotidian political economies. The same event may serve very different purposes in urban development in different areas of a given city or for different governmental agendas. While London may have harnessed the Olympics for urban redevelopment, the Olympic Games in Sochi served to lubricate a neopatrimonial political system (Müller, 2014) and Rio opened up spaces for development through public–private partnerships and accumulation by dispossession (Freeman, 2014).

Constituted through global networks and institutional relations, mega-events also epitomize the multiple mobilities at the heart of global urban research. Olympics, World Cups, World's Fairs, and other, smaller events both create and are captured by a vortex of global flows of capital, knowledge, policies, symbols, images, and people (Cook and Ward, 2011; Salazar et al., 2017). As such, they lend themselves to comparative research designs that explore the effects of the same intervention in different locations and trace the flows that bind, at first glance rather different, cities – Sochi and Pyeongchang, Rio and Tokyo – into common global circuits.

Challenges of researching global mega-events

Mega-events are a global phenomenon in multiple aspects: these large-scale, temporary spectacles travel to new locations around the world and feature international participants, but they are also broadcast to a global audience and each event is produced by a globalized network of actors – sponsors, construction companies, consultants, media companies, public relations firms, architects, banks, and so on. This fluid network is multi-local and temporary, dissolving once the mega-event is concluded and then reconstituting itself in new environments. A global urban researcher focusing on mega-events faces the challenge of making sense of the varying temporalities, spatialities, and articulations of this dynamic network.

Take, for example, the football World Cup: this mega-event is owned by the Fédération Internationale de Football Association (FIFA), a multinational association with 211 member nations, headquartered in Zürich, Switzerland. Nations that are interested in hosting a World Cup will create bidding committees to prepare and submit proposals for hosting. These committees typically involve members of the nation's governmental, sporting, and business elites, but also hire the expertise of international consultants and marketing firms who specialize in attracting mega-events (Hall, 2006).

Once FIFA grants the right to host a World Cup, the new host nation forms a national organizing committee, often composed of members from the bidding committee but also involving other actors, from both public and private entities (Andranovich et al., 2001). Since World Cup games are played in numerous venues around the host nation, the national organizing committee creates local organizing committees for each host city. Aside from governmental connections at the federal level, each host city is tied into a network of regional, national, and international construction companies, architects and planners, equipment suppliers, energy concerns, technology specialists, security firms, corporate sponsors, and consultants. This network begins the process of preparing the nation to host, launching infrastructure construction and rehabilitation projects and spearheading public relations initiatives.

These developments generate interest both locally and internationally, and are covered by an extensive media network that both reflects and shapes public attitudes. As the opening date approaches, media coverage increases in intensity until the games begin in earnest, at which point billions of people around the world tune in (Solberg and Gratton, 2014). Media is always present in global sport, but during mega-events the media concentration directs the world's attention to make the host city into a stage and the sporting event into global spectacle. Alongside traditional media coverage, social media and the internet represent another point of insertion into a global network, as individuals, organizers, and advertisers make use of new technologies to leverage the global attention paid to the World Cup (Karg and Lock, 2014).

After the closing ceremony, the international spotlight dims as the translocal, multi-scalar assemblage that imagined, produced, sold, and consumed the spectacle enters into a period of destructuring: fans switch off the television, internet groups go dormant, organizing committees dissolve, companies are disbanded, and sometimes workers join other mega-events as part of the international circuit of travelling consultants and policy experts (Prince, 2012; Wood, 2015). Meanwhile, preparations for the next World Cup are already under way; organizing committee members from future hosts observe the production and operational processes of previous World Cups. Though differing in the organizational details and urban footprint (number of venues and cities, for example, or length of the event), most mega-events follow similar patterns of development, incrementally building complex networks that are both translocal and temporary.

Mega-events do not just result from the emergence of global networks; they also draw the attention of an international network of researchers, each focusing on a particular aspect of the preparations, event dynamics, or impacts. Broadly speaking, these scholars have isolated and analysed a portion of the mega-event totality, discussing potential economic effects (Abelson, 2011; Baade and Matheson, 2004), environmental consequences (Karamichas, 2013), rationales behind bidding and hosting (Cornelissen, 2010; Wolfe, 2016), or the varying reactions of host populations, from nationalism to popular support to resistance and opposition (Hiller and Wanner, 2015). Other literature focuses more specifically on the built environment, for example on issues of urban regeneration (Coaffee, 2011; Smith, 2014), housing and gentrification (Blunden, 2012), the securitization of space (Bennett and Haggerty, 2011; Fussey et al., 2011), and white elephant infrastructure (Horne and Whannel, 2016: 42–47).

While the literature on mega-events is plentiful, it is dominated by case studies of individual events, and there is a need for more longitudinal and comparative research. This focus on case studies is partly due to the temporal and logistical challenges inherent in mega-events, where events might take place far from researchers' institutional bases, and where reliable information may be scarce, closely guarded, or only available in the host country's language(s). There are, however, some examples of comparative research between different host cities of one mega-event (Essex and Chalkley, 2004), a focus on a single city undergoing change from a series of different mega-events (Castro et al., 2015), and examinations of failed mega-event bidding across different cities (Lauermann, 2014a, Chapter 8). At the same time, the majority of mega-events literature – even the comparative research – tends to focus on the urban nodes of a global network while ignoring the flows and circulations between them.

Techniques for researching global mega-events

The techniques typically required for conducting mega-events research depend on which aspects of mega-events will be examined, as shown in Table 9.1. These aspects often overlap and multiple techniques can be employed in order to present a more robust picture.

Archival research is the backbone of studies that cover multiple iterations of the same event, such as a long-term analysis of Olympic urban development (Gold and Gold, 2011) or a detailed tracing of Olympic cost overruns (Flyvbjerg and Stewart, 2012; Zimbalist, 2015). Some researchers have used official archives, such as those at the Olympic Studies Centre in Lausanne (Lauermann, 2014b; Mascarenhas, 2013), but it is not necessary to have access to internal documents in order to pursue archival research. Many government documents and records are available online and bid committees sometimes make their urbanization plans and provisional budgets available. Archival research can also be used to trace the development of event coalitions or the history of event models, and it can provide researchers with material for discourse or statistical analysis.

Scholars employ statistical analysis in mega-events research to evaluate large volumes of data. It has been used to examine popular perception of

Table 9.1 Techniques and possible materials for researching mega-events

Research technique	Aspects of mega-events	Possible materials
Archival research	Urban development, planning methodologies, historical approaches	Planning documents, internal reports, media coverage
Statistical analysis	Population attitudes, image politics, economic impact assessments	Official statistics, opinion polls, surveys and other quantitative data
Grounded fieldwork	Urban development, identity questions, planning methodologies	Host cities, stadiums, airports, hotels, roads, construction sites, maps, blueprints
Interviews	Population attitudes, rationalities for hosting, planning methodologies	Event staff, government officials, planners, volunteers, residents, spectators, consultants
Discourse analysis	Image politics, geopolitics, identity questions, nation-building, rationalities for hosting	Bid documents, image brochures, media reports, press releases, ceremonies, websites
Participant observation	Urban development, planning methodologies, rationalities for hosting	Organizing committees, affiliated companies, host cities, volunteers

events among host populations (Zhou and Ap, 2009), to make sense of media reports collected via automated internet searches (Preuss and Alfs, 2011), and to measure the economic impact of hosting (Baade and Matheson, 2004). Analyses can be performed on primary data collected by the researcher, or they can be based on secondary data from governmental sources or polling firms. Statistical analysis can give weight to an argument that might otherwise be overly reliant on qualitative data and may allow the researcher to generalize trends and findings.

Ethnographic techniques are invaluable when conducting mega-event field research. Through fieldwork, (participant) observation, photography, recordings, field notes, interviews, and activist scholarship, researchers can achieve depth and nuance in their work, grounding the mega-event in local experience. Ethnographic research has been used to document protest against mega-events, from London (Giulianotti et al., 2015) and Poznań (Buchowski and Kowalska, 2015), and to illuminate the plight of homeless youth during the 2010 Vancouver Olympics (Kennelly, 2015). By embedding themselves in the host cities, researchers can provide a perspective grounded in lived experience. Scholars have used this perspective to answer questions of legacy on the local population after the mega-event is concluded (Waardenburg et al., 2015), and to explore the implications of hosting on the city's homeless youth (Kennelly and Watt, 2011).

Interviews provide depth and texture to mega-event research, bringing the human element squarely into focus. Scholars can make use of structured or semi-structured interviews, as well as informal conversations; transcribed or recorded, they can quote interview participants directly in their work or analyse interviews cumulatively to better communicate the lived experience of mega-events. In his examination of gentrification and the London 2012 Olympics, Watt (2013) includes interviews with residents of council housing, highlighting the human cost of mega-event ambition. Boykoff (2014) makes use of interviews with activists in order to explore dissent at the Olympics, and Alegi (2007) draws on interviews to understand the policy decisions behind Cape Town's controversial Green Point stadium. Other analyses use interviews to grasp the implications of creating securitized spaces through mega-events (Taylor and Toohey, 2011), and to unpack some of the rationales behind hosting the event (Bolsmann and Brewster, 2009).

Finally, mega-events are enmeshed in geopolitics, used by nations as a platform to convey messages and project power at multiple scales to different audiences. Researchers who wish to unpack this aspect of mega-events may find it useful to employ the tools of discourse analysis. Discourse analysis, used broadly here, is a range of techniques that can unpack texts, speech, maps, pictures, and other media (Caldas-Coulthard and Coulthard, 1996). As applied to mega-events, discourse analysis has been used to make sense of the development ideologies behind hosting the Olympics (Darnell, 2012), and to explore the nuances of national image creation through hosting (Alekseyeva, 2014). It can shine light on the symbolism in Olympic opening and closing ceremonies (Puijk, 1999; Qing et al., 2010), and has been used to problematize the Olympic torch relay (McGillivray and Frew, 2013) and to question organizers' discursive frameworks of environmental sustainability and legacy (Gaffney, 2013).

Case study: Brazil and Rio de Janeiro, 2003–16 (Christopher Gaffney)

In 2003, I was doing my dissertation fieldwork on the geography of football stadiums in Rio de Janeiro when the city was contracted to host the 2007 Pan American Games (Gaffney, 2008). Since that time, Rio has gone through the most extensive cycle of event hosting in the twenty-first century: 2007 Pan American Games, 2011 World Military Games, 2012 Rio+20 UN Conference on the Environment, 2013 Confederations Cup, 2013 World Youth Day, 2014 World Cup, and 2016 Summer Olympics. In addition to these events in Rio, the 2014 World Cup was realized in twelve cities across Brazil, each with localized processes and impacts (Santos Júnior et al., 2015). While these events were taking place in Brazil, the 2010 World Cup in South Africa and 2012 London Olympics were closely watched by Brazilians as models to follow (or not), allowing for comparative studies that increased the complexity and texture of research in the local context.

The most important first step that I took in preparing my initial research agenda was to contextualize the arrival of the contemporary wave of events in Brazil with previous events (Gaffney, 2010). In successive eras of accelerated globalization, Brazil had always sought to modify its infrastructure and image by hosting events that would push urban development agendas. For the 1922 centennial, for example, Rio de Janeiro demolished *favelas* and the hills on which they stood in the centre of town and built expansive, temporary structures to showcase Brazilian industry, agriculture, and the natural beauty of its then-capital city. In the aftermath of World War II, Brazil hosted the 1950 World Cup, building stadiums on a massive scale that were showcases for its cutting-edge architects, engineers, and designers. In the early twenty-first century, Brazil's economic and political fortunes were rising and they again sought to use the platform of mega-events to transform cities and to transmit political and governmental ideologies. Mega-events – although they may appear singular and exceptional – always need to be situated within larger historical, political, and economic contexts before setting out on an investigative path.

The second element of my research agenda was to reach out to local academics working on similar topics but from different disciplinary perspectives. Colleagues introduced me to sociologists, urban planners, architects, economists, and politicians who had an interest in collaborating on a large project. Through these connections, I worked with a team to develop a collaborative research project on the urban impacts of the 2014 World Cup that had nine research teams around Brazil. As a national co-coordinator of this project, I helped to set the agenda for research, communicated frequently with researchers around Brazil, and was able to make on-site visits to nearly all of the World Cup host cities. While there were inevitably some frustrations with the process of managing such a large, longitudinal, and diverse project, the learning experience was as important for me personally as the academic output. I had a ringside seat to the processes, problems, and possibilities of conducting mega-event research on a national scale. In this sense, I built a network of scholars to grapple with the network of the event, as outlined above.

My research was facilitated by the fact that I lived in the city I was researching and spoke fluent Portuguese; thus, every time I stepped out the door, I was engaging in fieldwork. I was teaching about the process of mega-event hosting and the historical context of the city and was able

(Continued)

to gather more information than I could possibly process on a daily basis. In addition to my role as an academic, I was a member of the foreign media and contributed my research to the burgeoning social movements that were resisting the implementation of mega-event governance paradigms and urbanization projects. This triple role as academic, journalist, and activist would make many researchers uncomfortable, but I found that it gave me a unique perspective on the various levels at which the event operates. For instance, my strong media presence forced the event organizers to pay attention to me in ways that they would not have had I only been writing academic articles. As a result, I was invited to 'exclusive' sports management conferences where I could talk face to face with event rights holders and their so-called stakeholders. On the other hand, I was on the streets holding protest banners and running from the tear gas and rubber bullets of Rio's notoriously violent military police. I maintained a blog for many years and became a conduit for translating what was happening on the ground, in the halls of power, and in the Brazilian media for foreign and Brazilian audiences.

This seemingly complex mix of research, media exposure, popular writing, and activism was inevitably influenced by my evolving knowledge of the urban transformations taking place in Rio. While I had started with a narrow range of focus, as I learned more about the city and event dynamics I began expanding my geographic and conceptual ranges. Of course, my disciplinary training as a geographer had encouraged a holistic view of my object of study, but as I learned more about the specificities of Rio's and Brazil's urban political economy, urban planning regimes, political machinations, and social struggles, I began to connect those in ever more complex and specific ways to my research. Eventually, I wrote academic articles on public security, gentrification, transportation, stadiums and sports venues, the political economy of Brazilian football, urban social movements, smart city technology, and corrupt practices in event organizing. I used a melange of all of the techniques we have enumerated above, choosing investigative implements from this toolbox as they suited the object of study. I had not set out to write about more than one or two of these elements, but as the events emerged on the urban landscape and I connected with an increasingly diverse and geographically diffuse public, my research interests shifted accordingly.

It is impossible for one person to have a totalizing conception of a mega-event, and this is perhaps what makes it such an attractive, elusive, and difficult research area. Gaining the kind of access that I had to documents, public meetings, rights holders, and the media, while being a part of social movements contesting the mega-events was uncommon, infusing my academic work with a texture, nuance, and intensity that may only be possible while living within the context of the event.

Much of the English-language literature that emerged out of the London 2012 Olympics was similarly situated, though perhaps less engaged with public pronouncements against the conjuncture of the events themselves. The close engagement with the local conditions is not, of course, a necessity for understanding and researching urban dynamics but we should always keep in mind the geographic and social positions from which we conduct, read, and communicate scholarship.

The academic consensus is that global mega-events are causing more harm than good, yet there seems to be very little public interest in halting the march of the white elephants across globalized and globalizing urban landscapes. Part of the problem lies in translating academic research to the broader public that consumes these events and in communicating directly with mega-event rights holders and local event coalitions that determine the urban futures of their host cities and countries. The role of researchers in the mega-event complex is under-theorized yet it is clear that many academics make their living on and off the mega-event industry as much as consultants, sports professionals, and stadium construction firms. Researchers have a role in shaping debates, public perception, and public policy – it is essential that we recognize this role and use it to minimize the damage that the current model of planning and execution of mega-events invariably brings.

The Brazilian experience of hosting mega-events was defined by massive public protest, endemic corruption, waste, incomplete, unnecessary, or ill-considered infrastructure, and some of the most exhilarating mega-parties on the planet. This 13-year cycle of hosting also brought unprecedented academic attention to the global phenomenon of mega-events – the Brazilian World Cup and Olympics produced record amounts of research, media reports, and documentation. As the dust settles after the 2016 Olympics and the global spotlight moves on, it will be important to maintain a focus on the long-term impacts of the events on Brazil and Rio de Janeiro. The forms that this research takes will be conditioned by the shifting dynamics on the ground but also by the interest of mega-event researchers in working outside the imminent epistemology of the event cycle.

Reflections on conducting global mega-events research

Mega-events are an attractive access point to doing global urban research: they manifest the global in one location, leaving traces of that interaction on the urban landscape and in the collective consciousness of hundreds of millions of people. In mega-events, the global is not just something that is abstract, floating around somewhere. It comes together in a city and it causes very visual, material changes: the swanky stadium by Calatrava; the new high rises, financed with pension funds, that replace old tenements; global migrants and local hipsters that drive gentrification (see also Shin, Chapter 10). In emerging economies, the mega-event is a mechanism for an accelerated insertion into the global, with the often-overplayed desire to join the club of rich countries and enjoy the recognition that comes with this.

But it would be misguided to conceive mega-events solely as global neoliberal steamrollers that flatten whichever city dares to host them. To really understand mega-events, one needs to see and research them as global phenomena, emerging from a web of relations, with very specific local articulations. As a consequence, one also needs to question any division between the global and the local. For while the Olympic Games may come with a standardized format that imposes similar requirements on hosts around the world, the social, political, and material outcomes of Beijing 2008, London 2012, and Rio 2016 are strikingly different. These differences result from the constant intermingling of the local and the global – a division erased as global processes become localized and local processes go global.

Recognizing that mega-events are global urban phenomena also means recognizing that they come with many of the same contradictions as globalization. They create winners and losers; they mobilize some things and people and immobilize others; they are vanguards in the global shift towards consumerism; they foster the most unreflexive nationalism while purporting to adhere to universalist ideals. While we can hone our analytical tools for doing global urban research with mega-events, we would do well not to forget that there is also a political side to these events that too often gets lost in the allure of the global spectacle.

References

Abelson, P. (2011) 'Evaluating major events and avoiding the mercantilist fallacy', *Economic Papers: A Journal of Applied Economics and Policy*, 30(1): 48–59.

Alegi, P. (2007) 'The political economy of mega-stadiums and the underdevelopment of grassroots football in South Africa', *Politikon*, 34(3): 315–31.

Alekseyeva, A. (2014) 'Sochi 2014 and the rhetoric of a new Russia: Image construction through mega-events', *East European Politics*, 30(2): 158–74.

Andranovich, G., Burbank, M.J. and Heying, C.H. (2001) 'Olympic cities: Lessons learned from mega-event politics', *Journal of Urban Affairs*, 23(2): 113–31.

Baade, R.A. and Matheson, V.A. (2004) 'The quest for the cup: Assessing the economic impact of the World Cup', *Regional Studies*, 38(4): 343–54.

Bennett, C.J. and Haggerty, K.D. (eds) (2011) *Security Games: Surveillance and Control at Mega-Events*. London: Routledge.

Blunden, H. (2012) 'The Olympic Games and housing', in H.J. Lenskyj and S. Wagg (eds), *The Palgrave Handbook of Olympic Studies*. Basingstoke: Palgrave Macmillan, pp. 520–32.

Bolsmann, C. and Brewster, K. (2009) 'Mexico 1968 and South Africa 2010: Development, leadership and legacies', *Sport in Society*, 12(10): 1284–98.

Boykoff, J. (2014) *Activism and the Olympics: Dissent at the Games in Vancouver and London*. New Brunswick, NJ: Rutgers University Press.

Buchowski, M. and Kowalska, M.Z. (2015) 'Doing ethnography and writing anthropology: A single-site-multiple-ethnography of a protest event against the 2012 UEFA European Championship in Poznań', in B. Alpan, A. Schwell and A. Sonntag (eds), *The European Football Championship: Mega-Event and Vanity Fair*. Basingstoke: Palgrave Macmillan, pp. 150–72.

Caldas-Coulthard, C.R. and Coulthard, M. (1996) *Texts and Practices: Readings in Critical Discourse Analysis*. London: Routledge.

Castro, D.G., Gaffney, C., Novaes, P.R., Rodrigues, J.M., Santos, C. and Santos Júnior, O. (eds) (2015) *Rio de Janeiro: Os Impactos Da Copa Do Mundo 2014 E Das Olimpíadas 2016*. Rio de Janeiro: Letra Capital.

Coaffee, J. (2011) 'Urban regeneration and renewal', in J.R. Gold and M.M. Gold (eds), *Olympic Cities: City Agendas, Planning and the World's Games* (2nd edition). London: Routledge, pp. 180–93.

Cook, I.R. and Ward, K. (2011) 'Trans-national networks of learning, mega-events and policy tourism: The case of Manchester's Commonwealth and Olympic Games projects', *Urban Studies*, 48(12): 2519–35.

Cornelissen, S. (2010) 'The geopolitics of global aspiration: sport mega-events and emerging powers', *The International Journal of the History of Sport*, 27(16–18): 3008–25.

Darnell, S.C. (2012) 'Olympism in Action, Olympic hosting and the politics of "Sport for Development and Peace": Investigating the development discourses of Rio 2016', *Sport in Society*, 15(6): 869–87.

Essex, S. and Chalkley, B. (2004) 'Mega-sporting events in urban and regional policy: A history of the Winter Olympics', *Planning Perspectives*, 19(2): 201–4.

Flyvbjerg, B. and Stewart, A. (2012) 'Olympic proportions: Cost and cost overrun at the Olympics 1960–2012', *Said Business School Working Paper*. http://dx.doi.org/10.2139/ssrn.2238053

Freeman, J. (2014) 'Raising the flag over Rio de Janeiro's favelas: Citizenship and social control in the Olympic city', *Journal of Latin American Geography*, 13(1): 7–38.

Fussey, P., Coaffee, J., Armstrong, G. and Hobbs, D. (2011) *Securing and Sustaining the Olympic City: Reconfiguring London for 2012 and Beyond*. Farnham: Ashgate.

Gaffney, C. (2008) *Temples of the Earthbound Gods: Stadiums in the Cultural Landscapes of Rio de Janeiro and Buenos Aires*. Austin, TX: University of Texas Press.

(Continued)

Gaffney, C. (2010) 'Mega-events and socio-spatial dynamics in Rio de Janeiro, 1919–2016', *Journal of Latin American Geography*, 9(1): 7–29.

Gaffney, C. (2013) 'Between discourse and reality: The un-sustainability of mega-event planning', *Sustainability*, 5(9): 3926–40.

Giulianotti, R., Armstrong, G., Hales, G. and Hobbs, D. (2015) 'Sport mega-events and public opposition: A sociological study of the London 2012 Olympics', *Journal of Sport and Social Issues*, 39(2): 99–119.

Gold, J.R. and Gold, M.M. (eds) (2011) *Olympic Cities: City Agendas, Planning and the World's Games* (2nd edition). London: Routledge.

Hall, C.M. (2006) 'Urban entrepreneurship, corporate interests and sports mega-events: The thin policies of competitiveness within the hard outcomes of neoliberalism', *The Sociological Review*, 54 (Supplement s2): 59–70.

Hiller, H.H. (2000) 'Toward an urban sociology of mega-events', *Research in Urban Sociology*, 5: 181–205.

Hiller, H.H. and Wanner, R.A. (2015) 'The psycho-social impact of the Olympics as urban festival: A leisure perspective', *Leisure Studies*, 34(6): 672–88.

Horne, J. and Whannel, G. (2016) *Understanding the Olympics* (2nd edition). London: Routledge.

Karamichas, J. (2013) *The Olympic Games and the Environment*. Basingstoke: Palgrave Macmillan.

Karg, A. and Lock, D. (2014) 'Using new media to engage consumers at the Football World Cup', in S. Frawley and D. Adair (eds), *Managing the Football World Cup*. Basingstoke: Palgrave Macmillan. pp. 25–46.

Kennelly, J. (2015) '"You're making our city look bad": Olympic security, neoliberal urbanization, and homeless youth', *Ethnography*, 16(1): 3–24.

Kennelly, J. and Watt, P. (2011) 'Sanitizing public space in Olympic host cities: The spatial experiences of marginalized youth in 2010 Vancouver and 2012 London', *Sociology*, 45(5): 765–81.

Lauermann, J. (2014a) 'Legacy after the bid? The impact of bidding to host Olympic Games on urban development planning', The Olympic Studies Centre. https://library.olympic.org/Default/doc/SYRACUSE/32532/legacy-after-the-bid-the-impact-of-bidding-to-host-olympic-games-on-urban-development-planning-john-?_lg=en-GB (accessed 19 September 2017).

Lauermann, J. (2014b) 'Competition through interurban policy making: Bidding to host megaevents as entrepreneurial networking', *Environment and Planning A*, 46(11): 2638–53.

Lauermann, J. (2018) 'Evaluating global urban sustainability', in J. Harrison and M. Hoyler (eds), *Doing Global Urban Research*. London: Sage, pp. 110–24.

Mascarenhas, G. (2013) 'Londres 2012 e Rio de Janeiro 2016: Conceito e realidade na produção da cidade Olímpica', *Revista Continentes*, 2(3): 52–72.

McGillivray, D. and Frew, M. (2013) 'The Olympic torch relay: Activating citizen-consumer discourses', *Lusophone Journal of Cultural Studies*, 1(2): 214–33.

Müller, M. (2014) 'After Sochi 2014: Costs and impacts of Russia's Olympic Games', *Eurasian Geography and Economics*, 55(6): 628–55.

Preuss, H. and Alfs, C. (2011) 'Signaling through the 2008 Beijing Olympics - using mega sport events to change the perception and image of the host', *European Sport Management Quarterly*, 11(1): 55–71.

Prince, R. (2012) 'Policy transfer, consultants and the geographies of governance', *Progress in Human Geography*, 36(2): 188–203.

Puijk, R. (1999) 'Producing Norwegian culture for domestic and foreign gazes: The Lillehammer Olympic opening ceremony', in A.M. Klausen (ed.), *Olympic Games as Performance and Public Event: The Case of the XVII Winter Olympic Games in Norway*. New York: Berghahn Books, pp. 97–136.

Qing, L., Boccia, L.V., Chunmiao, H., Xing, L., Fu, Y. and Kennett, C. (2010) 'Representing the opening ceremony: Comparative content analysis from USA, Brazil, UK and China', *The International Journal of the History of Sport*, 27(9–10): 1591–1633.

Salazar, N.B., Timmerman, C., Wets, J., Gato, L.G. and Van den Broucke, S. (eds) (2017) *Mega-Event Mobilities: A Critical Analysis*. London: Routledge.

Santos Júnior, O., Gaffney, C. and Ribeiro, L.C. (eds) (2015) *Brasil: Os Impactos Da Copa Do Mundo 2014 E Das Olimpíadas 2016*. Rio de Janeiro: Letra Capital.

Shin, H.B. (2018) 'Studying global gentrifications', in J. Harrison and M. Hoyler (eds), *Doing Global Urban Research*. London: Sage, pp. 138–52.

Smith, A. (2014) '"De-risking" East London: Olympic regeneration planning 2000–2012', *European Planning Studies*, 22(9): 1919–39.

Solberg, H.A. and Gratton, C. (2014) 'Broadcasting the World Cup', in S. Frawley and D. Adair (eds), *Managing the Football World Cup*. Basingstoke: Palgrave Macmillan, pp. 47–62.

Taylor, T. and Toohey, K. (2011) 'Ensuring safety at Australian sport event precincts creating securitised, sanitised and stifling spaces?', *Urban Studies*, 48(15): 3259–75.

Waardenburg, M., van den Bergh, M. and van Eekeren, F. (2015) 'Local meanings of a sport mega-event's legacies: Stories from a South African urban neighbourhood', *South African Review of Sociology*, 46(1): 87–105.

Watt, P. (2013) '"It's not for us": Regeneration, the 2012 Olympics and the gentrification of East London', *City*, 17(1): 99–118.

Wolfe, S.D. (2016) 'A silver medal project: The partial success of Russia's soft power in Sochi 2014', *Annals of Leisure Research*, 19(4): 481–96.

Wood, A. (2015) 'The politics of policy circulation: Unpacking the relationship between South African and South American cities in the adoption of bus rapid transit', *Antipode*, 47(4): 1062–79.

Zhou, Y. and Ap, J. (2009) 'Residents' perceptions towards the impacts of the Beijing 2008 Olympic Games', *Journal of Travel Research*, 48(1): 78–91.

Zimbalist, A. (2015) *Circus Maximus: The Economic Gamble behind Hosting the Olympics and the World Cup*. Washington, DC: Brookings Institution Press.

10

STUDYING GLOBAL GENTRIFICATIONS

Hyun Bang Shin

Why research global gentrifications?

It has been more than half a century since Ruth Glass's (1964) seminal essay that coined the term 'gentrification'. At the time, gentrification was about inner-city residential neighbourhoods that saw the incremental dwelling-by-dwelling upgrading of individual properties, which resulted in the replacement of original working-class families with middle classes. It was indeed a critical enquiry into class remake of urban space, while the urban context of north London determined the actual speed and form of how this class remake of urban space was carried out. Since then, gentrification studies have seen the proliferation of a large body of literature whose geographical coverage has gone global. Increasingly, we hear stories from non-usual suspects of gentrification about heritage conservation, transnational cityscapes, mega-projects and redevelopment of substandard and dilapidated neighbourhoods, and how these urban processes exacerbate place-specific socio-spatial injustices that accompany displacement of original land users. Despite some reservations among sceptics of the gentrification framework, as Ley and Teo (2014: 1296) assert, gentrification continues to offer 'a critical edge and some theoretical coherence to physical and social change incorporating eviction, displacement, demolition and redevelopment'.

Contemporary urban policies increasingly promote accumulation through the reorganization of the built environment (Cochrane, 2007; Harvey, 1989). This shifting attention has significant implications for the rise of gentrification, as real estate becomes a main source of not only public finance and business profits but also asset accumulation for individuals. Nowadays, we hear frequent reference to how gentrification has gone global (Smith, 2002), but instead of seeing the rise of gentrification as only having resulted from the dissemination of mobile capital and urbanism from the core to the peripheries of the world economy, it is important to see how the dependence on the secondary circuit of the built environment (real estate in particular) (Harvey, 1978; Lefebvre, 1970 [2003]) has become a general characteristic of capital accumulation. This has preconditioned the rise of gentrification as an endogenous (rather than imported) urban process, thus producing 'multiple gentrifications in a pluralistic sense rather than "Gentrification" with a capital "G"' (Lees et al. 2015: 442). It is in this regard that gentrification has become a planetary phenomenon (see Lees et al., 2016 for more discussions on planetary gentrification; also Sigler and Wachsmuth, 2016; Slater, 2017; Wyly, 2015).

In this chapter, I discuss some of the salient issues that are at the centre of planetary thinking of gentrification, examining how the inclusion of the urbanization experiences of non-usual suspects in the Global South helps us expand our horizon of gentrification research and reinterpret what has been learnt from the Global North. First, the chapter discusses how our understanding of displacement needs to actively take into consideration temporality, spatial relations and subjectivity. Second, the chapter ascertains the importance of locating gentrification in broader urban processes and also in the context of uneven development. Third, the chapter argues that gentrification is to be treated as a political and ideological project of the state and the ruling class in addition to it being an economic project. The concluding section sums up the arguments and provides some reflections on what it means to do comparative research on global gentrifications from a planetary perspective.

Challenges of doing global gentrification research: complicating displacement

At the heart of gentrification research is the attention to displacement. Any gentrification study that does not take displacement seriously can be regarded as an incomplete enquiry (see Slater, 2006). Nevertheless, despite the long history of gentrification research and enquiries into displacement from various disciplines, our understanding of displacement still remains limited. If we take into consideration the experience of the urbanizing world outside the Global North, then the picture gets even more complicated, but the complexity provides us with greater opportunities to advance our contemporary understanding of displacement.

Studies on displacement often focus on physical displacement concerning the last remaining residents only, who become subject to eviction when their properties are taken away by the government, developers, landlords and/or property agents. However, Peter Marcuse's (1985) seminal work provides a rich source of inspiration, for he reminds us that displacement is multidimensional and that its study needs to consider temporality, spatial relations and subjectivity. First of all, his reference to 'chain displacement' highlights the importance of processual approaches to the study of displacement, calling for the need to examine what happens to previous residents who decide to leave their neighbourhoods and whose empty dwellings get occupied eventually by last-remaining residents. This effectively asks us to think of displacement as a process that begins long before any official eviction notice is given to occupants.

While 'chain displacement' involves the succession of occupants, Mateja Celestina's (2016) insightful paper reminds us of the temporality of displacement embodied in an individual. Placed in the context of armed conflict and violence in Bolivian rural villages, Celestina (2016: 388) raises a penetrating question of 'when the "clock" of displacement starts'. When people are placed under heavy physical and psychological pressure that threatens their sense of belonging and security in their original place of residence, their perception of displacement already commences, even though their actual physical displacement is yet to arrive:

> [. . .] it is difficult to specify a precise starting point for displacement. Some events, like imprisonment and disappearance, might play a more prominent role than others and are indeed more memorable and have greater consequences. They therefore stand out. But alongside these events, the process of displacement can be traced back to a time when the negotiation of place became increasingly difficult; when witnessing the unmaking of one's place took on sufficient force, velocity and persistence that any attempts at resistance or other efforts to make the place more similar to what it used to be were perceived as futile. (Celestina, 2016: 388)

While the above statement reiterates the significance of a temporal understanding of displacement, it also highlights the importance of paying attention to various types of violence that displacees confront well before their actual moment of vacating their home, something that Marcuse (1985) was also trying to emphasize by coming up with the term 'displacement pressure'. Numerous studies point out that displacees are often threatened by legal and/or extralegal forces (for example, privately hired thugs), which can be immensely stressful and sometimes life-threatening (see for example, Gray and Porter, 2015; Shao, 2013; Shin, 2013). The importance of taking subjective feelings seriously is also underscored in the recent discussions about phenomenological or symbolic displacement (see Atkinson, 2015; Davidson and Lees, 2010; Shaw and Hagemans, 2015), which understand displacement to be more than physical displacement from a given space and call for the inclusion of psychological and emotional detachment or alienation from original places of residence even though residents stay put. Furthermore, the ordeal of domicide (the deliberate destruction of homes; see Porteous and Smith, 2001) has long-lasting effects on displacees' physical and psychological well-being: in this regard, in addition to the question of when the 'displacement clock' starts, we may also need to ask if the 'displacement clock' *will ever stop ticking*.

Displacement is also highly likely to be inherited across generations within a family, especially in countries of the Global South, where condensed urbanization is manifested (Shin, 2014). For instance, residents who are displaced to urban peripheral neighbourhoods as part of inner-city redevelopment to create a central business district (read gentrification) may become subject to another round of displacement in future, as rapid urban growth opens up opportunities to invite surplus capital for real estate and infrastructure development to urban peripheries. What used to be brand new (re-)developed neighbourhoods may also undergo new-build gentrification long before they reach their design building age, as they face obsolescence and thus a widening rent gap (see Weber, 2002). Under these circumstances, displacement becomes a repeated tragedy and disaster within a family, passed on from parents to their children's generation. The experience of an interviewee that I came across some years ago (in 2002) in Seoul very much testifies to the inheritance of displacement:

> I was in my second year of primary school when we were evicted and built a new house here. It's been more than 30 years since then, since 1968 [. . .] I came home after school, and my house was gone. I looked for my mom, and on a main road, there were my mom and dad, on a vehicle that resembled one of those garbage trucks. That night, we came here, and the life in Nangok began. (Female in her 40s, interviewed in Seoul; cited from Shin, 2006: 106)

In addition to temporality and subjectivity, Marcuse (1985) puts forward the notion of 'exclusionary displacement', which is concerned with the gentrification of a neighbourhood previously affordable to the poor and the impact of such gentrification on the poor living elsewhere.[1] Marcuse's conceptualization of exclusionary displacement compels us to retain a relational understanding of space, and to zoom out and consider what happens in those areas outside gentrified ones. Building on this perspective allows us to understand 'balloon effects' associated with mega-gentrification and displacement especially in the Global South (see Lees et al., 2016: chapter 7).[2] When an entire neighbourhood is subject to mega-gentrification as in a redevelopment project, the resulting displacement calls for a broader understanding about the relationship between the gentrified neighbourhood and the entire city (and beyond). For example, a number of substandard and informal settlements in the Global South are increasingly becoming subject to new-build gentrification, producing hundreds and thousands of displaced families looking for alternative housing.[3] For various reasons such as employment proximity and education of their children, families often end up finding a relocation dwelling in adjacent neighbourhoods, which get densified because of incoming displacees and experience pressure of rent increase. In short, there is a 'balloon effect' created by mega-displacement.

We need to understand what social and psychological impacts are experienced by those neighbourhoods that act as hosts to displacees, how the displacees adjust to the post-displacement lives and built environment, and if there are any embryonic signs of housing problems displaced to destination neighbourhoods.

The above discussions produce a set of huge policy implications as well. Governments often focus on last-remaining residents when estimating the costs of urban regeneration, and they often do this by limiting the enumeration to those residents eligible for compensation only in a project neighbourhood. In mainland China, for example, official publications usually omit migrant tenants from their estimation of the number of citizens affected by urban (re)development projects (see Shin, 2013), which results in huge underestimation of the real scale of displacement. If we include all dimensions of displacement such as chain and exclusionary displacement, the scale of displacement by any given urban regeneration programme would be much higher. Furthermore, the consideration of symbolic or phenomenological displacement means that any effort to rehouse original residents needs to go beyond simple rehousing and include the set-up of inclusionary measures that would allow rehoused original residents to feel at home and not alienated by the changed environment. Any discussions regarding the rehousing of original residents after redevelopment will need to be made with reference to (i) how much the original residents would retain a sense of belonging after regeneration; (ii) how much the original residents were in control of changes, meaning that original residents' views are to be taken on board from the early stage of designing a regeneration programme.

A more nuanced understanding of displacement is therefore an urgent task, especially in a rapidly urbanizing context such as that found in East Asia, where one may often come across viewpoints that exhibit a degree of positive understanding of neighbourhood changes, even if such changes incur wholesale clearance of existing dwellings and displacement of original residents: The justification is that original residents' poor dwelling conditions are improved by the redevelopment. For instance, Li and Song (2009: 1104) in their examination of changes to dwelling conditions among displacees in Shanghai conclude that displacees 'enjoy comparatively good housing' and 'are generally satisfied with their dwelling, if less so with their neighbourhood'. Because mainland China's redevelopment projects in major cities from the 1990s onward were focusing on those neighbourhoods that were deemed too dilapidated and structurally precarious to be subject to privatization (see Shin, 2007), and because of the socialist legacy built in the compensation system, most displacees are less likely to encounter worse housing conditions after displacement. Taking improved housing conditions as a reference point for evaluating displacees' satisfaction can therefore be limiting. More importantly, the focus on changed physical conditions of living overlooks the subjective feeling and various bodily threats that might imprint life-long scars in each displacee's mind and body. Here, Davidson and Lees (2010: 403) provide a helpful reminder: 'A phenomenological reading of dis*place*ment is a powerful critique of the positivistic tendencies in theses on replacement; it means analysing not the spatial fact or moment of displacement, rather the "structures of feeling" and "loss of sense of place" associated with dis*place*ment' (original emphasis).

Techniques for researching global gentrifications

In locating gentrification, the researcher needs to pay attention to other locally embedded urban processes that work in tandem with gentrification (Shin et al., 2016). In this section, I discuss some of the key approaches to carrying out research on global gentrifications, highlighting the importance of situating gentrification in wider urban processes and discussing how researchers working on the Global South and the Global North can learn from each other. Gentrification has been traditionally perceived as a neighbourhood-based urban process. As such, neighbourhood has often served as the main unit of analysis in gentrification research, with researchers zooming in to verify the presence (or absence) of gentrification. To some extent, this inward orientation and thinking of gentrification within a fixed boundary is inevitable, if any enumeration of displacees is to be carried out: it is vital to identify who used to live in a given area before finding out how many of them were displaced. For this reason, regeneration project sites subject to planning approval often become part of gentrification studies, as they usually provide opportunities to acquire official information on local populations, even if overly simplified. However, restricting one's enquiry into what goes on within a set boundary somewhat assumes that the urban space is a container of activities that unfold therein.

In the Global South in particular, it is necessary for gentrification research to take into consideration the particular contingent factors that produce 'mutated' forms of gentrification, deviating from more conventional forms of gentrification found in the Global North. Due to the ways in which contemporary urbanization produces city forms that co-exist or come into conflict with historic forms of human settlements, it is more likely for gentrification in the Global South to play out in a more complex legal, social, and physical environment than can be found in the Global North. For instance, it is probable to see the presence of a diverse range of extralegal tenure and informal property rights that determine the outcome of (speculative) property transactions in the Global South (Desai and Loftus, 2013). Informal building practices are often endorsed with the state turning a blind eye if such practices are deemed to be in the interests of influential private actors (Roy, 2005; Shatkin, 2008). The attention to such informality in the Global South can also feed into the study of gentrification in the Global North, shedding light on the extent to which cities in the Global North are not immune to informal building and tenure practices. As Bahar Sakızlioğlu (2014) has noted on her comparative study of state-led gentrification and displacement in both Dutch and Turkish neighbourhoods, researchers fail to study informality in Western cities in the same way as they do in non-Western cities.

Sceptics of gentrification usually assume that gentrification is largely associated with individualized tenure and involves transaction of formal private properties. Based on this understanding, they would argue that gentrification as a concept has a limited scope when transplanted to the Global South (see, for example, Ghertner, 2015; Maloutas, 2011). However, this is the same error as saying that the Western world sees capitalism as the only mode of production. It is not, and cannot be: different modes survive, albeit waning to varying degrees, and it is the prevalence of the capitalist mode of production, not the complete replacement of pre-capitalist modes, that warrants our attention for analysing capitalist society and economy.[4] Researchers working on gentrification in the Global North need to take into consideration how informality and non-market(ized) components of the economy and society influence the working of gentrification, and how multiple processes work together to determine the socio-spatial outcome that researchers come to observe. As Matthias Bernt (2016: 643) has ascertained, '[t]he commodification of housing and its decommodification are thus closely connected and need to be studied together, and this is true for both "northern" and "southern" experiences'.

I have tried to address some of the above concerns elsewhere (Shin, 2016), discussing how mainland China's particular land ownership structure produces a place-specific process of dispossession to create a pathway to gentrification. The argument was that in mainland China, both economic (land market) and extra-economic forces (the use of state apparatus and collective relations to coerce individual agreement to top-down redevelopment decision) are at play simultaneously. This perspective is not to be taken to indicate that the coercive use of state apparatus or extra-economic force are unique to mainland China or the Global South more broadly speaking, since the use of extra-economic force 'is a regular companion of gentrification, not only in the South, but everywhere' (Bernt, 2016: 642).

Additionally, there is a need to take political and cultural dimensions of urban change more seriously when discussing the reasons behind the rise of gentrification. When adhering to a critical political economic perspective (Lees et al., 2016), it is crucial to understand the extent to which material conditions mature, thus the need to examine the widening of the rent gap and the circulations of (real estate) capital (see López-Morales, 2011, 2016 and Shin, 2009 for some of the examples of rent gap in non-Western cities; and Slater, 2017 for rent gaps at planetary scale). However, this is not to prioritize the economics of gentrification (rent gap, exploitation of land rents, etc.) with no recourse for politics and culture to explain the rise of (or the absence of) gentrification in a given place. Even Neil Smith, who was frequently wrongly accused of being an advocate of an economically deterministic perspective, stresses that enlarged rent gaps do not act as a determinant of gentrification, but are simply indicating a greater possibility of gentrification to occur in that location:

> The whole point of the rent gap theory is not that gentrification occurs in some deterministic fashion where housing costs are lowest [. . .] but that it is most likely to occur in areas experiencing a sufficiently large gap between actual and potential land values. This is a fundamental distinction. Areas such as the central and inner city where the rent gap may be greatest may also experience very high land values and housing costs despite disinvestment from the built environment and the consequent rent gap. (Smith, 1987: 464)

Essentially, political struggles to turn material potentials into reality do matter. A neighbourhood experiencing gentrification would be a reflection of the imbalance of power relations skewed towards the rich and powerful. This is the conclusion also reached in my analysis (Shin, 2009) of how a substandard and informal neighbourhood in Seoul's periphery was redeveloped into an upscale housing estate that saw the displacement of the absolute majority of local tenants and owner-occupiers. Conversely, the importance of political struggles suggests that even if material conditions of gentrification mature, gentrification can be resisted if enough support for anti-gentrification can be mobilized.

Finally, gentrification researchers need to zoom out of neighbourhoods and be inclusive of wider processes of uneven development. As much as the global circuits of capital produce uneven development across the world, the ways in which surplus capital flows into cities and regions within a national territory and into different districts and neighbourhoods within a city are inevitably uneven. Therefore, it is highly possible that the prominence of gentrification in a city may come at the expense of urban decline elsewhere within and/or outside the city. For instance, in the UK, what does London's super-gentrification mean for the rest of the country? What does the domination of new-build gentrification in Seoul mean for other regional cities in South Korea? How does the inner-city gentrification of Beijing resulting from redevelopment projects reconcile with the concurrent processes of area-based conservation of the city's heritage sites and the suburbanization of new estate construction? What is the implication of 'splintering urbanism' for gentrification of cities in India? What does the construction of new 'urban utopias' (such as smart cities, eco-cities) for the middle- and upper classes in urban peripheries, a practice that is high on many government agendas in the Global South, mean for the future of historic urban cores? Reflecting diverse urban development trajectories in and outside cities around the world, there are endless questions that can be raised to help understand what kind of relationship gentrification of a given urban space establishes vis-à-vis other spatial processes at work. Here, a helpful reminder comes from Doreen Massey (1999: 281) who in her discussion of the space of politics points out that: '[a]n understanding of spatiality [. . .] entails the recognition that there is more than one story going on in the world and that these stories have, at least, a relative autonomy'. In addition to this perspective, Massey (1984) also highlights the persistent challenge every geographer faces; that is, the need to analyse the uniqueness of a place without losing sight of the general cause. For gentrification researchers and other urban scholars, it is essential to acknowledge the presence of multiple processes working simultaneously in a given space, and to discuss how these multiple processes – one of which may be gentrification – intersect, and what kind of compounding relationship they produce.

Rethinking gentrification as amalgamation of economic, political and ideological projects: An illustrated case study of Beijing

Gentrification as an economic project is a well-known argument (see Lees et al., 2008). The transformation of the demographic structure of a gentrified neighbourhood accompanied by upgrading or redevelopment of dilapidated dwellings is a welcoming change from the perspective of local government officials who equate the change with higher tax revenues, and of developers, financiers and property agents who welcome the new business opportunities (Betancur, 2002; Lang, 1986). In a place where land revenues are collected directly by local governments to be put into public finance for further development of infrastructure, gentrification is more than the beautification of the cityscape. This is the case in mainland China where under state ownership of urban construction land, land use rights are transferred from the state to developers in return for land use premium and other administrative charges (Hsing, 2010; Lin, 2015). Revenues collected in this way are known to account for a substantial share of municipal finance, sometimes exceeding the amount of other tax revenues (known as budgetary income as opposed to extra-budgetary income that land accounts belong to) (Hsing, 2010; Lin, 2015).

In addition to understanding gentrification as an economic project, gentrification is often part and parcel of political and ideological projects of the state and the ruling elites. Gentrification facilitates social cleansing, driving those deemed socially undesirable away from the urban space earmarked for those sought-after by the state. The retention of social order under the terms and conditions imposed by the ruling elites is an argument that Neil Smith put forward in his discussion of 'revanchist urbanism' (1996). With the growing economic and political power of major cities in the Global South, there is an increasing trend of urban policies aiming to convert an entire urban district into an exclusive space of development to cater for the needs of domestic and transnational elites and to showcase the power of the state and its legitimacy.

The example of China is an illustration of this, particularly the experience of Beijing, where the municipal government has strived to transform Beijing into a world city, following the hosting of the 2008 Summer Olympic Games.

Both urbanization itself and gentrification in a major city like Beijing have been the Chinese state's political, economic and ideological project (see Shin, 2014). In Beijing, one of the inner-city districts called Dongcheng District announced in 2011 that it would aim to reduce its population size substantially during the next 20 years so that the district population is to reach 650,000 people by 2030, which is 269,000 people less than the figure in 2011 (Dongcheng District Government, 2011). This was in line with the Beijing municipal government's effort to promote Beijing as world city, and was to help the Dongcheng District enhance its characteristic as a cultural, political and business centre of Beijing. The reduction of the district population was to be achieved by displacing those less desirable low-end services and industries (for example printing, garbage collection) and controlling the inflow of low-skilled migrant workers, while inviting highly talented professionals. The expected result is the production of an exclusive space that is earmarked for the consumption by domestic and transnational elites at the expense of the displacement of those workers deemed less desirable to fulfil the government's ambition. This is in fact mega-gentrification at city scale, driven by the municipal government (or the municipal branch of the party state) to fulfil their political ambition. Obviously, from the perspective of displacees, such transformation represents urban injustice, as they are being driven away from the city they helped to construct.

Reflections on doing global gentrification research

Despite various attempts by pro-business interests that try to depict gentrification as a positive urban process, gentrification remains a concept that highlights the looting and destruction of homes and neighbourhoods in order to advance the interests of the rich and powerful. As an urban process, gentrification is the class remake of urban space, entailing the exacerbation of urban socio-spatial injustice by the speculative desire to exploit the land rent gap and create an exclusive space that bars the poor and the marginalized from claiming their right to the city (Wachsmuth, Chapter 11). Doing global gentrification research is to understand the dialectical relationship between the particularity and the generality of gentrification processes (see Shin et al., 2016), and how this relationship is embodied in an individual case that gentrification as well as non-gentrification researchers study.

Is gentrification a useful concept for critically examining urban processes in both the Global North and the Global South? The conclusion of this chapter is an explicit yes, as long as both gentrification and non-gentrification researchers remain open-minded about multiple possibilities or combinations of urban processes that may work in tandem, and employ a relational perspective on space so that inquiries do not get confined to a single case or process under observation. Here, Doreen Massey's remark is a helpful reminder of this relationship between particularity and generality:

> The fundamental methodological question is how to keep a grip on the generality of events, the wider processes lying behind them, without losing sight of the individuality of the form of their occurrence. Pointing to general processes does not adequately explain what is happening at particular moments or in particular places. Yet any explanation must include such general processes. The question is how [. . .]. "General processes" *never* work themselves out in pure form. There are always specific circumstances, a particular history, a particular place or location. What is at issue – and to put it in geographical terms – is the articulation of the general with the local (the particular) to produce qualitatively different outcomes in different localities. (Massey, 1984: 9)

Doing global gentrification research is not to rule out cities in the Global South as if they possess distinctive urban processes that make them immune to gentrification. In so much as the cities in the Global South see the rising importance of the real estate industry and the secondary circuit of capital accumulation that is the built environment, they are prone to gentrification pressure. Borrowing from the words of Doreen Massey (1999: 281) again, doing global gentrification research is then to shed light on 'the possibility of the existence of a multiplicity of narratives' by acknowledging '[a] spatial (rather than a temporal) recognition of difference'. In this way, the urban processes in the Global South are not understood simply as part of the urbanizing Global South catching up with the Global North. This is what lies at the heart of a planetary perspective on studying global gentrifications.

Finally, it is important for researchers to think of why they carry out gentrification studies. Thinking about the purpose of one's research is closely related with the question of 'how to' do global gentrification research. On the one hand, there is the urgency of situating our understanding of gentrification in the concrete web of urban life, to give meaning to the struggles of displacees, and to think of the generality based on our own observations and review of empirical studies. With displacement of existing land users at its heart, gentrification research is essentially bound up with the question of social injustice (Lees, 2014; Smith, 1996). Devising local action plans to realize social justice and progressive urbanism requires the identification of place-specificities that produce injustice, while having a longer-term perspective on what cities after capitalism would look like. Gentrification research means to learn from the real struggles of displacees who open up new avenues of innovative anti-gentrification measures (Derickson and Routledge, 2015). This process of learning is what constitutes knowledge co-production in gentrification research, which would bring gentrification studies out of the entanglements about definitional disputes (Slater, 2006). Only then can we begin to think of place-specific strategies to fight urban injustice which is in part generated by gentrification. Global gentrification research, in this regard, is to inform locally embedded endogenous struggles against displacement in order for wider cross-regional alliances and solidarity to be formed so that social justice and cities after capitalism can be imagined collectively at planetary scale.

Notes

1. This type of displacement may result in the scarcity of remaining affordable housing units, preventing people from moving out of their current neighbourhoods even if their neighbourhoods experience rent hikes. Area-based poverty concentration may be one of the outcomes of exclusionary displacement.
2. Mega-gentrification is also increasingly popular in the Global North with the rise of mega-displacement; for example see Lees (2014) for the gentrification of council housing estates in London.
3. For example, in Seoul, about 720,000 people were known to have been affected by urban redevelopment projects between 1983 and 1988. Similar situations could be found in Beijing where 1.5 million people were estimated to have been affected by redevelopment projects between 2001 and 2008 (see ACHR, 1989; COHRE, 2007).
4. After all, the first line of *Capital,* Volume 1 says: 'The wealth of societies in which the capitalist mode of production prevails appears as an "immense collection of commodities"' (Marx, 1867 [1990: 125]). This is also similar to the ways in which we are to understand the rise of capitalism in a transitional economy, where socialist legacies create various frictions while colliding with capitalist development (Golubchikov et al., 2005; Hsing, 2010; Ma and Wu, 2005).

References

ACHR (Asia Coalition for Housing Rights) (1989) 'Evictions in Seoul, South Korea', *Environment and Urbanization*, 1(1): 89–94.

Atkinson, R. (2015) 'Losing one's place: Narratives of neighbourhood change, market injustice and symbolic displacement', *Housing, Theory and Society*, 32(4): 373–88.

(Continued)

Bernt, M. (2016) 'Very particular, or rather universal? Gentrification through the lenses of Ghertner and López-Morales', *City*, 20(4): 637–44.

Betancur, J.J. (2002) 'Can gentrification save Detroit? Definition and experiences from Chicago', *The Journal of Law and Society*, 4(1): 1–12.

Celestina, M. (2016) '"Displacement" before displacement: Time, place and the case of rural Urabá', *Journal of Latin American Studies*, 48(2): 367–90.

Cochrane, A. (2007) *Understanding Urban Policy: A Critical Introduction*. Oxford: Wiley-Blackwell.

COHRE (2007) *Fair Play for Housing Rights: Mega-Events, Olympic Games and Housing Rights*. Geneva: Centre on Housing Rights and Evictions.

Davidson, M. and Lees, L. (2010) 'New-build gentrification: Its histories, trajectories, and critical geographies', *Population, Space and Place*, 16(5): 395–411.

Derickson, K.D. and Routledge, P. (2015) 'Resourcing scholar-activism: Collaboration, transformation, and the production of knowledge', *The Professional Geographer*, 67(1): 1–7.

Desai, V. and Loftus, A. (2013) 'Speculating on slums: Infrastructural fixes in informal housing in the global South', *Antipode*, 45(4): 789–808.

Dongcheng District Government of Beijing (2011) Comprehensive Development Strategic Planning of Dongcheng District, Beijing (2011–2030). http://zhengwu.beijing.gov.cn/ghxx/qxgh/t1148628.htm (accessed 20 September 2017).

Ghertner, D.A. (2015) 'Why gentrification theory fails in "much of the world"', *City*, 19(4): 552–63.

Glass, R. (ed.) (1964) *London: Aspects of Change*. London: MacGibbon & Kee.

Golubchikov, O., Badyina, A. and Makhrova, A. (2005) 'The hybrid spatialities of transition: Capitalism, legacy and uneven urban economic restructuring', *Urban Studies*, 51(4): 617–33.

Gray, N. and Porter, L. (2015) 'By any means necessary: Urban regeneration and the "state of exception" in Glasgow's Commonwealth Games 2014', *Antipode*, 47(2): 380–400.

Harvey, D. (1978) 'The urban process under capitalism: A framework for analysis', *International Journal of Urban and Regional Research*, 2(1–3): 101–31.

Harvey, D. (1989) *The Urban Experience*. Baltimore, MD: Johns Hopkins University Press.

Hsing, Y-T. (2010) *The Great Urban Transformation: Politics of Land and Property in China*. Oxford: Oxford University Press.

Lang, M. (1986) 'Measuring economic benefits from gentrification', *Journal of Urban Affairs*, 8(4): 27–39.

Lees, L. (2014) 'The urban injustices of New Labour's "new urban renewal": The case of the Aylesbury Estate in London', *Antipode*, 46(4): 921–47.

Lees, L., Shin, H.B. and López-Morales, E. (eds) (2015) *Global Gentrifications: Uneven Development and Disparity*. Bristol: Policy Press.

Lees, L., Shin, H.B. and López-Morales, E. (2016) *Planetary Gentrification*. Cambridge: Polity Press.

Lees, L., Slater, T. and Wyly, E. (2008) *Gentrification*. New York: Routledge.

Lefebvre, H. (1970 [2003]) *The Urban Revolution*. Trans. R. Bononno. Minneapolis, MN: University of Minnesota Press.

Ley, D. and Teo, S.Y. (2014) 'Gentrification in Hong Kong? Epistemology vs. ontology', *International Journal of Urban and Regional Research*, 38(4): 1286–1303.
Li, S-M. and Song, Y-L. (2009) 'Redevelopment, displacement, housing conditions, and residential satisfaction: A study of Shanghai', *Environment and Planning A*, 41(5): 1090–1108.
Lin, G.C.S. (2015) 'The redevelopment of China's construction land: Practising land property rights in cities through renewals', *The China Quarterly*, 224: 865–87.
López-Morales, E. (2011) 'Gentrification by ground rent dispossession: The shadows cast by large-scale urban renewal in Santiago de Chile', *International Journal of Urban and Regional Research*, 35(2): 330–57.
López-Morales, E. (2016) 'Gentrification in Santiago, Chile: A property-led process of dispossession and exclusion', *Urban Geography*, 37(8): 1109–31.
Ma, L.J.C. and Wu, F. (eds) (2005) *Restructuring the Chinese City: Changing Society, Economy and Space*. Abingdon: Routledge.
Maloutas, T. (2011) 'Contextual diversity in gentrification research', *Critical Sociology*, 38(1): 33–48.
Marcuse, P. (1985) 'Gentrification, abandonment, and displacement: Connections, causes, and policy responses in New York City', *Journal of Urban and Contemporary Law*, 28: 195–240.
Marx, K. (1867 [1990]) *Capital: A Critique of Political Economy* Volume 1. Trans. B. Fowkes. London: Penguin.
Massey, D. (1984) 'Introduction: Geography matters', in D. Massey and J. Allen (eds), *Geography Matters! A Reader*. Cambridge: Cambridge University Press, pp. 1–11.
Massey, D. (1999) 'Spaces of politics', in D. Massey, J. Allen and P. Sarre (eds), *Human Geography Today*. Cambridge: Polity Press, pp. 279–94.
Porteous, J.D. and Smith, S.E. (2001) *Domicide: The Global Destruction of Home*. Montreal: McGill-Queen's University Press.
Roy, A. (2005) 'Urban informality: Toward an epistemology of planning', *Journal of the American Planning Association*, 71(2): 147–58.
Sakızlioğlu, B. (2014) 'Confessions of a doorstep researcher: Reflections on a comparative study of displacement experiences', Field Research Method Lab at LSE (14 October 2014). http://blogs.lse.ac.uk/fieldresearch/2014/10/14/confessions-of-a-doorstep-researcher (accessed 20 September 2017).
Shao, Q. (2013) *Shanghai Gone: Domicide and Defiance in a Chinese Megacity*. Lanham, MD: Rowman & Littlefield.
Shatkin, G. (2008) 'The city and the bottom line: Urban megaprojects and the privatization of planning in Southeast Asia', *Environment and Planning A*, 40(2): 383–401.
Shaw, K.S. and Hagemans, I.W. (2015) '"Gentrification without displacement" and the consequent loss of place: The effects of class transition on low-income residents of secure housing in gentrifying areas', *International Journal of Urban and Regional Research*, 39(2): 323–41.

(Continued)

Shin, H.B. (2006) 'Transforming urban neighbourhoods: Limits of developer-led partnership and benefit-sharing in residential redevelopment, with reference to Seoul and Beijing'. Unpublished PhD thesis, London School of Economics and Political Science. http://etheses.lse.ac.uk/996/ (accessed 20 September 2017).

Shin, H.B. (2007) 'Residential redevelopment and social impacts in Beijing', in F. Wu (ed.), *China's Emerging Cities: The Making of New Urbanism*. London: Routledge, pp. 163-84.

Shin, H.B. (2009) 'Property-based redevelopment and gentrification: The case of Seoul, South Korea', *Geoforum*, 40(5): 906–17.

Shin, H.B. (2013) 'The right to the city and critical reflections on China's property rights activism', *Antipode*, 45(5): 1167–89.

Shin, H.B. (2014) 'Contesting speculative urbanisation and strategising discontents', *City*, 18(4–5): 509–16.

Shin, H.B. (2016) 'Economic transition and speculative urbanisation in China: Gentrification versus dispossession', *Urban Studies*, 53(3): 471–89.

Shin, H.B., Lees, L. and López-Morales, E. (2016) 'Introduction: Locating gentrification in the Global East', *Urban Studies*, 53(3), 455–70.

Sigler, T. and Wachsmuth, D. (2016) 'Transnational gentrification: Globalisation and neighbourhoood change in Panama's Casco Antiguo', *Urban Studies*, 53(4): 705–22.

Slater, T. (2006) 'The eviction of critical perspectives from gentrification research', *International Journal of Urban and Regional Research*, 30(4): 737–57.

Slater, T. (2017) 'Planetary rent gaps', *Antipode*, 49(S1): 114–37.

Smith, N. (1987) 'Gentrification and the rent gap', *Annals of the Association of American Geographers*, 77(3): 462–5.

Smith, N. (1996) *The New Urban Frontier: Gentrification and the Revanchist City*. New York: Routledge.

Smith, N. (2002) 'New globalism, new urbanism: gentrification as global urban strategy', *Antipode*, 34(3): 427–50.

Wachsmuth, D. (2018) 'Researching the global right to the city', in J. Harrison and M. Hoyler (eds), *Doing Global Urban Research*. London: Sage, pp. 153–68.

Weber, R. (2002) 'Extracting value from the city: Neoliberalism and urban redevelopment', *Antipode*, 34(3): 519–40.

Wyly, E. (2015) 'Gentrification on the planetary urban frontier: The evolution of Turner's noösphere', *Urban Studies*, 52(14): 2515–50.

11

RESEARCHING THE GLOBAL RIGHT TO THE CITY

David Wachsmuth

Why research the global right to the city?

In March 1968, the French sociologist Henri Lefebvre published a short book called *Droit à la ville* [*Right to the City*]. Lefebvre was a professor at the suburban University of Nanterre, located on the periphery of the Paris region. Two months later, students from Nanterre were occupying universities across Paris, leading general strikes, and bringing the entire French economy to a halt with their demands for a radical transformation of French society and state. These students were the instigators of the famous May 1968 movement. Their banners and graffiti featured slogans such as 'Be realistic, demand the impossible', 'Boredom is counterrevolutionary', and 'It is forbidden to forbid'.

Some of the student leaders of the May 1968 movement were students of Lefebvre; as he himself described it, 'the movement began in a big, crowded amphitheatre where I was giving a course' (Ross, 1997: 82). And the movement as a whole can be understood as a collective attempt to claim a right to the city – what Lefebvre (1968 [1996: 158]; emphasis in original) called 'a cry and a demand [. . .] a transformed and renewed *right to urban life*'. In the fifty years since Lefebvre first published *Right to the City*, the concept has served as a rallying cry for social activism, an inspiration for urban policymaking, and an organizing concept for critical urban research. It unites questions of inclusion and exclusion, social reproduction, the use of public space, social movements and urban development.

And, in the wake of the worldwide urban upheavals of the last decade – from the Arab Spring to Occupy Wall Street, from the *indignados* of Spain and

Greece to Black Lives Matter in the United States – the right to the city has arguably taken on new, more urgent and more global dimensions. The global right to the city also now faces more formidable foes, from the profiteers and austerians of the worldwide financial crisis of 2008 to the more recent surge of far-right nationalist politics in the United States and Europe. So, what does the right to the city mean today, for political practice or scholarly research?

Challenges of researching the global right to the city

Over its fifty-year history as an intellectual, political, and policy concept, the right to the city has served as a container for many different specific ideas and agendas. But there has arguably been a relatively stable core within this diversity: a connection between, on the one hand, 'agentic' questions of urban social movements and political struggles, and, on the other, 'structural' questions of political economy, the state and power relations. We see this core within the three major 'eras' of right to the city scholarship and activism (Table 11.1).

Although this academic and policy discourse on the global right to the city has defined a reasonably coherent object of analysis and political practice, there are nevertheless a number of challenges or tensions inherent to the concept. These can be productively analysed by scrutinizing each of the keywords in the phrase 'global right to the city'. To begin with, as critical legal scholars have long recognized (Kennedy, 2002; Olsen, 1984), the concept of 'rights' is problematic to the extent that it elides questions of who has rights, who grants them, and which rights get priority. As David Harvey (2003: 940) has remarked, 'We live in a society in which the inalienable rights to private property and the profit rate trump any other conception of inalienable rights you can think of'. And, as Karl Marx (1867 [1976: 344]) famously argued, 'Between equal rights, force decides'. So who grants the right to the city? The state, in some capacity, as the international policy community would have it?

Table 11.1 Major 'eras' of right to the city scholarship and activism

Era	Emerged	Key references
Concept development	1960s	Henri Lefebvre (1968) *Right to the City*; Manuel Castells (1977) *The Urban Question*
Neo-Marxist and post-Marxist renewal	2000s	David Harvey (2003/2008) 'The right to the city'; Neil Brenner et al. (2012) *Cities for People, Not for Profit*
International urban policy debates	Mid-2000s	UNESCO (2006) *International Public Debates: Urban Policies and the Right to the City*; UN-Habitat (2010) *The Right to the City: Bridging the Urban Divide*

Or inhabitants on their own behalf, as radical urban scholars and social movements claim? This is a tension that remains to be properly explored in research and in practice.

Less recognized outside the community of critical urban studies, the concept of the 'city' is in some senses just as problematic as 'rights'. Contemporary public discourse is pervaded with variants of the 'urban age' idea – whereby the quantitative expansion of human settlement space, particularly across some putative '50% of the world now lives in cities' threshold, is meant to signal a profound global social transformation. But, paradoxically, this urban age discourse tends to simultaneously overemphasize the significance of this demographic shift while underplaying the extent to which urban regions, apparently non-urban hinterlands, and the relations between the two have been politically, socially and economically restructured in recent decades – what some scholars now call 'planetary urbanization' (Brenner, 2014; Brenner and Schmid, 2014; Katsikis, Chapter 2; Wachsmuth, 2014). Just two years after writing *Right to the City*, Lefebvre (1970 [2003: 57]) argued in *The Urban Revolution* that 'The concept of the city no longer corresponds to a social object. Sociologically it is a pseudoconcept.' Reconciling the truth of this statement with the idea of the right to the city remains a significant tension in scholarship on the latter concept.

Finally, 'global' as a modifier of the right to the city contains several tensions of its own. The right to the city is generally interpreted as pertaining to 'local' struggles over social reproduction and daily life. There are some systemic structures which potentially unite such struggles (Harvey, 2008), but even these structures are variegated. The result is that the global right to the city needs to be understood in the context of uneven spatial development: even 'global' processes take concrete form in highly differentiated ways.

These tensions concern the right to the city as a concept for research rather than a slogan to motivate political action. As a political slogan, the power of the right to the city in fact lies in these ambiguities, which allow it to evoke different dimensions of urban justice and struggle in different specific circumstances. From a research perspective, however, the conclusion is that the right to the city is an evocative concept that needs to be specified precisely if it is to have analytical traction.

Techniques for researching the global right to the city

So how can we productively research the global right to the city? A wide variety of specific methods (for example interviews, participant observation, or spatial analysis) are appropriate for specific research questions, but in this section I want to argue in favour of a common set of underlying methodological approaches.

Just as each of the keywords in the phrase reveals certain theoretical and methodological tensions, each also suggests some principles for resolving those tensions in empirical investigation and analysis. The first principle – implied by the word 'right' – is to focus on contested claims for rights, rather than rights which have already been achieved. After all, in Lefebvre's original formulation, the right to the city is 'a cry and a demand'. Since rights are always tied up in power relations and social struggles, and since the city is a key site of social reproduction and 'collective consumption' (Castells, 1977) in the contemporary world, the right to the city can be a helpful concept for analysing and decoding competing conceptions of social justice and social priorities. Concretely, urban researchers can investigate the claims that social actors make over urban space, and the actions they take in support of those claims. The political actions that individuals and groups undertake to contest the production of urban space can reveal what they believe the right to the city should be. Lefebvre (1968 [1996: 178–9]) himself thought of the right to the city in these terms: he described it as one of a number of 'rights in the making [...] rights which define civilization (in, but often *against* society – *by*, but often *against* culture)'.

The second principle is implied by the word 'city'. In the face of the ongoing transformation of urban regions into larger, polycentric and more suburbanized forms (Keil, Chapter 12) – as well as the ongoing transformation of spatial divisions of labour, consumption and regulation which have changed the relationship between urban centres and their hinterlands and frontier zones – it is increasingly difficult to answer the questions of 'what city?' or 'whose city?' implied in the concept of the right to the city. I have elsewhere argued that it is therefore more tenable to approach the concept of the city as a *category of practice* instead of a *category of analysis* (Wachsmuth, 2014). The 'city' is how people make sense of their everyday spatial practice; it is a phenomenological category. Urban researchers should take this idea seriously – that the city is a meaningful concept for everyday life – but that does not mean naturalizing the city as an adequate *analytical* concept. Urban researchers can investigate how the city is constructed as a social entity through social action, and how that entity in turn constrains individual and collective action undertaken in the name of the 'right to the city'. After all, as Robert Park (1967: 3) declared, 'if the city is the world which man [sic] created, it is the world in which he is henceforth condemned to live. Thus, indirectly, and without any clear sense of the nature of his task, in making the city man has remade himself'.

Research that uses the concept of the city as an analytical lens for understanding processes of urban transformation which are not limited to the city (in other words, a focus on the city as a site, as opposed to urbanization as a process) falls into the trap of 'methodological cityism' (Angelo and Wachsmuth, 2015). Accordingly, the final principle – suggested by the word 'global' – is not to artificially limit research on the right to the city to the boundaries of the city itself. This means, first of all, that researchers should investigate the more-than-city geographies and social networks which are co-produced with the city through urban political action. Many of the things which constrain city inhabitants' ability to enjoy the right to the city originate outside city borders (global financial markets, national political structures, regional economic restructuring), and many of the resources which inhabitants can draw upon to claim their right to the city reach outside the city too. Methodologically, this means that research on the right to the city must often travel along relatively far-flung pathways despite the apparently 'local' nature of social reproduction, daily life and urban public space which the right to the city tends to evoke.

Secondly, a global approach to researching the right to the city should explore its *variegation* across contexts (Brenner et al., 2010; Peck and Theodore, 2007), which is to say the *systematic* unevenness in how the right to the city is claimed and contested worldwide. One of the distinctive features of the right to the city as a political demand is that it has found prominence in cities and regions across both the Global North and Global South. It does not follow that the right to the city is some sort of aspatial and ahistorical universal; but this fact does establish the importance of investigating both the convergences and divergences across these contexts, and the social, political, economic and cultural factors which give rise to each (Morange and Spire, 2015).

In sum, the methodological approach to researching the global right to the city which I am advocating is one which focuses on (i) competing claims social actors make over the production of urban space; (ii) the different practical conceptions of the city which social actors articulate through the claims they make; and (iii) the more-than-city geographies which are mobilized in claims for the right to the city, and the globally variegated forms that these claims take.

Case study: The Vancouver housing crisis

How can we put these various analytical considerations into practice in concrete research into the global right to the city? In order to illustrate some of the possibilities, I offer here a brief case study of ongoing research into the crisis of housing affordability in Vancouver, Canada. The results so far are based on 18 interviews conducted with policymakers, community leaders and real estate agents in 2016; documentary and media analysis; and GIS spatial analysis.

Thanks in part to its temperate climate and natural amenities, Vancouver frequently tops lists of the most livable cities in the world (for example, Economist Intelligence Unit, 2016). But this 'livability' has paradoxically made it difficult to afford to live in Vancouver; relative to

(Continued)

household incomes, Vancouver is currently among the world's three most expensive cities (Demographia, 2016). Indeed, three distinct housing crises can be observed in contemporary Vancouver. The first is a longstanding crisis of homelessness and poverty, which has its roots in 1980s federal cuts to social housing programmes and the deinstitutionalization of the mentally ill, and has intensified in the following decades. The second is a crisis of homeownership affordability for the middle class in the Vancouver region, apparently driven by high-end housing purchases from speculative overseas investors in China. The third is a general shortage of rental housing in Vancouver – the region-wide rental vacancy rate was a shocking 0.8% in 2015, almost an order of magnitude under the 5% vacancy rate which is usually taken to indicate a healthy rental market (the rate in the city itself was even lower).

Partially corresponding to these crises, three distinct social movements have mobilized around housing affordability issues in Vancouver. First of all, there is a longstanding poor people's housing movement in Vancouver. Focused mainly on the city's Downtown Eastside, this movement has advocated for the homeless, struggled against private developers and the government to resist gentrification, and argued for the construction of new social housing (Blomley, 2004). Second, there is a loose movement organized under the hashtag #donthave1million, referring to the minimum amount of money necessary to buy a house in Vancouver. Initiated in 2015 by a Vancouver resident (and renter) in her late 20s, this movement has drawn attention in particular to the intergenerational implications of Vancouver's rising housing prices, which can be interpreted as a massive transfer of wealth to the house-owning older population from the house-renting younger population. The #donthave1million movement has also sought to frame Vancouver's housing affordability problems as an economic drain because it is driving talented young professionals out of the city. Finally, an organic opposition to speculative housing investment has emerged in Vancouver, aimed above all at the spectre of foreign ownership of housing. The major target of outrage here has been absentee property owners from China, who have bought houses in Vancouver as financial investments but keep them empty, relying on rising property values rather than tenants to achieve their rate of return.

What we find in Vancouver, in short, is not a single affordable housing movement, or even a single 'cry and demand' for affordable housing. Instead, a diverse set of groups and actors are attempting to articulate a right to the city in opposition to the commodification and financialization of housing, but in ways which sometimes fail to overlap and other times are directly contradictory.

To establish the basic historical parameters of Vancouver's housing problems, my research team analysed the full text of 1,146,061 articles in the *Vancouver Sun* and the *Province*, the two main Vancouver newspapers, between 2000 and 2015. Figure 11.1 shows the proportion of these articles which include the terms 'housing affordability', 'housing crisis', 'foreign ownership' and 'vacant housing'. What this figure indicates is that, while there was a general uptick in media discussion of housing problems in the run-up to the 2008 global financial crisis (which originated in housing markets), since 2011 there has been an explosion of discussion about housing affordability in general, and about the problems of foreign ownership and speculation in vacant houses more specifically. There has also been a smaller but noticeable increase in discussion of Vancouver's housing problems as a 'crisis' - very strong language which is rare to encounter in the mainstream media.

From a mainstream perspective, therefore, the story of Vancouver's housing problems is effectively a story of the last five years. There is undeniable truth to this perspective; as Figure 11.2 shows, since 2011 housing prices have risen to incredible heights across the region. Of particular note are the west side of the City of Vancouver and the inner suburbs to the south. The former is where absolute house prices are the highest and where there is general agreement that overseas Chinese

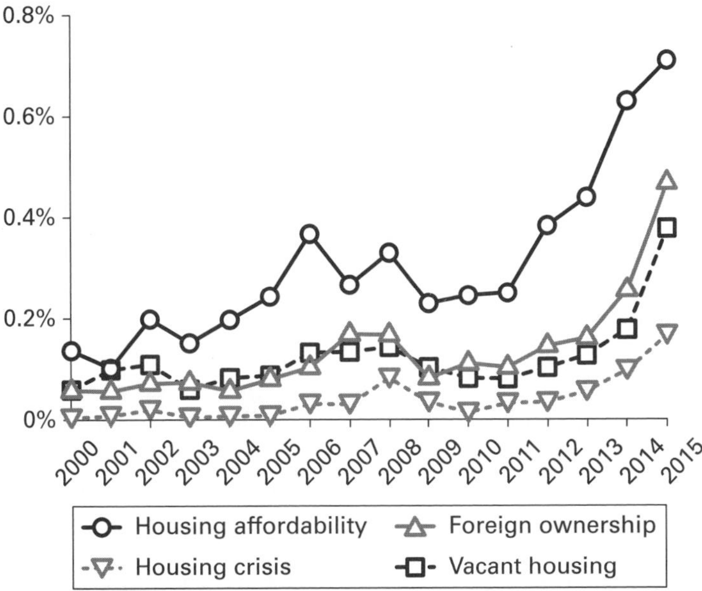

Figure 11.1 Proportion of articles in Vancouver newspapers referencing housing problems

Source: David Wachsmuth and Shunyao Chen

(Continued)

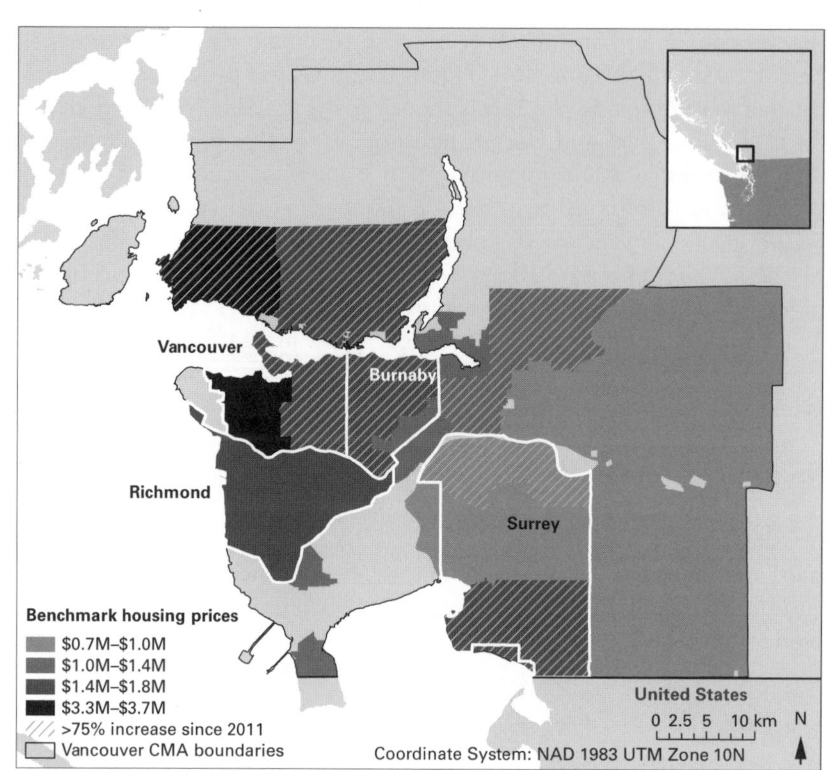

Figure 11.2 Benchmark house prices by neighbourhood in Vancouver, August 2016

Source: Real Estate Board of Greater Vancouver and Fraser Valley Real Estate Board; map by David Wachsmuth and Shunyao Chen

ownership of housing has surged in recent years. The latter, however, is where the homeownership affordability problem is arguably most acute. Unlike the west side of Vancouver, where prices have increased from already extremely high baselines, houses in the inner suburbs of Richmond and Surrey here have historically been reasonably affordable for middle-class and even working-class families. The high benchmark housing prices combined with the large percentage increase in prices in the last five years demonstrates that this is no longer true, and this fact has been particularly important for motivating the #donthave1million protests.

However, another perspective on Vancouver's housing affordability issues can be seen in Figure 11.3, which shows the incidence of 'core housing need' across the region. A household is in core housing need if it is unable to afford decent housing, and the map shows that there are census tracts where more than a third of the population is in this situation. They are concentrated in the Downtown Eastside (where a majority

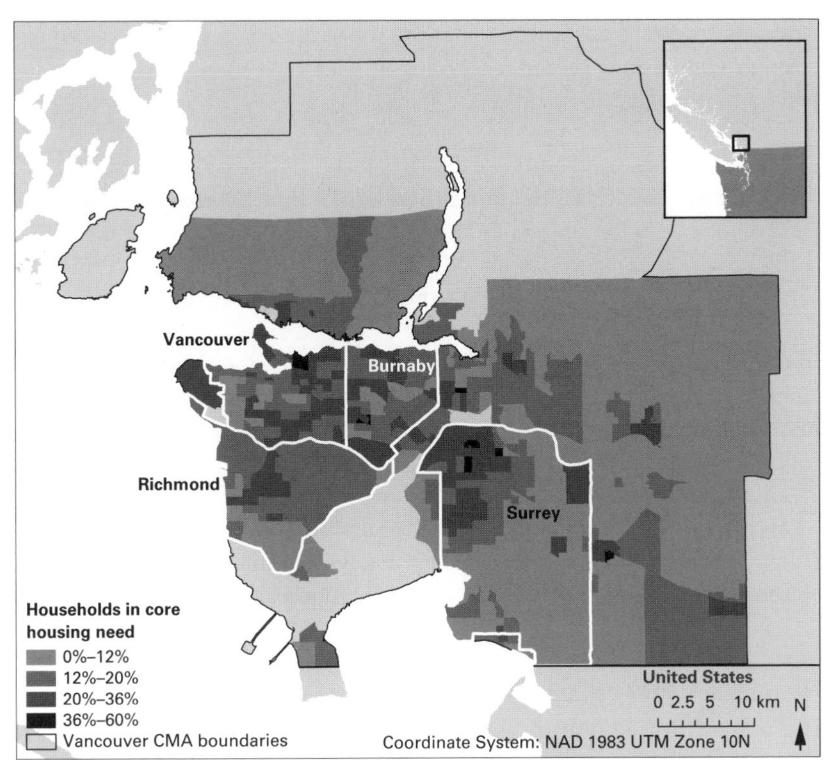

Figure 11.3 Incidence of core housing need by census tract in Vancouver, 2011

Source: Statistics Canada; map by David Wachsmuth and Shunyao Chen

of households are in core housing need), in the east of the city, and in the eastern suburbs – a very different geography from the high house prices portrayed in Figure 11.2.

The research director at a large British Columbia housing non-profit organization explained one way that these apparently distinct housing crises are related through governmental housing policy:

> As long as we've had housing policy, it's always prioritized home-ownership [. . .]. But I think that's starting to change a little bit municipally where we're seeing [. . .] the City of Vancouver and the City of New Westminster [. . .] incentivizing rental development [. . .]. You know, we also look at policy around homelessness, and a shift towards housing first philosophy within a lot of funding programmes. Well that requires a fairly strong [rental] vacancy rate.

(Continued)

And yet in the popular imagination these housing problems remain strongly compartmentalized, according to a staff member from a province-wide anti-poverty organization:

> Vancouverites tend to think that [poverty] [. . .] is only an issue for the Downtown Eastside, and are in denial that poverty is actually in all of our communities in Vancouver, in Metro Vancouver and in BC. Even in somewhere like West Vancouver that we would think it's protected from poverty, it's there for sure.

In part as a result of this fact, she went on to explain, different groups claiming a housing-based right to the city have not yet managed to connect their struggles:

> Last year there was this rally in Vancouver for #donthave1million and it was all focused on home ownership. The low-income community felt excluded; they weren't involved in the organizing or on the day speaking. I would say there is an opportunity here but we haven't managed to take it yet.

Housing and anti-poverty organizing continue to look for creative ways to connect low-income housing problems to broader (global) issues, though. The Syrian refugee crisis, to which the Canadian government responded in part by accepting 25,000 refugees in 2015, created an unexpected opportunity in this regard, as the staffer from the BC Poverty Reduction Coalition explains:

> In some ways the refugee housing issue has given us a bit of a way to talk about the issues of homelessness and housing for the folks that are here [. . .]. Everyone's been welcoming refugees in to either their own private homes or recognizing the government needs to play a role in this. And it's been dicey because some homeless folks have been angry about this, and there is a potential for tension obviously. But there is also an opportunity to say, okay if we can do this for refugees [. . .] then we can also make these commitments and kick in government resources for the folks that we have here that are homeless. So I have seen those conversations, and they seem to have been more productive.

A major fault line that has emerged in public discussions of Vancouver's housing problems is the spectre of anti-Chinese racism. On the one hand, there is ample evidence that Vancouver's local housing market is being distorted by inflows of foreign capital, and that the overwhelming majority of this capital is coming from mainland China. Particularly galling to many housing observers is that a sizeable portion of this investment appears to be taking the form of absentee ownership of vacant houses, which is a perfectly rational strategy in a city where any potential cash flows from renting the house would be dwarfed by the appreciation from property prices increasing by 30% or more a year. But this speculative ownership has the double impact of first driving up housing prices through competing demand for existing inventory and second driving up housing prices further by reducing the effective supply of housing in the city when an occupied house becomes unoccupied.

On the other hand, even if one accepts the role of Chinese buyers in driving a large portion of Vancouver's housing unaffordability problems (and, to be clear, some observers do not accept this), there is no necessary reason why nationality should be a major point of policy or political interest. The real problem is a disjuncture between Vancouver's labour market and housing market. Housing prices are rising thanks to demand coming from outside the local economy, and local economic growth is not keeping up with the cost of living. From the local perspective, there is not much difference if the demand comes from Beijing or from Toronto, from Hong Kong or from Seattle. The result has been a fierce and at times acrimonious debate about, effectively, who should be able to claim a right to the city, and at whose expense.

One Vancouver real estate agent (a relatively recent Chinese immigrant who works mainly with the Chinese population in the city) downplayed the impact foreign ownership has had on Vancouver housing prices, while stressing instead consumer choice and the realities of the free market:

> I think the media exaggerates the impact of Chinese people for its own benefit. The percentage of homeowners among the Chinese is high because they save their money for buying a house, while local white residents tend to spend all their income every month or even go into debt. So they can't afford the down payment. Housing prices are high in Vancouver, but people don't have to choose to live here. They can go somewhere else with lower prices. If people really want to live here, they need to earn it; they should work hard for it. Vancouver is a beautiful place where everyone wants to stay, but only those who can afford the living cost can stay.

But another Chinese real estate agent, while also arguing that Chinese immigrants should not be blamed for the housing crisis, inverted the free-market script to make this argument by raising the agency of *sellers* as well as buyers.

(Continued)

> It is not reasonable to blame the Chinese. It is [the existing residents] who decide to sell their houses; they could decide to keep them instead. And they gain huge profits from selling their house because one little house on the west side of Vancouver can sell for 3 million. They think selling their house is profitable, and they prefer to get the money instead of staying in the City of Vancouver.

A community organizer who works with the low-income Chinese population in Vancouver's Chinatown made a similar point, while also identifying the real cost of racism in current discourse over Vancouver's housing problems:

> A lot of people in my group have lived here a long time – decades – but to someone walking down the street, they're not going to know, they're going to assume, "oh you don't speak English, you must have come here recently", just driving this issue of a lot of racism [...]. I think as the media continues to play on this sort of thing and keep bringing it up and signalling a particular ethnic group's [responsibility for the housing crisis] [...] you're going to have these stereotypes where when you see Chinese people you think they're going to be rich, and you're not going to associate Chinese people needing social housing [...]. I think this stereotyping is more divisive, whereas I think the main issue is just look at the market and look at the money. There are people that speculate here that are residents and what difference does that make? Are they off the hook because they're residents?

A common charge among progressive critics of Vancouver's development-gone-wild urban growth politics is that developers have attempted to aggressively reframe any criticism of unrestrained foreign money in Vancouver real estate as racist criticism of foreigners. But this racism discourse has made actual productive discussion of issues of foreign ownership difficult, according to a prominent newspaper columnist who has covered real estate connections between China and Vancouver for a number of years:

> Cries of racism have helped muzzle that debate [...]. I think there are very valid concerns about racism, but to an extent, I think that by muzzling the conversation about foreign money as opposed to foreigners, what is happening is that the only people left in the discussion are going to be racists [...]. I think that Vancouver in particular – although it's probably a Canada-wide problem – struggles to talk about race and ethnicity and immigration without being seen

> as a confrontation about racism. And I think you can particularly see it in Vancouver, and particularly when you're talking about real estate. Because it's an all too easy thing for wealthy, white property developers to quickly say "Oh, this is racist".

The middle-class crisis of homeownership and its accompanying tensions around foreign ownership generated sufficient political pressure that in the fall of 2016 both the provincial and municipal governments introduced sharp new financial controls on housing which would have seemed unthinkable just a year or two earlier. In August, the provincial government introduced a 15 per cent transaction tax on foreign nationals buying property anywhere in the Vancouver region. And then in November, the City of Vancouver passed a $10,000-a-year fee on owners of vacant properties in the city as a means to discourage speculative ownership. And, as it turns out, a senior member of the mayor's office had told me several months earlier that one of the appeals of a vacancy tax as a means to address housing supply was that it avoided any appearance of racism:

> It appeals to a lot of people because it's not seen as potentially xenophobic, it's whoever. It doesn't matter where you're from, you know, citizen, non-citizen.

It is too soon to know if these measures will significantly alter dynamics of housing affordability in the region, but at a minimum they make it clear that the cries and demands for a right to the city are not going unheard.

Reflections on researching the global right to the city

Returning one more time to the three keywords of 'right', 'city' and 'global', the Vancouver case study shows, first of all, multiple conflicting claims for the right to the city through the housing system. The longstanding anti-homelessness and anti-poverty movement has found some new resources for its struggle from the advent of middle-class housing problems, but has not been able to significantly broaden its basis of support into the middle class. Meanwhile, the rising cost of homeownership in Vancouver has created a new demand for the right to the city on behalf of the middle class, and *against* the right of foreign nationals to buy property as speculative investments. We thus see something like a spectrum of housing-based claims on the right to the city, from a right to shelter to a right to property ownership to a right to property investment.

This Vancouver case study also demonstrates multiple 'cities' – as imaginative communities or categories of practice – at work in these different claims on the right to the city. Is the city a community of Canadian homeowners? A region where people who work for a living should be able to afford a decent place to live? A destination for foreign immigrants, or foreign capital? With Vancouver's housing affordability problems now extending deep into the city's hinterland, where can we draw the city's boundaries?

Lastly, as the case study makes clear, the right to the city in Vancouver is in part a function of the operations of Chinese capital originating overseas, and researching this right thus takes us far outside the boundaries of the city. While my research team has only begun to explore the Vancouver housing crisis as it is experienced and interpreted in mainland China, it is already clear that a resolution to the crisis does not lie only within the control of 'local' political and economic interests in Vancouver.

These characteristics, I believe, could offer some inspiration for research into the right to the city in other sociospatial contexts. At the same time, this brief case study was unable to address other important dimensions to the right to the city. Above all, many inhabitants claiming a right to the city worldwide do so in the face of violence or the strong threat of violence. While there has been significant state and police repression of anti-poverty activists in Vancouver over the years, the severity of that repression is not comparable to the circumstances confronting African American communities and Black Lives Matter activists in the United States today, to say nothing of communities facing off against authoritarian regimes and corporate power elsewhere in the world.

In fact, it is precisely this interface between urban social movements on the one hand and capital and the state on the other which the right to the city calls on us to attend to – both for researchers seeking to better integrate politics into their study of urban space, and for the activists claiming this right as 'a cry and a demand' in public spaces, streets, and the halls of power.

Acknowledgements

I would like to thank Shunyao Chen for invaluable research assistance on this chapter, including the conduct of interviews with real estate agents and the translation of those interviews from Mandarin, analysis of media sources and GIS analysis. I would also like to thank Payvand Razaghizad and Derrick Swallow for assistance transcribing interviews.

References

Angelo, H. and Wachsmuth, D. (2015) 'Urbanizing urban political ecology: A critique of methodological cityism', *International Journal of Urban and Regional Research*, 39(1): 16-27.

Blomley, N.K. (2004) *Unsettling the City: Urban Land and the Politics of Property*. New York: Routledge.

Brenner, N. (ed.) (2014) *Implosions/Explosions: Towards a Study of Planetary Urbanization*. Berlin: Jovis.

Brenner, N. and Schmid, C. (2014) 'The "urban age" in question', *International Journal of Urban and Regional Research*, 38(3): 731–55.

Brenner, N., Peck, J. and Theodore, N. (2010) 'Variegated neoliberalization: Geographies, modalities, pathways', *Global Networks*, 10(2): 182–222.

Brenner, N., Marcuse, P. and Mayer, M. (eds) (2012) *Cities for People, Not for Profit: Critical Urban Theory and the Right to the City*. London: Routledge.

Castells, M. (1977) *The Urban Question: A Marxist Approach*. Trans. A. Sheridan. Cambridge, MA: MIT Press.

Demographia (2016) *12th Annual Demographia International Housing Affordability Survey*. Belleville, IL: Demographia. http://demographia.com/dhi2016.pdf (accessed 20 September 2017).

Economist Intelligence Unit (2016) *A Summary of the Liveability Ranking and Overview*. London: The Economist. www.eiu.com/public/topical_report.aspx?campaignid=liveability2016 (accessed 20 September 2017).

Harvey, D. (2003) 'The right to the city', *International Journal of Urban and Regional Research*, 27(4): 939–41.

Harvey, D. (2008) 'The right to the city', *New Left Review*, 53: 23–40.

Katsikis, N. (2018) 'Visualizing the planetary urban', in J. Harrison and M. Hoyler (eds), *Doing Global Urban Research*. London: Sage, pp. 12–33.

Keil, R. (2018) 'Constructing global suburbia, one critical theory at a time', in J. Harrison and M. Hoyler (eds), *Doing Global Urban Research*. London: Sage, pp. 169–81.

Kennedy, D. (2002) 'The critique of rights in critical legal studies', in W. Brown and J. Halley (eds), *Left Legalism/Left Critique*. Durham, NC: Duke University Press, pp. 178–228.

Lefebvre, H. (1968) *Le droit à la ville*. Paris: Anthropos.

Lefebvre, H. (1968 [1996]) 'Right to the city', in *Writings on Cities*. Trans. E. Kofman and E. Lebas. Malden, MA: Blackwell, pp. 61–181.

Lefebvre, H. (1970 [2003]) *The Urban Revolution*. Trans. R. Bononno. Minneapolis, MN: University of Minnesota Press.

Marx, K. (1867 [1976]) *Capital: A Critique of Political Economy*, Volume 1. Trans. B. Fowkes. London: Penguin.

Morange, M. and Spire, A. (2015) 'A Right to the City in the Global South?' *Metropolitics*. www.metropolitiques.eu/A-Right-to-the-City-in-the-Global.html (accessed 20 September 2017).

Olsen, F. (1984) 'Statutory rape: A feminist critique of rights analysis', *Texas Law Review*, 63(3): 387–432.

Park, R. (1967) *On Social Control and Collective Behavior*. Chicago: University of Chicago Press.

(Continued)

Peck, J. and Theodore, N. (2007) 'Variegated capitalism', *Progress in Human Geography*, 31(6): 731–72.

Ross, K. (1997) 'Lefebvre on the Situationists: An interview', *October*, 79: 69–83.

UNESCO (2006) *International Public Debates: Urban Policies and the Right to the City*. Paris: UNESCO.

UN-Habitat (2010) *The Right to the City: Bridging the Urban Divide*. Rio de Janeiro: World Urban Forum, United Nations.

Wachsmuth, D. (2014) 'City as ideology: Reconciling the explosion of the city form with the tenacity of the city concept', *Environment and Planning D: Society and Space*, 32(1): 75–90.

12

CONSTRUCTING GLOBAL SUBURBIA, ONE CRITICAL THEORY AT A TIME

Roger Keil

Why do suburban research?

Most of what we call urbanization in this so-called century of the 'urban revolution' (Lefebvre, 1970 [2003]) is in form and process suburbanization. On a planet that may eventually house ten billion humans, this includes the hundreds of millions who are expected to continue the original rural-to-urban migration and those who leave established cities for the periphery – both displaced populations and privilege seekers. These are worldwide processes that involve a large variety of phenomena from gated communities to squatter settlements, and from single-family home subdivisions to suburban high-rise hubs (Keil, 2013, 2018). Suburbanization includes complex processes of post-suburbanization through which the city folds in on itself as common perceptions of centre and periphery, and densities and morphologies are inverted (Charmes and Keil, 2015; Phelps, 2015; Phelps and Wu, 2011; Sieverts, 2003). Suburbanisms as suburban ways of life are an integral part of the spread of the urban fabric (Moos and Walter-Joseph, 2017), of infrastructures of and for the suburbs (Filion and Pulver, forthcoming), and the making of suburban land (Harris and Lehrer, 2018). Forms of suburban governance that combine modalities of state, capital accumulation and private authoritarianism are part of the problematique (Hamel and Keil, 2015). In sum, suburbanization is the prime process shaping the urban experience and life in the twenty-first century.

Although suburbs as places, suburbanites as people who work, live and play in the periphery, and suburbanisms as typically suburban ways of life are now dominant realities around the globe, we have not been well prepared to study these places, populations, processes and pastimes. This is partly a consequence of a preoccupation of the multidiscipline of urban studies with the *centre* and the *core*. But it is also a function of the deficits in suburban studies itself, a sub-discipline that has been predominantly concerned with empirical research. In this chapter, I will discuss both and present the case for integrating suburban research into the mainstream of urban inquiry, including critical theory. Suburban studies, as they are, have a reputation as a sub-region, a lesser domain of general urban studies. This can be laid at the feet less of those engaged in the study of urban peripheries than of those who have historically looked at the margins from the centre. In the long century during which we have now been involved in taking the studies of urbanization seriously, 'the suburban' as a real event has figured prominently while it has led a life in the shadows in the mainstream of urban analysis. Critical urban studies in particular have shown no love for suburbanization, which has been looked at as a deviation of sorts, a strategy of capital shifting, a Haussmannian plan to expel the proletariat from the centre, or its inverse, the production of elite escape spaces, a process of cultural and ecological atrophication, and so on. The subfield itself has often reacted with a defensive strategy, and has delivered myriad historico-empirical studies, but has remained out of the core theoretical debates that have driven urban studies overall.

The suburbs have been around in our collective mind for a century at least. In North America, in particular, they have been the place of what Robert Fishman calls 'bourgeois utopias'. He cites Mumford's famous quip that the suburbs are 'a collective effort to live a private life' (1987: x). We are aware, of course, that this assumed right to a private life ended up being more often like a nightmare than a utopian dream. The right was codified in the lasting institution of the restrictive covenant, a neighbourhood-based contract of self-defined communities to limit access of the Other to somebody's assumed home turf. Those covenants, Robert Fogelson writes, tell us about the suburbanites' 'fear of others, of racial minorities and poor people, once known as "the dangerous classes," and their fear of people like themselves. About their fear of change and their fear of the market, of which they were among the chief beneficiaries' (2005: 24).

In Fishman's view, as he wrote about them in the 1980s, the suburbs were there to stay. While speaking about the 'fall of suburbia', he explicitly noted that he was 'not predicting a return to the cities' nor did he 'foresee grass growing in the gently-curving streets of abandoned subdivisions, nor the wind whistling through empty shopping malls' (1987: xi). Instead, the fall of the suburbs, in Fishman's view, was equivalent to resulting in 'a new form of city' (1987: xi). This city was a collective elite creation and, in his definition, a place of residential privilege. The claim Fishman is making about 'a new form of city' is important as an attempt to remove the suburb from its marginality.

Suburban 'accidental cities' of homes, malls and office parks, the 'boomburbs' that often get overlooked in the urban landscape of North America, are in a process of mainstreaming, an awakening in the public mind. The 'suburban city', as Dolores Hayden (2003) called the phenomenon, is a form of normalization of what previously was outside of the core both geographically and cognitively. It also is an attempt to give space and credibility in research to aspects of suburbanization that had historically often been overlooked.

While Fishman (1987), for example, is clear in his narrow definition of traditional suburbia as residential and single family home based, others have noted that suburbanization was diverse from the start and included industrial, commercial and other forms of suburbanization that usually are underrated or ignored in histories of suburbia (Lang and LeFurgy, 2007: 10–11; Lewis, 2004). Walker and Lewis consequently enlarge the definition of the suburban city to include more than residential land uses long before the birth of the technoburb: 'At the burgeoning edges of the metropolis we find a full panoply of workplaces, homes, infrastructure, and commerce that make up the economy and life of the city' (2004: 31). Walker and Lewis also stand out from conventional suburban research in rolling their observations about the diversity of suburban histories into a more general quest for urban theory. They argue 'the combination of geographical industrialization, land development, and metropolitan politics and planning is a theoretical framework that offers a means to advance beyond previous theories at the disposal of urban scholars' (2004: 31). While such broadening of the historical and empirical base for suburban studies is an important step and will yield relevant theoretical insights, it actually does not go far enough. My thesis in this chapter, and in fact in our research initiative on global suburbanization, about which I will say more below, is that the suburbs are not just the future city, but that we can learn from the suburbs and their study something more general, perhaps even universal, about the urban overall, without writing the suburban merely back into the political economy logics of urban economic development theories.

As the owl of Minerva once again flies over suburbia, we can say in hindsight that Fishman was both right and wrong with his predictions about the fall of suburbia: the wind does now in fact blow through the malls of North America and grass grows in the yards of a post-subprime suburbia. And the fact that suburbia is now the city of record is not so much a consequence of its success as a particular form, but because it is now more than a mere residential place of privilege: the suburbs are, in fact, a composite of all urban forms as they age into a post-suburban complex.

Challenges of doing suburban research

Suburban studies (for an overview see Forsyth, 2012, 2014; Harris, 2010; Jauhiainen, 2013; Keil, 2018; Rubey, 2009) have largely shared the fate of their object as being seen as something of lesser importance. For every urban centre of relevance, there is a de(p)rived periphery. For each important work of urbanization, there exists a less weighty study of suburbanization. While commentary on urbanism as a way of life fills libraries and introductory lecture classrooms, suburbanisms as ways of life are barely recognized in their own right. We might object, immediately, that this is surely an exaggeration. Suburban studies, as a field, have been around for a while, have made noted contributions and have produced masterful contributors. It has, many may argue, been as influential as the settlement form itself, the suburbia, has been for the study of cities of the twentieth century in particular. Yes, certainly, the 'suburban solution' to capitalist overproduction crises, named so by Richard Walker in the 1970s, the suburbs have been at the core of not just how capitalist urbanization works, but also how it fails (1977). For many in the field, capitalism cannot be understood without its outlet in so much acreage of single home subdivisions, and urbanization cannot be understood without its (planned) Other at the periphery: sprawling suburbanization.

While Fishman stands out among suburban researchers in his broad and visionary approach to the subject, he is not alone. The most systematic examination of the suburban phenomenon has perhaps been performed by Canadian historical geographer Richard Harris. In his comprehensive life's work, he has subjected both the idiosyncratic self-built working-class suburbanism of the East End of Toronto, and the ubiquitous mass-produced housing of the post-World War II years to detailed scrutiny (Harris, 1996, 2004). More recently, he has expanded his perspective to the global scale as he has examined not just 'the material world' as Fishman would have it (1987: 9) of postcolonial South Africa and India, but also the discursive reach of the concept of the suburban itself (Harris and Vorms, 2017; see also Lang and LeFurgy, 2007 on naming new suburban spaces). Harris (2010) offers a typology of suburbanization, starting with a reference to Jennifer Robinson's appeal that '[c]onsideration needs to be given to the difference [that] the diversity of cities makes to *theory*' (2002: 549; emphasis added). This appeal is both specifically postcolonial in its substantive significance and general in its call for a theory of urbanization that defies the normative pull of the dominant, the centre, the core, the citadel. In his own effort to challenge 'theory with diverse realities' Harris, quite in step with Robinson's original formulation, focuses on how 'the experience of the Global South [bears] upon our conceptualization of suburbs' and puts forth that there is a tendency, first identified by Robinson herself, to contextualize urban and suburban change there in a developmental frame (2010: 20).

While there is much emerging literature in and on peripheral urbanization in the Global South (including work on peri-urban relations, informal marginal settlements such as *favelas* and *gecekondu*, and 'rurban' landscapes such as *desakota*), there is a) little connection with the traditional suburban studies literature in the West and b) surprisingly rare overlap among the burgeoning work on squatter settlements, gated communities, new middle-class suburbanization and so forth in the Global South (Harris, 2010: 22–3). Invoking, then, a 'worldwide frame of reference', Harris proposes a pre-theoretical typology of suburbs which differentiates in the first instance 'those who had some choice from those who did not, and those moving towards as opposed to those leaving the city' (2010: 33–4). Harris's categories are immensely helpful to structure the kind of comparative work Robinson and others identify as non-negotiable parts of a theory-building based on ordinary sub/urbanization. For Harris, this work flows into empirical or taxonomic research questions but not necessarily into theory per se.

For that, suburban research needs to make connections to larger questions of social change, including the ones asked by critical urban theory that sees itself as social theory. This work has often been identified in recent decades with a Marxist, especially a Lefebvre-inflected approach to complete urbanization, or put differently, urban society. In his thinking, Lefebvre embraced the suburbanization process observed in Paris in the 1960s and 1970s as 'precisely the occasion for finding a larger theory of the city, and not a pretext for abandoning the problem' (Lefebvre and Ross, 2015). Importantly for Lefebvre, then, as Walks has argued, 'the suburban is conceptually an extension of urbanism', but at the same time since suburbanization has appeared on the scene as a massive phenomenon, it becomes the basis for a new and more comprehensive theory of the city, and ultimately society (2013: 1477). This shift in perspective has forced us, as Andy Merrifield has put it, to call out the false dichotomies in urban studies (2012). Yet it remains necessary, as we consolidate the dichotomous fragmentation of non-related categories into dialectical syntheses, to understand the merit of individual processes that make up the overall dynamic of the planet's move towards complete urbanization. In this dynamic, distinct processes of suburbanization contribute to the overall push towards an urbanized world. Those processes can be understood in the foundational categories of governance, land and infrastructure, and can be studied empirically in those contexts, but they also need to be seen as important differentiated elements from which to draw theory (Robinson, 2002).

Techniques for doing suburban research

The work discussed in this chapter is based on a Major Collaborative Research Initiative (MCRI) on *Global Suburbanisms: Governance, Land and Infrastructure in the 21st Century*. This MCRI has been based at York University in Toronto and has been funded by the Social Sciences and Humanities Research Council of Canada. It ran from 2010 to 2018 and I have been the initiative's Principal Investigator. The project was designed in a multidisciplinary manner and involved various quantitative and qualitative research techniques and methods.

Some of the most insightful interventions in theory-building from suburbanization come from work done less on urban form, economic structure or political economy in the classical sense, but from the study of suburban ways of life. In the research cluster on suburbanisms as part of our MCRI, two very different approaches to suburban ways of life have produced an impressive body of work with a large spectrum of methodological and conceptual approaches. At one end of the spectrum, we have systematic quantitative analyses of Canadian suburbanization using general categories of what might be seen as 'suburban'. These categories have been mapped out in an atlas of suburbanisms that shatters and shifts our understanding of suburbanization processes in many ways (Moos and Walter-Joseph, 2017). More important, perhaps, in the context of the current chapter, has been the theoretical provocation that was at the basis of this large-scale empirical exercise. This provocation was best summarized by Alan Walks (2013). Walks focuses on the aspect of suburbanism in his examination of Lefebvre's implosion/explosion dialectics (1970 [2003]) and conceptualizes it 'as an inherent aspect of urbanism that is both distinct yet inseparable from it – urbanism's internal ever-present anti-thesis that, in dialectical fashion, stands in productive tension with it, producing interleaved dimensions of "urbanism-suburbanism"' (2013: 1472). Importantly, Walks sees suburbanism therefore as 'a multidimensional evolving process within urbanism that is constantly fluctuating and pulsating as the flows producing its relational forms shift and overlap in space' (2013: 1472). Walks draws from this theoretical discussion six dimensions of urbanism-suburbanism, which also lie at the basis of his and his colleagues' work on the quantitative analysis of Canadian suburbanization (Moos and Walter-Joseph, 2017).

At the other end of the methodological spectrum, Lisa Drummond and Danielle Labbé have proposed a theoretical approach to everyday suburbanism that is less based in quantitative data and shifting categories of general suburban and urban divides but an in-depth, anthropological and ethnographic view of suburban life at the global frontier of urbanization. Drummond and Labbé suggest that '[o]ur studies of suburban everyday life [. . .] will require attention to the practices and the spaces of social interaction across the spectrum of suburban places and forms' found increasingly all around the world and especially outside the Anglo-Saxon suburban heartland, '[a]cross the global south, [where] cities are experiencing the construction, on outer urban edges, of informal periurban areas, new commercial developments, industrial compounds, and middle-class housing estates which often sit cheek-by-jowl' (2013: 51).

In addition to and in concert with an expansion of critical suburban research into everyday suburbanisms, we have seen an acknowledgment that suburbanization has become a global phenomenon (Keil, 2013). A conceptual study of governance in suburbanization processes around the world has found that we now have conjugations of state, market and private authoritarian modalities of governance in the production and governance of suburbs around the globe, which have become the frontiers of urbanization everywhere (Hamel and Keil, 2015). This work builds on an explosion of regionally specific studies on peripheral urbanization in the conventional cases of North America, Australia, Eastern and Western Europe. The tremendous suburbanization of China, India, Africa and Latin America are crucial elements of the ongoing and emerging research. In this work, we see a growing tendency of linking theoretical debates relevant to societal change more generally to the suburban phenomenon. For Stanilov and Sýkora, for example, 'confronting suburbanization has become a mirror of confronting the wider societal challenges that need to be addressed in order to construct a sound framework for a sustainable future development' in post-socialist countries (2014: 22).

Suburban studies generally have been too Anglo-American in flavour and origin and too mainstream and empiricist in their techniques. Our project was initially no exception. Most of the authors of the original application were professionally active in the English-speaking world and for those who were not English remained the *lingua franca* of sub/urban research. Still, the cultural-linguistic divides are tremendous in this research area. Our focus here is, however, less in the linguistic problematic itself, but on the actual literatures of different national and regional discourses. Workshops on suburban *governance* in Leipzig, Germany, suburban *land* in Montpellier, France and suburban *infrastructures* in Waterloo, Canada have yielded a kaleidoscope of results in these foundational areas of global suburban research (Filion and Pulver, forthcoming; Hamel and Keil, 2015; Harris and Lehrer, 2018). Thematic and regional cooperation has been the subject of workshops in Delhi, India on South Asian suburbanization; in London, UK (Phelps, 2017); in Shanghai, China on Asian suburbanization; Istanbul on massive suburbanization in that Turkish city and elsewhere; Belo Horizonte, Brazil on boundaries and green-blue landscapes that define suburbanization, and Johannesburg, South Africa on African suburbanization. In all of these encounters a new 'invisible college' of suburban researchers around the globe is gaining contours. This 'college' is home to plural epistemologies and ontologies combining and engaging with many traditions of suburban research and urban theory, as well as with Eastern and Western European, Chinese, Indian, African, Australian, North and Latin American practices and traditions of doing research. Joint publications have made explicit use of and have cross-fertilized theory-building.

Doing (global) suburban research

In this following section, rather than focus on one particular empirical case study, I make the argument that our work in the global suburbanisms research initiative takes on both common urban studies and conventional suburban research by claiming new ground for research on suburbanization and suburbanisms, especially by making it the basis from which to advance the field conceptually, theoretically and methodologically. As it stands, the literature in the field of new suburban research tends to be specializing rather than generalizing. No big claims are made. There is rather a tendency to advocate more local, specific and thematic approaches: 'individual voice', habitation and suburban imaginaries (Crawford, 2015: 383–7). While these three areas fulfil to a degree Robinson's and Harris' call for more ordinariness in urban research, and cast light on 'suburbia's long and varied histories and the ways people have inhabited, revised, and reinterpreted sub-urban areas over time' (Archer et al., 2015: viii), they do not readily contribute to theory-building.

In our research initiative, we have begun to change that perspective. In an influential paper on the changing geographies of urban theory, Ananya Roy (2009) mentions suburbs and peripheries in several occasions, but never specifically as a basis for theory-building as such. When she makes the case for a worlding of urban studies, she talks about peripheries and 'the emergence of core–periphery structures within the global South' (2009: 825). From this, ultimately, comes an appeal to break open the static core–periphery (or more specifically also city–suburb) relationships in theoretically and conceptually meaningful ways. In a subsequent contribution, Roy suggests just that: 'This is the task of de-centring (sub)urban theory, of not only fostering a sense of global urbanism but also of attending to the geopolitics of such globality. This too is at stake in the charting of global suburbanisms' (Roy, 2015: 345).

The group of international scholars in the research initiative on global suburbanisms centred around the City Institute at York University deliberately made suburbanization and suburbanisms the focus of their joint work. Applying critical theoretical thinking to, and gaining theoretical insights from, the process of suburbanization and the everyday lives lived in the urban periphery, this programme has been multi-disciplinary and multi-method as would be expected. The initiative has lived by the stated postulation that such work, as Parnell and Pieterse have formulated, must 'embrace divergent methods, not just concepts and values, in order to ensure greater representivity' (2015: 244). In fact, it has been specific to Global Suburbanisms and new to the overall endeavour of critical suburban studies that the approach would be global. The intended globality was going to be established through four related processes: (i) the team of ultimately 50 associated scholars was to be roughly representative of some of the major existing literatures and ongoing research efforts worldwide of peripheral urbanization; (ii) while it would be impossible to cover the actual global multitude of cases of suburbanization and suburbanisms, Global Suburbanisms made a sincere effort to be as geographically inclusive as possible; (iii) the thematic areas of the research were chosen with an eye towards relevance in suburbanization processes around the globe; (iv) and most importantly, the researchers pledged not to make this an exercise in applying preordained 'Western' theory to multiple case studies elsewhere. The inclusion of suburbanization in the Global South was not a mere addition of more empirical cases to an existing script of peripheral expansion, but a core requirement for theory-building.

Reflections on doing global suburban research

I will end this chapter with some speculations on how critical urban theory and research have benefitted from prioritizing the peripheral, and how a dialectical approach has, in turn, helped transcend the urban and suburban divide in theory and practice. It is today possible to distinguish two critiques of suburbanization. One is systemic, the other one symptomatic. The systemic critique sees suburbanization as an outgrowth of contradictions caused by capitalist urbanization processes and intrinsically entwined with them. The symptomatic critiques largely disregard the systemic issues of suburbanization and see suburbs as a technical constellation that can be reformed and rebuilt into more economically appropriate, socially productive and environmentally sustainable forms. This second strand is largely driven by urbanist considerations. It makes a fundamental difference whether one studies suburbanization and suburbanisms as processes and relationalities of systemic significance (related to contradictions of capital accumulation, state formation, neoliberalization, racialization, etc.), or of mere symptomatic value (easily manipulated by choices in urban form, community economics, citizen behaviour, etc.).

There is no single global suburbanism. It is a precondition of this research to not assume convergence. For ethical and conceptual reasons, the North American experience as a model for all suburbanization cannot be taken as guiding for all suburbanisms. Empirical inclusivity is the key to examining the dazzling and puzzling diversity of the suburban process, form and function. In terms of the general formation of overarching theory, historically, the form of suburbanization has been tied to three dynamics: property ownership (Anglo-America), industrialization (mass housing) and displacement (Haussmannization). In the current period, suburbanization is driven by a different set of dynamics: post-Fordist regional economies, globalization and neoliberalization. These are themselves open-ended processes. Suburbanization and suburbanisms will evolve and articulate with those change dynamics. In fact, suburbanization is enabled by and enables those three processes at the same time. What is more, the urban society Henri Lefebvre (1970 [2003]) envisioned emerging as a global phenomenon now has a decidedly suburban feel to it. This has epistemological and ontological consequences that need the same treatment as the erstwhile urban theorists in the past gave to centralized urbanization. This adds up to a de-centring of the geopolitics of the urban narrative. New processes originating from the margins and peripheries defy the traditional dependencies of outsides from insides, suburbs from cities, and expand our understanding of the dialectic of the urban process. In discussing these dynamics, our project contributes to a 'reloaded urban studies' (Merrifield, 2012), creating openings beyond the traditional dichotomies. Finally, suburban studies allows for a more radical theoretical inversion of urban theory. This leads back to a central point our MCRI has insisted on: it is from the emerging geographies of non-European and non-American (sub)urbanity that the architectures of urban theory await rebuilding (for a longer discussion of these themes see Keil, 2018).

One way in which we have begun this journey is to work deliberately on the discursive constructions that undergird processes of suburbanization and suburban ways of life. For now, we have settled for hybrid terminologies. Some of us speak of the peri-urban, others have subscribed to more mixed concepts such as *Zwischenstadt* (in-between city) or post-suburbanization. At the tail end of those iterative and inductive travels through suburbia, we will at one point come across new languages that will adequately describe and allow us to analyse the urban world in which we now live (Harris and Vorms, 2017). That, then, will engender direct engagement questions such as 'why suburbs now?' and 'why suburbs in this form and shape?' and lead to a number of explanations that tell us clearly what the suburbanizing world is like that we live in. The grammar of the suburbanized landscape, which is rolled out across the globe, is as good an indicator of where, and who we are, as Manchester was to Frederick Engels in his famous reflections on urban life in industrial capitalism in the middle of the nineteenth century. This works in much the same way as Chicago represented the screen for the researchers in the School of the same name in the 1920s and 1930s, or Los Angeles was the blueprint, for a while, for the Los Angeles School of urbanists who predicted a quite different sub/urban future. The causalities, such as the 'whys', will then become transparent through the comparative, multi-site, multi-disciplinary, multi-method empirical and conceptual research we are involved in, and will lead to theoretical and conceptual insights that will guide further research on the topic. Our team was assembled in 2009 from many of the best suburban researchers we could find around the world. This network built on previous engagements, joint projects and longstanding research collaborations. It also however, assembled new groups, and created crossover among many previously unconnected themes, intellectual traditions and methodological approaches.

Through our conceptual and empirical work in close to a decade we produced a remarkable output from tweets to books, from teaching syllabi to maps, from a suburban atlas to reports on policy work (Keil and Hertel, 2015). In this process, our team not only created new substantive (conceptual and positive) knowledge, but also moved the perspective beyond the previously established boundaries. This entailed both a seismic move from the dichotomies of city/suburb, North/South, centre/periphery, etc. and a reimagining of the place of suburban studies (theoretical and empirical) in the overall project of urban scholarship and practice. Having frontloaded Global Suburbanisms in the early years with big 'foundational' questions, researchers have subsequently engaged with very empirical, concrete and practical subprojects – informed by sophisticated conceptual frameworks and characterized by methodological diversity and rigour. Through this work, it will be possible to develop domains of collective inquiry. This implies the acknowledgement of the existence of continuing intertwined spirals of theoretical and empirical work in the specialized field of suburban studies. Those will be tied together in a matrix that displays the original elements – governance, land and infrastructure – but that also points beyond, as each turn of the spiral keeps repositioning the standpoint of the researcher. Global Suburbanisms seeks to exchange key thinkers inside and outside of the initiative, and with whom we will continue to reflect on the outcomes in a thorough and incisive manner. In this exchange, ultimately, a set of post-suburban constellations may reveal themselves.

References

Archer, J., Sandul, P.J.P. and Solomonson, K. (2015) 'Introduction: Making, performing, living suburbia' in J. Archer, P.J.P. Sandul and K. Solomonson (eds), *Making Suburbia: New Histories of Everyday America*. Minneapolis, MN: University of Minnesota Press, pp. vii–xxv.

Charmes, E. and Keil, R. (2015) 'The politics of post-suburban densification in Canada and France', *International Journal of Urban and Regional Research*, 39(3): 581–602.

Crawford, M. (2015) 'Afterword', in J. Archer, P.J.P. Sandul and K. Solomonson (eds), *Making Suburbia: New Histories of Everyday America*. Minneapolis, MN: University of Minnesota Press, pp. 381–7.

Drummond, L. and Labbé, D. (2013) 'We're a long way from Levittown, Dorothy: Everyday suburbanism as a global way of life', in R. Keil (ed.), *Suburban Constellations: Governance, Land and Infrastructure in the 21st Century*. Berlin: Jovis, pp. 46–51.

Filion, P. and Pulver, N. (eds) (forthcoming) *Global Suburban Infrastructure: Social Restructuring, Governance and Equity*. Toronto: University of Toronto Press.

Fishman, R. (1987) *Bourgeois Utopias: The Rise and Fall of Suburbia*. New York: Basic Books.

Fogelson, R.M. (2005) *Bourgeois Nightmares: Suburbia, 1870–1930*. New Haven, CT, and London: Yale University Press.

Forsyth, A. (2012) 'Defining suburbs', *Journal of Planning Literature*, 27(3): 270–81.

Forsyth, A. (2014) 'Global suburbia and the transition century: Physical suburbs in the long term', *Urban Design International*, 19(4): 259–73.

Hamel, P. and Keil, R. (eds) (2015) *Suburban Governance: A Global View*. Toronto: University of Toronto Press.

Harris, R. (1996) *Unplanned Suburbs: Toronto's American Tragedy, 1900 to 1950*. Baltimore, MD: The Johns Hopkins University Press.

Harris, R. (2004) *Creeping Conformity: How Canada Became Suburban, 1900–1960*. Toronto: University of Toronto Press.

Harris, R. (2010) 'Meaningful types in a world of suburbs', in M. Clapson and R. Hutchinson (eds), *Suburbanization in Global Society*. Bingley: Emerald, pp. 15–50.

Harris, R. and Lehrer, U. (eds) (2018) *The Suburban Land Question: A Global Survey*. Toronto: University of Toronto Press.

Harris, R. and Vorms, C. (eds) (2017) *What's In a Name? Talking about Urban Peripheries*. Toronto: University of Toronto Press.

(Continued)

Hayden, D. (2003) *Building Suburbia: Green Fields and Urban Growth, 1820–2000*. New York: Pantheon Books.

Jauhiainen, J.S. (2013) 'Suburbs', in P. Clark (ed.), *The Oxford Handbook of Cities in World History*. Oxford: Oxford University Press, pp. 791–809.

Keil, R. (ed.) (2013) *Suburban Constellations*. Berlin: Jovis.

Keil, R. (2018) *Suburban Planet*. Cambridge: Polity.

Keil, R. and Hertel, S. (2015) '"Erst reden, dann handeln" – Die Greater Toronto Suburban Working Group und der (Um-)Bau der städtischen Peripherie in Kanadas boomender Metropole', in J. Jessen and F. Roost (eds), *Refitting Suburbia: Erneuerung der Stadt des 20. Jahrhunderts in Deutschland und in den USA*. Berlin: Jovis, pp. 151–72.

Lang, R.E. and LeFurgy, J.B. (2007) *Boomburbs: The Rise of America's Accidental Cities*. Washington, DC: Brookings Institution Press.

Lefebvre, H. (1970 [2003]) *The Urban Revolution*. Trans. R. Bononno. Minneapolis, MN: University of Minnesota Press.

Lefebvre, H. and Ross, K. (2015) 'Finding a larger theory of the city: Henri Lefebvre und die Situationistische Internationale', *Dérive*, 58: 45–50.

Lewis, R. (ed.) (2004) *Manufacturing Suburbs: Building Work and Home on the Metropolitan Fringe*. Philadelphia, PA: Temple University Press.

Merrifield, A. (2012) 'Whither urban studies?', *Cities@Manchester* (10th December 2012). http://citiesmcr.wordpress.com/2012/12/10/whither-urban-studies (accessed 20 September 2017).

Moos, M. and Walter-Joseph, R. (eds) (2017) *Still Detached and Subdivided? Suburban Ways of Living in 21st Century North America*. Berlin: Jovis.

Parnell, S. and Pieterse, E. (2015) 'Translational global praxis: rethinking methods and modes of African urban research', *International Journal of Urban and Regional Research*, 40(1): 236–46.

Phelps, N.A. (2015) *Sequel to Suburbia: Glimpses of America's Post-Suburban Future*. Cambridge, MA: MIT Press.

Phelps, N.A. (ed.) (2017) *Old Europe, New Suburbanization? Governance, Land, and Infrastructure in European Suburbanization*. Toronto: University of Toronto Press.

Phelps, N.A. and Wu, F. (eds) (2011) *International Perspectives on Suburbanization: A Post-Suburban World?* Basingstoke: Palgrave Macmillan.

Robinson, J. (2002) 'Global and world cities: A view from off the map', *International Journal of Urban and Regional Research*, 26(3), 531–54.

Roy, A. (2009) 'The 21st-century metropolis: New geographies of theory', *Regional Studies*, 43(6): 819–30.

Roy, A. (2015) 'Governing the postcolonial suburbs', in P. Hamel and R. Keil (eds), *Suburban Governance: A Global View*. Toronto: University of Toronto Press, pp. 337–47.

Rubey, D. (ed.) (2009) *Redefining Suburban Studies: Searching for New Paradigms*. Hofstra University: The National Center for Suburban Studies.

Sieverts, T. (2003) *Cities Without Cities: An Interpretation of the Zwischenstadt*. London: Spon Press.

Stanilov, K. and Sýkora, L. (eds) (2014) *Confronting Suburbanization: Urban Decentralization in Postsocialist Central and Eastern Europe*. Oxford: Wiley-Blackwell.

Walker, R. (1977) 'The suburban solution: Capitalism and the construction of suburban space in the United States'. PhD dissertation, Johns Hopkins University.

Walker, R. and Lewis, R. (2004) 'Beyond the crabgrass frontier: Industry and the spread of North American cities, 1850-1950', in R. Lewis (ed.), *Manufacturing Suburbs: Building Work and Home on the Metropolitan Fringe*. Philadelphia, PA: Temple University Press, pp. 16-31.

Walks, A. (2013) 'Suburbanism as a way of life, slight return', *Urban Studies*, 50(8): 1471-88.

13

COMPARATIVE ETHNOGRAPHIC URBAN RESEARCH

Tim Bunnell

Why do comparative ethnographic urban research?

As recently as only a decade ago readers of a volume such as this would likely have been surprised to see ethnographic approaches proffered as means of doing urban research that is either *global* or *comparative*. Ethnography has conventionally connoted in-depth, human-centred study of cultural groups, communities and institutions in more-or-less bounded localities. As such, while ethnographic work has long been recognized as yielding richly textured accounts of people-in-places, it has equally been criticized for failing to generate findings that can be compared meaningfully with other studies (Jackson, 1985). The foundational urban ethnographies of the Chicago School of sociology were determinedly microscale, ahistorical and atheoretical – and those three traits arguably continued to be imagined as the defining features of ethnography for much of the twentieth century, despite the relative extroversion of subsequent schools. Michael Burawoy (2000) has elaborated how from the middle decades of the twentieth century the Manchester School of anthropology expanded the contextual and theoretical scope of urban ethnography, most famously through Max Gluckman's 'extended case method'. It is Burawoy himself who has demonstrated that even 'global ethnography' is not necessarily an oxymoron. There is nothing necessarily or specifically 'urban' about the global ethnography practised by Burawoy or fellow contributors to his influential edited volume – an issue that I will return to in the final section of this chapter – but other scholars have shown how Burawoy's globalized version of the extended case method can be adopted/adapted for research on urban policy mobilities (McCann, 2010; Peck and Theodore, 2012). It is increasingly widely accepted not only that ethnography is far from 'irrevocably local' (Burawoy, 2000: 2), but that global ethnography is very well suited for examination of spatially extended human practices and associated urban processes (Clarke, 2012). Ethnographic approaches are also recognized as a potentially important part of 'relational' and 'relational comparative' urban studies (Jacobs, 2012; Ward, 2010).

While the upscaling and relational unbounding of ethnographic work in recent decades have made it appear more suited to doing *global* urban research, it is possible to identify three further responses to the 'why' question that frames the opening section of this chapter. The first has to do with the very attention to territorial detail and human lifeworld immersion that, for some, might be precisely what makes traditional forms of ethnography appear unfit for working at the global scale. In particular, ethnographic approaches may be embraced as a means of counterbalancing the focus of existing global urban studies on inter-city connections rather than their territorial grounding. The by now highly diverse range of scholarship on global/world cities, for example, has certainly included consideration of the importance of co-proximity among the specialized service firms that are understood to produce the capacity for global economic control (Sassen, 1991). However, subsequent strands of world/global city scholarship that have focused on transnational intra-firm networks, and sought to map the 'metageography' of a World City Network (WCN) (Taylor and Derudder, Chapter 3), have given correspondingly much less attention to the territorial urban geographies of producer service activity (for example Beaverstock et al., 2000). The names of cities – certain global/world cities – feature very prominently in such work, but they are understood largely as nodes. Put another way, the outcome has been that 'in some WCN analyses, the city appears to be simply a point in Cartesian space' (Coe et al., 2010: 145). This is significant because there is an ongoing need to consider situational or territorial as well as relational aspects of cities in an era of globalization (McCann and Ward, 2010). In work on world city networks, this might mean giving more attention to the dynamics of sub-nodal localities (places as well as institutions/organizations) that could be examined through ethnographic approaches. Meanwhile, in the currently burgeoning field of urban policy mobilities, ethnographic approaches are well suited to examination of the intertwining of cultural history and city politics that can have profound implications for how, where and why policies are (not) imported, adopted or adapted (Temenos and Ward, Chapter 5). Attending to the human lifeworlds of relationality/territoriality also implies possibilities for extending beyond the kinds of elite and expert actors who have featured most prominently in both urban policy mobilities and WCN work.

A second reason for 'why ethnography?' in global urban research concerns the diversity of relational geographies that are anchored in urban territories. The problem with proffering territorialized ethnographic approaches as a means of bringing non-elite actors into global urban research is that this implies a dichotomy between globe-trotting policy, producer services or 'intelligence corps' (Olds, 2001) elites on the one hand, and place-bound, ordinary or even subaltern urbanites on the other. Many far-from-elite groups pass through cities at some point in their transnational movements (Smith, 2001), making use of established inter-urban connections and forging new ones as they do so. Today, a bewildering array of people and economic activities are bound up in globe-spanning urban networks that extend well beyond the realms of advanced producer services, policy mobilities or real estate development (which have tended to dominate the academic urban research usually cast as 'global'). It is also important to recognize that even relatively immobile city-dwellers and city-makers frequently operate in relation to global (and sometimes 'counterglobal') imaginations and aspirations (Appadurai, 1996; Burawoy, 2000).

A third rationale follows on from this and has to do with seeking to incorporate a wider range of lives and experiences into so-called global urban research. Among the most influential work in Anglophone urban studies over the past decade or so have been postcolonial calls to make the field 'more cosmopolitan' and 'more global' through the incorporation of a wider range of cities and regions (Robinson, 2006, 2013). While I believe that this call remains valid, I also contend that unsettling inherited biases needs to be about more than expanding 'geographies of theory' (Roy, 2009); it should also be about incorporating the voices, experiences and aspirations of a wider range of city-makers (Bunnell, 2016). This could be achieved through ethnographic examination of an expanded range of people and places in established global cities as much as through spatial diversification of urban studies research to cities that have conventionally been left 'off the map' (Robinson, 2002). Proceeding in this way, the aim would not merely be to carry out localized Chicago School-style ethnographies of more and more city-based groups, but could be to consider how diverse urban lives are shaped through relations with a variety of elsewheres, or ways in which different kinds of inter-urban relations might form the basis for comparative studies. It is also worth noting that (ordinary) people in places can be resources for, as well as objects of, global urban comparison (Bunnell and Kathiravelu, 2016).

Challenges of doing comparative ethnographic urban research

Doing ethnography often requires commitments that many scholars are unable or unwilling to make, especially in terms of time. There are differences across disciplines and between national scholarly contexts as to how much time and even what kinds of practices are necessary before a piece of work could legitimately be labelled 'ethnographic'. John Brewer (2000) has even distinguished between 'big' and 'little' definitions of ethnography, the former encompassing qualitative research methods in general, the latter denoting a more delimited form based around intensive fieldwork including participant observation.

Even in anthropology, traditionally and stereotypically the disciplinary bastion of ethnography in its purer 'little' form, it is no longer necessarily expected that scholars conduct years of fieldwork in a single stretch. With regard to researching sites overseas, the relative ease of long distance travel and communications by historical standards opens possibilities for ways of sustaining ethnographic engagement other than through an extended period 'away'. Meanwhile, the possibility of studying sites, groups or institutions at (or close to) home extends right back to the founding (sociological) traditions of the Chicago School. Nonetheless, significant commitments of time are still necessary for immersion into others' lifeworlds (including, in some cases, to learn their languages), to build up trust with gatekeepers, to negotiate power relations (especially, but not only, when studying 'down') and to develop ethically sound collaborative relations. These essential investments are arguably at odds with the accelerated expectations for research output demanded and incentivized by the neoliberalizing academy. There may of course be very good scholarly (and political) reasons for wanting to take the ethnographic route, but it is also tempting to follow much less time-consuming, alternative pathways to doing and publishing global urban research (see also Goh et al., 2015).

If it is difficult for the urban scholar to justify or make time for ethnographic study of a specific site or city, then what more for the often multi-sited and relational phenomena that may interest would-be global urban scholars and extend possibilities for comparative study? Even aside from issues of time, conventional area studies partitions of knowledge production and training mean that it is very rare to find scholars with the capacity to engage ethnographically with multiple urban elsewheres. Although there are certainly important exceptions (for example Simone, 2010) most urbanists attempting to undertake relational and/or comparative work across cultural contexts will not be able to work proficiently alone. As such, as Garth Myers (2014: 115) has put it, '[. . .] it is of the utmost importance to develop collaborative energies that can build beyond the inevitable circumscription of the lone researcher'.

Collaboration among ethnographers who may traditionally have been disposed to working alone may be welcomed by institutions and funding agencies, but scaling up research projects brings its own challenges. At a practical level, there is the challenge of coordinating research schedules so as to allow effective cooperation among researchers working in different sites. There is also a danger that efforts channelled into working effectively with fellow academics result in a corresponding diversion of energy away from collaborative responsibilities and commitments in the field. More fundamentally, the largely inductive and iterative nature of ethnographic work precludes the kinds of standardized or cumulative data collection that may traditionally have been expected of multi-sited comparative research. One team of anthropologists have noted that the kind of 'strong collaboration' required of collaborative ethnography is not so much about making the project work; 'it is the work of continually remaking the project' (Matsutake Worlds Research Group, 2009: 198). While this continual reworking can undoubtedly make for a better project (or projects), it can also be troubling both for principal investigators (who are often tied to timelines for deliverables set by their home institutions or external funding agencies) and for more junior collaborators (who might have academic labour market-related preferences for swifter and more clear-cut ways of developing material for publication).

Techniques for doing comparative ethnographic urban research

It is difficult to elaborate a 'how to' set of comparative ethnographic techniques, not least because both 'comparative' and 'ethnographic' mean so many different things to different researchers within as well as across disciplinary boundaries. It should also be noted that if there is one commonality across most existing methodological reflections, it is the presumption that ethnographers work alone rather than as part of wider collective and/or comparative scholarly initiatives. What is more, even when merely seeking to guide the lone future researcher, more experienced scholars have sometimes considered that ethnography defies codification. A chapter by Kate Swanson on urban ethnographic research published in a pedagogically oriented urban studies text recounts one distinguished professor advising his students that the first thing they should do when they begin fieldwork is to throw away any prior plan: '[n]ow that you've seen the field, it obviously won't work anyway' (Bernard Nietschmann, cited in Swanson, 2013: 58). Swanson's reflections on her own experiences of doing ethnographic research with street vendors and beggars in cities in Equador (see Swanson, 2010) are rather more hopeful. While acknowledging that projects may change radically in the field, she flags the importance of: 'a carefully planned proposal, with core research questions' (Swanson, 2013: 58); a useful 'gatekeeper'; informed consent (especially when working with young people and marginalized groups); taking extensive field notes every single day in the field; and being disciplined in writing up experiences and observations so as to connect them up to 'larger and more self-reflexive issues' (2013: 63). These reflections relate most closely to participant observation and qualitative interviews – perhaps the methodological core of ethnographic research – but, as Swanson notes, those techniques are often combined with a variety of others (ranging from photography and focus groups to diary keeping and participatory action research), as well as with the collection of secondary data. Such reflections are helpful for ethnographers working as part of collaborative teams as much as for the lone ethnographer, not least because efforts to work comparatively – 'beyond the inevitable circumscription of the lone researcher' (Myers, 2014: 115) – are likely to build upon material initially collected by individual researchers.

How does one go about doing the almost inevitably collaborative aspects of comparative ethnographic work? The first and most straightforward suggestion is to plan regular meetings to facilitate sharing of field-based findings, and to bring contextually specific insights into conversation with other(s') sites, concepts and understandings. It is in such meetings that the work of strong collaboration (literally) takes place. Unless collaborators happen to be based at the same institution, however, face-to-face meetings can be very difficult to arrange, not to mention prohibitively expensive in the absence of funding for dedicated workshops. A (slightly) less expensive option then becomes the synchronization of attendance at international conferences to bring together dispersed collaborators. A second set of suggestions follows on from this and concerns electronic alternatives to co-present collaborative exchange. This could include communication through widely used software such as Skype, but another, as yet less common, option is to develop digital platforms for the collaborative interweaving of ethnographic material. Here there are possibilities for exchanging not merely what individual ethnographers say about their own findings, but also for exchanging specific ethnographic texts, notes, images, etc. Third, and very much at the other end of the spectrum from virtual ethnographic collaboration, is the possibility of individual researchers physically visiting each other's field sites. Benedict Anderson (2016: 18) noted that 'good comparisons often come from the experience of strangeness and absences'. Visiting a collaborator's research site is not only a good way of learning about somewhere different (or perhaps unexpectedly similar), but may also give rise to new and different questions, rendering both 'here' and 'there' strange while drawing them into comparative relation.

Case study of doing comparative ethnographic urban research

The as yet unspecified background to the previous three sections of this chapter is a multi-sited collaborative ethnographic research project on *Aspirations, Urban Governance and the Remaking of Asian Cities* that ran between 2013 and 2016. I was principal investigator for this initiative that I will refer to henceforth as the Urban Aspirations project. Based at the National University of Singapore (NUS), the project included eleven collaborators in total, mostly anthropologists, geographers and sociologists. What we had in common at the outset, apart from a shared institutional base at NUS, was a background of conducting in-depth, mostly qualitative research on or in cities in Asia. There was big variation, however, in the degree to which team members considered themselves as having done ethnography prior to our collaborative project (and, indeed, there is variation in the extent to which we see ourselves as having done 'big' or 'little' ethnography in the project itself). The main scholarly motivation for the Urban Aspirations collaboration was to

(Continued)

draw our knowledges of different parts of urban Asia into a comparative constellation – to try to generate collaborative insights that might not have emerged had we each merely continued to work on discrete case studies from our own separate field sites. Arjun Appadurai's conceptualization of aspiration as a navigational capacity (Appadurai, 2004), and, more specifically, a concern with the way in which the aspirations of both urban elites and everyday city dwellers are variously (re)formed, realized and impeded, provided an umbrella framing for the project. The intention was that this would allow individual collaborators to continue ongoing work in our respective sites while also allowing us to foster relational and comparative cross-site perspectives through regular face-to-face meetings and a digital platform for sharing ethnographic text, images and other artefacts.

For reasons that I will reflect upon in the final section, a majority of the published research outputs from the Urban Aspirations project were individually authored, site-specific contributions, thus conforming to conventional ethnographic norms (for example, Elinoff, 2016; Gillen, 2015). In the remainder of the current section, however, I will focus on two examples of cases where it did prove possible, in different ways, to realize the project's collaborative and comparative objectives. The first is a case where team members' different areal knowledges enabled in-depth analysis of both destinations for and the site of origin of urban policy models. For several years prior to the Urban Aspirations collaboration, the small city of Surakarta (or Solo) in Central Java, Indonesia, had been vaunted as an exemplar of 'good practice' for various aspects of urban development and governance in post-Suharto Indonesia, and I had examined the emergence of Solo-as-model as part of other small-scale collaborative projects (Bunnell et al., 2013). Yet as soon as policies and models travelled beyond Indonesia (through international donor initiatives) to municipalities in Cambodia or Thailand, they also exceeded my individual areal or ethnographic capacity. As such, I specifically encouraged another member of the Urban Aspirations project to conduct fieldwork in Pak Kret, a municipality in Thailand which was at the receiving end of a Solo-as-model policy transfer initiative. My anthropologist colleague Eric C. Thompson already planned to carry out research in Bangkok, and that city's extended metropolitan region encompasses Pak Kret municipality. While this cross-site collaborative possibility was built into the grant from the outset – and so was an 'expected' relational comparison (Myers, 2014) – other unanticipated or unexpected possibilities for examining the travel of Solo-as-model arose during the project. At the time when our Urban Aspirations proposal was under review, the mayor who had overseen Solo's rise to model status, Joko Widodo ('Jokowi'), left the city to become governor of Indonesia's national capital region, Jakarta. Another colleague, Rita Padawangi, already planned to work on

Jakarta as part of the Urban Aspirations project (see Padawangi, 2018), and so was well placed to examine ways in which 'Solo' travelled through Jokowi's political upward mobility. Thus, through a mixture of planning and happenstance, our collaborative constellation of cities enabled in-depth, field-based examination of Solo-as-model that neither Eric, nor Rita, nor I could have carried out alone (Bunnell et al., 2017).

The second example is not to do with constitutive interrelations between urban sites that were covered by the project, but instead about how insights from dispersed field sites were brought into collective conversation with wider conceptual debates. During discussion with my two fellow human geography collaborators in the Urban Aspirations project, it emerged that in each of our respective field sites – in China, Vietnam and Indonesia – the people with whom we had been working had (in different ways) engaged 'the future' through relations with elsewhere(s). Elaine Ho had been working with African students in the Chinese cities of Guangzhou and Wuhan. For the young men and women that she has interviewed, China's accelerated economic modernization presented a glimpse into what they thought Africa's urban future might look like if the right moves are made, including through their own migration and associated acquisition of knowledge and skills. Jamie Gillen, in contrast, had been working with Vietnamese Americans who had moved to Ho Chi Minh City to realize entrepreneurial ambitions. Here, a Vietnamese city that had previously been imagined as (developmentally and biographically) a place of the past had become a site for (re)imagining alternative futures where business goals intermingled with a diasporic reclaiming of cultural roots. My own fieldwork in Solo had centred upon people's experiences of relocating from along the banks of a flood prone riverbank, and what this meant for their individual and collective relations with the future. The relocation itself was another of the developments during Jokowi's time as mayor that had been documented and circulated as national good practice, but was also bound up with wider normative imaginings of what a city river should look like. Interweaving our individual ethnographic insights Elaine, Jamie and I sought to conceptualize the future-oriented ways in which people seek to remake themselves and their urban milieus beyond Appadurai's metaphor of aspiration as a navigational capacity. Instead, we proffer conceptualization around the *prospect* of (urban) elsewheres, where prospect is operative both as a noun (suggesting a mental image of the future) and as a verb (suggesting practices of seeking, searching – and the possibility of finding opportunities not only different from a priori imaginings, but beyond what had previously even been imaginable or deemed possible). In sum, conversations taking place across cities in three different nation-states in Asia enabled reconceptualization beyond the ethnographic preoccupations of our respective sites of study (Bunnell et al., 2018).

Reflections on doing comparative ethnographic urban research

While the two rather different examples of cross-site ethnographic collaboration that I have just recounted were in line with the broadly comparative aims of the Urban Aspirations project, many other aspects of the project did not correspond with the original plans or timeline. To a large extent this had to do simply with individual collaborators (myself included) finding it difficult to commit sufficient time to the project – clearly a challenge that is not unique to comparative forms of ethnographic urban research. Yet there are aspects of ethnographic research that are particularly time-consuming. These have to do not merely with expectations about the amount of time spent conducting fieldwork, but also the openness of ethnographic approaches to unforeseen possibilities in the field that compel individual researchers to venture along unexpected pathways. Pursuit of such divergent pathways demands collaborative investments in order to make the wider project work, but is also part of the reason why individual researchers often do not have time to meet up or to work collaboratively in other ways. Our project's digital platform for ethnographic collaboration did not compensate for the difficulty of assembling collaborators in face-to-face meetings. In part, this was due to technical delays – which meant that some individual collaborators had already begun to analyse their ethnographic material before the platform was up and running – but also because some colleagues saw the platform more generally as adding an unnecessary stage to the process of developing field-based material into publishable writing. Junior colleagues, especially those with tenure clocks ticking in their heads, understandably preferred to take the tried-and-tested route to publication rather than experimenting with new technologies of ethnographic collaboration or participating in cross-site writing initiatives that would inevitably only proceed at the pace of the slowest collaborator. It is this preference, above all, that explains why so many of the published outputs from the Urban Aspirations project took the form of individually authored pieces on specific ethnographic sites. And yet several of the colleagues concerned have acknowledged that their site-specific case studies were shaped to varying degrees through cross- or trans-site discussions that occurred as part of the wider project – and so bore traces of comparativism after all (on such 'implicit' comparativism, see also McFarlane, 2011: 18–9).

Recognition that even single-authored papers based on empirical research in a single site or city may have been inflected by discussion of various urban elsewheres in the project raises wider questions about what is – and what is not – comparative, as well as about the extent to which different forms of comparative urban studies might be considered 'global'. Among the range of existing comparative methods discussed by Jennifer Robinson (2011) is the 'detailed case study', or what she terms 'individualizing' comparison. Although this might sound like what urban ethnographers have been doing for almost a century, it is important to highlight the specifically comparative and theory-oriented aspects of the kind of case study Robinson has in mind, as compared to say some of the classic Chicago School ethnographies: '. . . research on one city is brought into comparative relief through careful engagement with a wider literature, either in relation to generalized statements, or theories, about urban experiences or in terms of specific other individual experiences that might throw light on the case study in question' (2011: 6). Some of the other forms of comparativism that Robinson covers may require case studies in multiple sites, therefore demanding collaborative initiatives similar to the one I have discussed in this chapter. But, to connect to the wider framing of this volume, what makes a multi-sited collaboration *global*? To what extent does or should the answer to this question have to do with the spatial reach of the cases/sites concerned, or perhaps with their spread across multiple world regions? As I was asked in Loughborough at the conference where I presented an earlier version of this chapter, in what ways can a project including cities in Asia – *only* in Asia – be considered global? To me, the scope, regional distribution and even the number of cases/sites are not of paramount importance (although I do appreciate the political significance of efforts to build collaborative networks that incorporate urban scholars from institutions and parts of the world that are much less well-resourced than those of us based at NUS in Singapore – see Sheppard et al., 2015). It has long been accepted that studies of particular cities can be matters of global significance (Sassen, 1991), and urban scholars have demonstrated that it is not only so-called global cities that articulate global-scale political economic shifts and processes (see Glick Schiller and Çağlar, 2011; McCann, 2004). In my Solo-based component of the Urban Aspirations project, I have been concerned with how that city formed part of efforts by policymakers, donor agencies and individual citizens to 'scan' globally for urban policy models (McCann and Ward, 2010: 177), and with how the transformation of its waterways was bound up with a global aesthetics of city-building (cf. Ghertner, 2015; Harms, 2012). More widely, my own and my collaborators' efforts to bring both new cities and an expanded range of human voices, experiences and aspirations into the orbit of Anglophone urban theory (Bunnell and Goh, 2018) may be couched as a contribution to a 'more global' urban studies (Robinson, 2013).

A final, and concluding, set of reflections has to do with the urban in (global) urban ethnographic research. In a review article published more than three decades ago, geographer Peter Jackson (1985: 171) contended that '[e]thnography has yet to establish a firm place in urban studies precisely because it is not yet clear what is specifically "urban" about urban ethnography'. Central to the problem according to Jackson, was that much ostensibly urban ethnography 'has been *in* the city rather than *of* the city'. This distinction would call into question the urban credentials of much of the work undertaken as part of the Urban Aspirations project, including that concerned with patterns of migration to or through Asian cities, and on religious engagement with futurity in the city (for example, Ho, 2017; Low, 2016; Sinha, 2016). However, scholarship on planetary urbanization that rose to prominence in urban studies during the time when our NUS-based collaboration was running, has, in turn, called into question the centrality of the city to conceptualization, definition and territorialization of the urban (Brenner, 2014a; especially Angelo and Wachsmuth, 2014; Brenner 2014b; see also Katsikis, Chapter 2). Building upon some of the later works of Henri Lefebvre, planetary urbanization research has drawn attention to territorial configurations of urbanization beyond cities and other conventional urban territories. At one level, the focus of this work on the political economy and ecology of 'operational landscapes' means that ethnographic approaches may be one way of adding consideration of socio-cultural meanings and human experiences into the burgeoning mix of research on urban studies beyond methodological cityism. Yet one might also argue that such ethnographic perspectives already exist. Ethnographic work in/on Asia, for example – including by one of my colleagues who collaborated on the Urban Aspirations project – has examined 'rural' villages as 'socially urban' (Thompson, 2007). The fact that such work has (so far) not travelled nearly as far as Lefebvre-inspired urban theory may say something about the ongoing limitations of ethnography as a means of (re)building theory, or in speaking beyond areal partitions of knowledge. But it may also say something about a scholarly politics of who is emboldened to speak at planetary or global urban levels, and from where – both geographically and institutionally.

References

Anderson, B. (2016) 'Frameworks of comparison', *London Review of Books*, 38(2): 15–18.

Angelo, H. and Wachsmuth, D. (2014) 'Urbanizing urban political ecology: A critique of methodological cityism', in N. Brenner (ed.), *Implosions/Explosions: Towards a Study of Planetary Urbanization*. Berlin: Jovis, pp. 372–85.

Appadurai, A. (1996) *Modernity at Large*. Minnesota, MN: University of Minnesota Press.

Appadurai, A. (2004) 'The capacity to aspire: Culture and the terms of recognition', in V. Rao and M. Walton (eds), *Culture and Public Action*. Stanford, CA: Stanford University Press, pp. 59–84.

Beaverstock, J.V., Smith, R.G. and Taylor P.J. (2000) 'World-city network: A new meta-geography', *Annals of the Association of American Geographers*, 90(1): 123–34.

Brenner, N. (ed.) (2014a) *Implosions/Explosions: Towards a Study of Planetary Urbanization*. Berlin: Jovis.

Brenner, N. (2014b) 'Urban theory without an outside', in N. Brenner (ed.), *Implosions/Explosions: Towards a Study of Planetary Urbanization*. Berlin: Jovis, pp. 14–30.

Brewer, J. (2000) *Ethnography*. Buckingham: Open University Press.

Bunnell, T. (2016) *From World City to the World in One City: Liverpool through Malay Lives*. Chichester: John Wiley & Sons.

Bunnell, T. and Goh, D. (eds) (2018) *Urban Asias: Essays on Futurity Past and Present*. Berlin: Jovis.

Bunnell, T. and Kathiravelu, L. (2016) 'Extending urban liveability: Friendship and sociality in the lives of low-wage migrants', *International Development Planning Review*, 38(2): 201–20.

Bunnell, T., Miller, M.A., Phelps, N.A. and Taylor, J. (2013) 'Urban development in a decentralized Indonesia: Two success stories?', *Pacific Affairs*, 86(4): 857–76.

Bunnell, T., Padawangi, R. and Thompson, E.C. (2017) 'The politics of learning from a small city: Solo as translocal model and political launch pad', *Regional Studies*. doi: 10.1080/00343404.2017.1298087.

Bunnell, T., Gillen, J. and Ho, E. (2018) 'The prospect of elsewhere: Engaging the future through aspirations in Asia', *Annals of the American Association of Geographers*, 108(1): 35–51.

Burawoy, M. (2000) 'Introduction: Reaching for the global', in M. Burawoy, J.A. Blum, S. George, Z. Gille, T. Gowan, L. Haney, M. Klawitter, S.H. Lopez, S. Ó Riain and M. Thayer, *Global Ethnography: Forces, Connections, and Imaginations in a Postmodern World*. Berkeley, CA: University of California Press, pp. 1–40.

Clarke, N. (2012) 'Urban policy mobility, anti-politics, and histories of the transnational municipal movement', *Progress in Human Geography*, 36(1): 25–43.

Coe, N.M., Dicken, P., Hess, M. and Yeung, H.W.-C. (2010) 'Making connections: Global production networks and world city networks', *Global Networks*, 10(1): 138–49.

Elinoff, E. (2016) 'A house is more than a house: Aesthetic politics in a Northeastern Thai railway settlement', *Journal of the Royal Anthropological Institute*, 22(3): 610–32.

Ghertner, D.A. (2015) *Rule by Aesthetics: World-Class City Making in Delhi*. Oxford: Oxford University Press.

Gillen, J. (2015) 'Bringing the countryside to the city: Practices and imaginations of the rural in Ho Chi Minh City, Vietnam', *Urban Studies*, 53(2): 1–14.

Glick Schiller, N. and Çağlar, A. (eds) (2011) *Locating Migration: Rescaling Cities and Migrants*. Ithaca, NY: Cornell University Press.

Goh, D.P.S., Bunnell, T. and van der Veer, P. (2015) 'Introduction: Doing Asian cities', *Ethnography*, 16(3): 287–94.

Harms, E. (2012) 'Beauty as control in the new Saigon: Eviction, new urban zones, and atomized dissent in a Southeast Asian city', *American Ethnologist*, 39(4): 735–50.

Ho, E.L.E. (2017) 'The geo-social and global geographies of power: Urban aspirations of "worlding" African students in China', *Geopolitics*, 22(1): 15–33.

Jackson, P. (1985) 'Urban ethnography', *Progress in Human Geography*, 9(2): 157–76.

(Continued)

Jacobs, J.M. (2012) 'Urban geographies I: Still thinking relationally', *Progress in Human Geography*, 36(3): 412–22.

Katsikis, N. (2018) 'Visualizing the planetary urban', in J. Harrison and M. Hoyler (eds), *Doing Global Urban Research*. London: Sage, pp. 12–33.

Low, K. (2016) 'Migrant warriors and transnational lives: constructing a Gurkha diaspora', *Ethnic and Racial Studies*, 39(5): 840–57.

Matsutake Worlds Research Group (2009) 'Strong collaboration as a method for multi-sited ethnography: On mycorrhizal relations', in M.-A. Falton (ed.), *Multi-sited Ethnography: Theory, Praxis and Locality in Contemporary Research*. Farnham: Ashgate, pp. 197–214.

McCann, E. (2004) 'Urban political economy beyond the "global city"', *Urban Studies*, 41(12): 2315–34.

McCann, E. (2010) 'Urban policy mobilities and global circuits of knowledge: Toward a research agenda', *Annals of the Association of American Geographers*, 101(1): 107–30.

McCann, E. and Ward, K. (2010) 'Relationality/territoriality: Toward a conceptualization of cities in the world', *Geoforum*, 41(2): 175–84.

McFarlane, C. (2011) *Learning the City: Knowledge and Translocal Assemblage*. Chichester: Wiley-Blackwell.

Myers, G. (2014) 'From expected to unexpected comparisons: Changing the flows of ideas about cities in a postcolonial urban world', *Singapore Journal of Tropical Geography*, 35(1): 104–18.

Olds, K. (2001) *Globalization and Urban Change: Capital, Culture, and Pacific Rim Mega-Projects*. Oxford: Oxford University Press.

Padawangi, R. (2018) 'Excavating the ruins of aspirational urban futures in Bukit Duri, Jakarta', in T. Bunnell and D. Goh (eds), *Urban Asias: Essays on Futurity Past and Present*. Berlin: Jovis, pp. 205–18.

Peck, J. and Theodore, N. (2012) 'Follow the policy: A distended case approach', *Environment and Planning A*, 44(1): 21–30.

Robinson, J. (2002) 'Global and world cities: A view from off the map', *International Journal of Urban and Region Research*, 26(3): 531–54.

Robinson, J. (2006) *Ordinary Cities: Between Modernity and Development*. London: Routledge.

Robinson, J. (2011) 'Cities in a world of cities: The comparative gesture', *International Journal of Urban and Regional Research*, 35(1): 1–23.

Robinson, J. (2013) 'The urban now: Theorising cities beyond the new', *European Journal of Cultural Studies*, 16(6): 659–77.

Roy, A. (2009) 'The 21st-century metropolis: New geographies of theory', *Regional Studies*, 43(6): 819–30.

Sassen, S. (1991) *The Global City: New York, London, Tokyo*. Princeton, NJ: Princeton University Press.

Sheppard, E., Gidwani, V., Goldman, M., Leitner, H., Roy, A. and Maringanti, A. (2015) 'Introduction: Urban revolutions in the age of global urbanism', *Urban Studies*, 52(11): 1947–61.

Simone, A. (2010) *City life from Jakarta to Dakar: Movements at the Crossroads*. London: Routledge.

Sinha, V. (2016) 'Marking spaces as "sacred": Infusing Singapore's urban landscape with sacrality', *International Sociology*, 31(4), 467–88.

Smith, M.P. (2001) *Transnational Urbanism: Locating Globalization*. Oxford: Wiley-Blackwell.

Swanson, K. (2010) *Begging as a Path to Progress: Indigenous Women and Children in the Struggle for Ecuador's Urban Spaces*. Athens, GA: University of Georgia Press.

Swanson, K. (2013) 'Urban ethnographic research', in K. Ward (ed.), *Researching the City*. Los Angeles: Sage, pp. 54–69.

Taylor, P.J. and Derudder, B. (2018) 'Exploring the world city network', in J. Harrison and M. Hoyler (eds), *Doing Global Urban Research*. London: Sage. pp. 34–51.

Temenos, C. and Ward, K. (2018) 'Examining global urban policy mobilities', in J. Harrison and M. Hoyler (eds), *Doing Global Urban Research*. London: Sage. pp. 66–80.

Thompson, E.C. (2007) *Unsettling Absences: Urbanism in Rural Malaysia*. Singapore: NUS Press.

Ward, K. (2010) 'Towards a relational comparative approach to the study of cities', *Progress in Human Geography*, 34(4): 471–87.

14

DOING LONGITUDINAL URBAN RESEARCH

Katherine V. Gough

Why do longitudinal urban research?

The launch of the UN's New Urban Agenda in October 2016 has set global standards of achievement in sustainable urban development, rethinking the way we build, manage and live in cities (Acuto, Chapter 7). This agenda, together with the adoption of an urban Sustainable Development Goal (SDG 11) to 'Make cities inclusive, safe, resilient and sustainable' (UN, 2016: n.p.), has highlighted the need for innovative research on urban issues. Much conventional urban research is unable to capture the fluid dynamics of cities and their inhabitants since it is conducted within the framework of a specific research project, typically of around three years' duration. Consequently, time spent in the field collecting empirical data is limited and rarely spans more than 12 months. The data that are used to provide empirically grounded accounts of a wide range of urban processes, and feed into conceptualizations and theorizations of global urban complexity, thus only provide a snapshot of the urban at a specific point in time.

Longitudinal urban research, which entails collecting data over extended periods of time, has the advantage over short-range projects of introducing a temporal element to the data increasing the explanatory power of empirical analysis (Ruspini, 1999). Such analysis facilitates distinguishing between transient and enduring processes occurring across all scales – from local to global – thus enabling identification of the changes that matter. In relation to global urban research, adopting a longitudinal approach can shed new light on issues such as: the impact of the global labour market and associated remittances; responses to global economic booms and crises; the influence of aspirations for and actual international mobility; the impact of rising global inequality; as well as changing urban–rural ties and trajectories of social and economic change in general.

Although 'longitudinal' is a rather imprecise term, longitudinal data can be defined as 'data gathered during the observation of subjects on a number of occasions over time' (Ruspini, 2002: 3). There are several different research designs within longitudinal research: repeated cross-sectional studies, prospective studies and retrospective studies (Ruspini, 1999). In repeated cross-sectional studies, typically surveys are conducted at two or more points in time with a new sample population selected each time enabling a time trend to be incorporated into the analysis. Prospective longitudinal research typically involves panel surveys which trace individuals (often part of a cohort) at regular points in time enabling the nature of individual change to be analysed. Retrospective studies in contrast involve recording data in continuous time typically by conducting retrospective life histories over the entire life course.

Longitudinal research can thus take on a range of differing characteristics. It may involve: continuous research in the same society over a number of years; re-studies that take place periodically either at regular or irregular intervals in 'waves'; or return to a place/people after an extended period of time has elapsed. Whilst some longitudinal research is planned from the start as such, in other instances it emerges subsequently as a result of a researcher's curiosity to discover how people and places have changed over time in contexts they once knew well (see, for example, Blaikie et al., 2002; Gugler, 1991; Moser, 2009; Perlman, 2010; Rigg and Salamanca, 2015; Ward, 2012). The fieldwork itself may entail the collection of quantitative data, qualitative data or combine the two in a mixed methods approach. Regardless of the specific research design, however, longitudinal research has the ability to 'provide a glimpse into both the life histories of the individuals who make up a segment of a population, and the broader patterns of change that make up the social landscape' (Brock and Knowles, 2012: 16). Thus a key strength of longitudinal research is the ability to link analysis of micro and macro processes over time. As Neale and Flowerdew claim:

> It is *through time* that we can begin to grasp the nature of social change, the mechanisms and strategies used by individuals to generate and manage change in their personal lives, and the ways in which structural change impacts on the lives of individuals. Indeed, it is only through time that we can gain a better appreciation of how the personal and the social, agency and structure, the micro and macro are interconnected and how they come to be transformed. (Neale and Flowerdew, 2003: 190, italics in original)

This, it can be argued, is especially important in an urban context as cities and their inhabitants are in a constant state of flux due to the interaction of global and local processes, which longitudinal research is best able to capture.

Longitudinal research is conducted in a range of disciplines but especially in health studies, psychology, education, sociology, childhood and youth studies, criminology and anthropology. Within an urban arena there are some classic longitudinal studies which adopted the ethnographic tradition of anthropologists (Holland et al., 2006). These include Lynd and Lynd's (1937) pioneering study of how the social structure of the town they called 'Middletown' in Indiana had changed from their original study in the 1920s due to the Great Depression. The urban ethnographic tradition of the Chicago School was important in promoting qualitative longitudinal methods such as Whyte's (1943) study of Italian Americans in Boston. More recently, in a Latin American context in her book *Favela*, Janice Perlman (2010) provides a fascinating account of how the fortunes of families living in Rio de Janeiro's *favelas* have evolved over a period of almost 40 years. This enables her to shed light on the transgenerational transmission of poverty, inequality and exclusion, and explore issues of social mobility within a society characterized by high inequality. In a similar manner, drawing on data collected over a period of 30 years, Caroline Moser (2009) recounts the struggles of families, who initially built their homes in a mangrove swamp in the Ecuadorian city of Guayaquil, to get out of poverty from the late 1970s to early 2000s. In all of these studies, the global is seen to affect the urban in myriad ways.

Key themes which emerge as being especially appropriate for longitudinal research in an urban context include: studying transitions over the life course; analysing how pathways are experienced and negotiated; understanding mobility over space and time; exploring the impact of particular events, interventions or traumas; and the evaluation of policies and programmes (drawing on Holland et al., 2006). In all of these instances, adopting a temporal perspective adds greatly to our understanding of urban places and processes, and can make important contributions to urban theory. The importance of time, it can be argued, has become increasingly significant with the rapid social change that has occurred under later modernity (Neale and Flowerdew, 2003), partly due to globalization, which is especially evident in urban areas around the globe.

Challenges of doing longitudinal urban research

Whilst all urban research is full of challenges, it can be argued that these are amplified when engaging in longitudinal research. These challenges are multifarious and will be discussed here under the following types: theoretical, methodological and ethical.

Theoretical challenges regarding longitudinal urban research include conceptualizations of time and the ways in which the passing of time can change previous interpretations of data by both the researcher and informants (Miller, 2015). Miller (2015: 300) illustrates how 'powerful discourses shape what is felt to be permissible to say (when) and what remains unspoken, such that earlier theorizations can be confirmed, re-evaluated and refined'. Consequently, theorizing the urban from longitudinal research may be a messy endeavour, as not only do urban places and people change over time but so too do informants' accounts of their lives, experiences and aspirations. Another theoretical conundrum, highlighted by Blaikie et al. (2002: 1257), is the risk of longitudinal research being 'imprisoned' in the theories and epistemologies of the original study, and whether if follow-up research is freed from its intellectual genealogy it really is a re-study.

An additional theoretical challenge is linking events and processes from the local to the global which, despite being one of the strengths of longitudinal urban research, in practice is far from straightforward. As Perlman (2010: xxii) writes in the preface to her book on life in Brazilian *favelas*, rather than discovering convincing links between macro-level political and economic changes and the life stories of her interviewees, what she found was 'a much more complex situation, with contradictory implications that did not lead to simple conclusions or solutions'. This highlights the importance of not making simple cause and effect claims when generating urban theory, which may be especially tempting for researchers having invested extensive time and energy in conducting longitudinal research.

Methodologically, as Holland et al. (2006) argue, there is always a tension between *comparability* and *innovation* in longitudinal research. Especially in the case of quantitative methods, where consistency is at a premium, innovation has to be kept to a minimum but may be necessary in instances where old questions or ways of measuring become obsolete. In qualitative research this is less of an issue and researchers have the advantage of being able to respond to innovation resulting in the questions being 'tailored' as circumstances change and new findings come to light (Holland et al., 2006: 38). This highlights one of the key challenges of longitudinal research, which is 'the absence of analytic closure, with new rounds of data always threatening to render interpretations redundant' (Thomson and Holland, 2003: 243). Unless a decision is made to stop at a certain point in time, data collection and analysis are never finished hence interpretation is always provisional. Moreover, new data may generate contradictory versions of previous findings, which prompts questions regarding which version of events is trustworthy (Miller, 2015).

Tracing participants, especially after an extended period of time, can be a constant headache in all longitudinal research. This is typically a greater challenge in an urban compared with rural context due to the frequency with which many urban residents change their place of abode, especially if they are tenants, and due to weaker social networks. As Perlman (2010: 341) writes regarding the challenges of finding research participants again, in her case after a gap of 30 years: 'It was like being a detective, searching out clues, going to places where I had last seen each person, following up leads, running into dead ends, and trying alternative tacks.' She highlights, however, how the tracking process itself was enlightening as through it she discovered how strong and long lasting the ties within the communities she studied were, as in many instances people knew where their former neighbours and friends had gone and how to get hold of them. Whilst this was also my experience in a low-income neighbourhood in a Zambian urban context, it is much less likely to be the case in higher-income neighbourhoods and in cities located in the Global North where neighbourly ties tend to be weaker.

Keeping in contact with and tracking down participants, however, has become easier in today's world with almost universal access to mobile phones, the internet and social media. This in itself can result in new challenges emerging as Miller (2015: 294) indicates, claiming that at times it can 'feel analogous to stalking'. Despite new ways of staying in touch with participants, there will always be some who either decline to be re-interviewed or who cannot be traced. Potential bias resulting from unknown differences between people re-interviewed and those not traced is an additional challenge for longitudinal research since it cannot be assumed that nonresponse occurs completely randomly (Ruspini, 1999). This will inevitably affect the empirical claims made and consequent theorizing about the urban.

An additional challenge that can emerge from making repeat visits to informants, especially in low-income urban settlements, is the raising of their expectations that some form of support will be coming their way. In relation to research I conducted on home-based enterprises in Accra, Ghana, for which I made a return visit to the same 30 enterprises on an annual basis for 10 years, I wrote:

> Whilst most informants are pleased when researchers return, as it shows they have not been forgotten, making return visits does raise expectations and at times I had to deal with complaints along the lines of "You keep on coming back here and asking more questions but nothing changes, nothing improves. When are we going to see any benefits?" (Gough, 2010: 52)

Whilst the expectation of material benefits is one challenge a longitudinal researcher may face, another is handling the relationships that develop over time between participant and researcher. In particular, researchers need to be aware of how participation in a particular study can inadvertently alter an informant's views of themself and other people and places. As both researchers and informants themselves change over time, this can also affect how they relate to each other, how informants react to certain questions asked, and the responses they provide. Moreover, changes in the nature of the community and in the wider urban landscape can present additional challenges. Again Perlman's (2010) study is illustrative here as the increasing control of drug gangs in the communities in Rio de Janeiro she studied made access to some of her participants difficult.

Ethical issues, whilst paramount in all research, tend to be amplified in longitudinal research due to the extended timeframes and intensive research relationships (Taylor, 2015). As Holland et al. (2006) highlight, key ethical issues in longitudinal research revolve around consent, confidentiality, anonymity, intrusion, dependency, emotional involvement and distortion of experiences through intervention. A study by Jellinek (1997), in which she followed one woman, Sumira, over a period of 14 years until her death, as well as providing graphic detail of the trials and tribulations of living and working in Jakarta, Indonesia, highlights many of these ethical issues. In previous publications Jellinek had anonymized Sumira by calling her Bud for fear that the authorities could harm her for telling her story to a foreigner but following her death Jellinek decided she deserved her own name. Writing more broadly on anonymity in longitudinal research, Taylor (2015: 282) highlights how it can be 'hard to anonymize in a way that does not also lose contextual richness and the coherent narrative of the case'.

Jellinek (1997) also writes about her dilemma regarding advising Sumira when faced with the decision of whether to take up the offer of a government apartment following the demolition of her home, and her shock when Sumira subsequently used her compensation money to renovate the apartment rather than banking it and living off the interest. As she writes, 'I deeply regretted that I had ever meddled in her life. How could I, a secure middle-class Australian, hope to understand the values, the dreams, the pressures, and especially the unpredictability of the life of a Jakarta kampong dweller?' (Jellinek, 1997: 149). This highlights how power relations can affect longitudinal research as participants view researchers as knowledgeable actors and may seek their advice which, given the nature of the relationship that evolves over time, researchers can feel compelled, and even wish, to give. Finally, through a series of footnotes, Jellinek (1997) highlights the ways in which this last account of Sumira's life differs from previous ones due to new information emerging. Despite all these challenges, the article itself provides a fascinating account of Sumira's life, offering real insight into how processes spanning from the global to the body affect urban living across the life course.

Techniques for doing longitudinal urban research

As in all research, it is the nature of the research questions and the substantive research area, combined with the epistemological and ontological orientations of the researcher, which determine the most appropriate methods to adopt. Within longitudinal urban research, quantitative methods are more common though qualitative methods have become increasingly recognized as being important tools. Most longitudinal studies combine extensive (quantitative) and intensive (qualitative) data collection in a mixed methods approach.

A key decision to make at an initial stage of a research project is the unit of analysis. Potential units for longitudinal urban research include: communities, organizations, groups (including families, households, social networks, age cohorts, etc.), individuals, events, physical settings and time periods (Holland et al., 2006). The unit selected affects the nature of the study as well as having cost, ethical and analytical implications. The individual is the most common unit of analysis followed over time especially in quantitative longitudinal studies, which typically start by selecting a random sample of respondents; either the same sample is followed over time (as in cohort studies) or new samples are selected each time (as in repeated cross-sectional studies). The ability to select a random sample within an urban area depends on the availability and accessibility of population data; where this data is not available, alternative sampling has to take place, such as interviewing in every fifth house. Within qualitative approaches, longitudinal studies tend to either follow communities – including individuals within these communities – or follow individuals over time (Holland et al., 2006).

In deciding the scale of a particular study, longitudinal approaches not only need to consider the size but also the duration. Larger samples over longer time periods will generate more reliable data (Holland et al., 2006), though funding constraints play a role in limiting both. The main quantitative method used to collect data is a questionnaire survey. Whilst devising a large-scale questionnaire survey is always challenging, particular to longitudinal research is the dilemma of formulating a revised questionnaire comparable to the original but relevant to the current moment in order to best facilitate comparison. As Rigg and Salamanca (2015) found in a 25-year panel study from Thailand, markers of poverty and prosperity are especially likely to change over time.

A wide range of qualitative methods are used in longitudinal urban research. The most common is in-depth interviews which are conducted with the same individuals at various points in time. For this type of interviewing it is considered especially important for the same interviewer to conduct the return interviews due to the nature of the bonds that develop between researcher and participant. Diaries are another useful method. These are usually written by the participants to record events and thoughts between interviews. Miller (2015) highlights how by inviting her participants to write a post-interview 'diary' this generated valuable insights as they were able to add any additional thoughts that had occurred to them after the interview. Especially in ethnographic longitudinal research, field diaries written by the researcher can also be very informative alongside participant observation.

Caroline Moser's (2009) longitudinal research in the *barrios* of Guayaquil can be drawn on to illustrate how these various methods can be combined within one study. As is the case in much unintended longitudinal research, her methodology did not follow a pre-established plan but evolved over the course of extended field visits – seven in total – stemming from 1978 to 2005. Living within the community, she engaged in extensive participant observation which enabled her to better understand the political negotiation of basic services as well as gain an insight into household dynamics. Key informant interviews were held on each visit with members of five families followed in detail throughout the study, as well as political and community leaders. These were complemented with many informal conversations held in kitchens and on back patios. Moser (2009: 266) also kept field diaries during all of her visits in which she recorded her 'insights into events, seemingly mundane and parochial, that had an impact on people's lives'. She explains how some of the early entries gained greater significance over time shedding light on events that form a key part of her narrative.

Supplementing these qualitative methodologies, Moser (2009) also carried out household surveys; a census survey was conducted in the initial research in 1978 in six blocks followed by a random sample survey in 1988, 1992 and 2004 in the same six blocks. The precise combination of qualitative and quantitative data collection varied between field visits depending on the focus of the research. For example, she describes how her insight into women's community-managing roles, and hence their triple roles in reproduction, production and community affairs, emerged from her evolving research methodology illustrating how 'an understanding of such multidimensionality necessitates complementary data collection techniques and instruments in order to undertake the required comprehensive analysis' (Moser, 2009: 266). Moreover, starting from the 1992 fieldwork she integrated local people into all aspects of data collection, which she claims enhanced the level of detail of the information collected. The resultant analysis of this extensive quantitative and qualitative data set have enabled Moser (2009: xvi) to make an important contribution to the global urban literature adding to existing understandings of urban poverty and challenging the 'pervasive, persistent, and embedded stereotypes and myths about urbanization'.

Turning to analysis of longitudinal data, there are two distinct but interrelated approaches that are adopted: cross-sectional analysis of the data collected at one particular point in time across the sample and longitudinal analysis of the data over time typically following individual cases (Thomson and Holland, 2003). As there is also a subsequent stage of examining the articulation between the two, this has been referred to as a tripling of the analytical burden (Holland et al., 2006: 35). For quantitative data, the analysis may involve conducting time-series techniques for repeated cross-section data, logistic and log-linear models (Ruspini, 1999). For qualitative data, narrative analyses of individual cases enable researchers to explore change over time including bringing in their personal reflections, whilst a software programme such as NVivo can be useful for conducting cross-sectional analysis. As Thomson and Holland (2003: 238–9) argue, in the latter the 'focus on text allows for complexity and is open to a more grounded approach to theorizing' but it also poses challenges for 'maintaining the integrity of individual narratives, cutting data up into small chunks of text'. Combining longitudinal quantitative and qualitative data analysis, both cross-sectionally and over time, whilst highly labour intensive can generate real insight into processes of global urban change.

Case study: Doing longitudinal urban research in Pereira, Colombia

My own engagement in longitudinal urban research stems initially from a desire to discover the changes that were taking place in the low-income urban settlements (*barrios*) that I had studied in my PhD research in the intermediate-sized city of Pereira, Colombia. Focussing on the construction of 'self-help' housing, my initial research design attempted to incorporate a temporal perspective by studying settlements of differing ages; I selected two settlements where households were in the initial stages of constructing their homes and three settlements where the houses were around 8–10 years old. The research being a reflection of its time (1980s), I conducted a questionnaire survey with randomly selected households all of whom were homeowners, 243 of which I was able to use. I also tracked some households during the 12 months (1986/87) I spent in Pereira, noting their progress building their homes over time through conducting numerous informal interviews, and even built a house myself in an attempt to better understand the process (Gough, 1992). This research enabled me to discover how the inhabitants of low-income settlements access land and building materials and to analyse the processes of construction, consolidation and commodification of their homes (Gough, 1996a, 1996b, 1996c, 1998, 1999). It soon became clear, however, that relying on people's memory for recalling past events was fairly inadequate and, as I had got to know some of these households well, I was curious to find out how they had faired over time.

Consequently, 10 years later and living in Denmark, I succeeded in obtaining a small amount of funding from the Carlsberg Foundation to return to Colombia for one month to revisit all of the houses where I had initially held interviews. The aim of the research was to investigate how the houses and the households living in these houses had changed over time; hence, unlike the other studies discussed in this chapter, the unit I am tracking is the house. By working flat out I managed to conduct the slightly modified questionnaire survey in 221 (91%) of the same houses as in 1987 (some houses had been demolished whilst a few new households declined to participate). This revealed that two-thirds of the households were the same as in 1986/87, the remaining third being new, mainly tenant, households. Where the same households were encountered, most could remember me – not many young Western women enter low-income settlements in Colombia – and amazingly some could even produce the postcard of London I had given them 10 years previously. They saw my return visit as an indication that they had not been forgotten and interpreted the fact that I still had copies of the original questionnaires as an indication of the importance of the research project, which they were proud to be part of. As Perlman (2004, 2010) also found from her longitudinal research in Brazil, most people were eager to update their stories.

Whilst the return fieldwork was in many ways enjoyable and gratifying, it was also very challenging on numerous fronts. Although I knew the settlements would have consolidated, I was unprepared for the extent of the changes; places where I had felt very at home 10 years earlier were almost unrecognizable and initially I wandered around in rather a daze. I soon discovered that whilst the material living conditions of the inhabitants had greatly improved, their lives had become much more fragile in a situation of increasing insecurity as paramilitary groups as well as guerrillas and the military had become involved in drug-related battles over territory. One of my study settlements had acquired the status of having the worst reputation in Pereira with taxi drivers being reluctant to take me there and social workers who knew the settlement well warning me to take care or I could be 'disappeared'. When participants told me that people were '*limpiando el barrio*' (literally, cleaning the settlement) I naively understood this as clearing away the garbage until I realized that it meant assassinating those (usually young men) who were considered to be undesirable residents due to their (sometimes prior) involvement in drugs and violence. I became acutely aware that I too had changed during the intervening decade to being in my early 30s, rather than early 20s, and having become the mother of two young daughters. Not only did I have a heightened awareness of the importance of my own safety but the impact of a woman breaking down when telling me that her son had been murdered on her doorstep during the intervening 10 years was considerably greater. Such incidences also highlighted the ethical implications associated with conducting longitudinal urban research as unwittingly painful memories can be evoked when asking about the intervening period.

The findings from this first return visit revealed that the average housing standard had risen in all of the settlements, though not all households had managed to consolidate their dwellings. A more consolidated house increases the possibilities of generating income from the home, either through renting out rooms or setting up a home-based enterprise. By 1997 almost a third of households were operating the latter, illustrating the symbiotic relationship between housing and work: economic activities provide income which enables housing improvements to take place, and as the houses are consolidated this improves the potential for setting up home-based enterprises (Gough and Kellett, 2001).

Although on leaving Colombia safely in 1997 I promised myself I would not return, just over a decade later in 2010 the situation was much more

(Continued)

stable and I had become curious once again to discover how the settlements had changed and the people I knew were getting on. On this occasion I took my elder daughter with me – by this time aged 22 and just graduated in anthropology. I was able to tell the participants that I had returned not only to find out how their houses and lives had changed but also so that they could meet my daughter, which was a real hit. I started off with the intention of conducting interviews in the same houses in all five settlements, again within one month, but after a couple of days my daughter declared she was not prepared to work non-stop plus questioned why I was always rushing on when I could learn more by stopping and talking for longer with people who wanted to. Accepting her rationale I restricted my data collection to the two newer settlements, which by this stage were already 20 years old, and supplemented my questionnaire survey with in-depth interviews whenever participants were willing to talk for longer. Thus my sample size halved (to 110 households) but the qualitative data is much stronger. I discovered that by 2010 most of the houses and settlements were well consolidated with good services and people felt much more secure. The key problem that emerged was the lack of employment, as a result of which many Pereiranos had emigrated to Spain, which has had interesting implications for the settlements. Through receiving remittances from Spain, some households had consolidated their homes to a higher quality than I had expected, and some households who had emigrated to Spain were renting out their homes increasing the number of tenant households. This highlights how longitudinal research can reveal the ways in which urban settlements are affected by both local and global processes.

One of the challenges of this type of longitudinal research supported by small research grants, which facilitate the data collection but nothing more, is finding the considerable time needed to analyse the data and write up the findings, especially in the current academic climate where researchers are constantly under pressure to bring in research money. Having not managed to publish from my previous round of data collection, I subsequently returned to Pereira in 2016 to update my knowledge of the situation by conducting some follow-up in-depth interviews with core families and key informants in the two settlements. Despite this being my intention, I ended up using a shorter version of the questionnaire for two reasons: first, it was what people were accustomed to me doing hence expected – once I had conducted the questionnaire they considered the work done and we could chat; second, I had been spotted in the settlements and people I had not planned to visit asked me when I was coming to their house. To not visit them and conduct an interview would have been considered an insult. This illustrates how participants' expectations can influence the nature of longitudinal urban research.

I now have a unique quantitative and qualitative data set that spans over 30 years consisting of more than 700 questionnaires and numerous in-depth interviews, all of which I have collected personally, as well as extensive participant observation. This is enabling me to answer questions including: How has the consolidation process of the houses progressed? Which households have the highest quality dwellings and which have failed to improve their homes? How is the space in the home used for living and income generation changing? Are multiple generations cohabiting and if so how are they sharing the space in the home? What are the inheritance arrangements of low-income housing? Who is selling and who is buying the houses? Is gentrification occurring in low-income settlements? How is the proportion of owners and tenants changing over time? This should enable me to shed new light on the capacities of, and challenges faced by, the urban poor in their attempts to create decent housing and show how these are the consequence of the interaction of processes occurring both locally and globally. Conceptually, important contributions will be made to several key debates including housing consolidation and commodification, gentrification, migration and mobility, and intergenerationality, thus responding to calls to develop urban theory, policy and practice from a Global South perspective (Pieterse, 2011). All I need is to find the time!

Reflections on doing longitudinal urban research

Without a doubt, conducting longitudinal research has been the most rewarding, both intellectually and emotionally, that I have engaged in. Similarly, the urban research I have found most stimulating to read has been based on longitudinal data which has drawn out the links between local and global processes. As this chapter has shown, doing longitudinal urban research can generate a wealth of empirical data, including on housing, enterprises and families, which adds real insight into our understanding of global urban complexity at a range of spatial and temporal scales. This in turn can feed into ways in which the urban is theorized and conceptualized by adding an important temporal perspective to our understanding.

Whilst some longitudinal studies are devised as such, many (like my own) are not, rather evolving over time as researchers develop an interest in returning to places where they have previously conducted research. In recognition of this, even if a research design does not include plans to conduct follow-up interviews, it is advisable to manage data and keep informants' contacts should the desire and possibility to return subsequently arise. In the days of mobile phones, email addresses and Facebook, it is possible to keep track of informants (with their consent) in ways that previously were much more difficult. Ironically, however, as Miller (2015) argues, increasing ethical regulation may mean that doing return interviews or extending a study may become more difficult due to recent requirements regarding data storage and protecting confidentiality. As she argues, it is important that 'ethics committees and researchers are able to sensitively respond to more fluid notions of informed consent, research participation and data collection' (Miller, 2015: 303) for unplanned longitudinal research to still be possible.

Looking forward, in these days of greater concern about 'impact' it is encouraging that policymakers are increasingly interested in the findings of longitudinal research. This can be at any stage of the policy cycle including policy formulation, policy implementation and policy accountability. Whilst the value of quantitative longitudinal research has long been recognized in policy circles, there is also a rising awareness of the value of qualitative longitudinal research and its ability to 'generate unique insights into the ways that social policies and interventions are "lived" and "survived" by individuals, families, communities and organisations' (Thomson and McLeod, 2015: 244).

Some of the most exciting developments in longitudinal research appear to be within qualitative longitudinal research. In a recent paper setting out an agenda for this approach, Thomson and McLeod (2015: 246) claim that as well as offering the potential to follow individuals, groups and institutions, they see an 'emergent and exciting frontier' for the method being the possibility to 'engage with durational practices, inheritances, flows and interruptions'. Such research could shed new light on the dynamic and processual dimensions of urbanism and urbanization, and the theorization of social and spatial mobility at all scales. Generating empirically informed theorizations of the urban based on insights gained from longitudinal research is important for understanding our increasingly urban and globally connected world, as reflected in the SDG 11 and the New Urban Agenda.

References

Acuto, M. (2018) 'Engaging with global urban governance', in J. Harrison and M. Hoyler (eds), *Doing Global Urban Research*. London: Sage, pp. 96–109.

Blaikie, P., Cameron, J. and Seddon, D. (2002) 'Understanding 20 years of change in west-central Nepal: Continuity and change in lives and ideas', *World Development*, 30(7): 1255–70.

Brock, K. and Knowles, C. (2012) 'Doing longitudinal research: Opportunities and challenges in a study of childhood', in J. Boyden and M. Bourdillon (eds), *Childhood Poverty: Multidisciplinary Approaches*. Basingstoke: Palgrave Macmillan, pp. 15–23.

Gough, K.V. (1992) 'From bamboo to bricks: Self-help housing and the building materials industry in urban Colombia'. Unpublished PhD thesis, University of London.

Gough, K.V. (1996a) 'Linking production, distribution and consumption: Self-help builders and the building materials industry in urban Colombia', *Third World Planning Review*, 18(4): 397–414.

Gough, K.V. (1996b) 'Self-help housing in urban Colombia: Alternatives for the production and distribution of building materials', *Habitat International*, 20(4): 635–51.

Gough, K.V. (1996c) 'Home-based enterprises in low-income settlements: Evidence from Pereira, Colombia', *Danish Journal of Geography*, 96: 95–102.

Gough, K.V. (1998) 'House for sale? The self-help housing market in Pereira, Colombia', *Housing Studies*, 13(2): 149–60.

Gough, K.V. (1999) 'Affording a home: Strategies adopted in low-income settlements in urban Colombia', in G. Jones and K. Datta (eds), *Housing and Finance in Developing Countries*. London: Routledge, pp. 119–35.

Gough, K.V. (2010) 'Continuity and adaptability of home-based enterprises: A longitudinal study from Accra, Ghana', *International Development Planning Review*, 32(1): 45–70.

Gough, K.V. and Kellett, P. (2001) 'Housing consolidation and home-based income generation: Evidence from self-help settlements in two Colombian cities', *Cities*, 18(4): 235–47.

Gugler, J. (1991) 'Life in a dual system revisited: Urban-rural ties in Enugu, Nigeria, 1961–87', *World Development*, 19(5): 399–409.

Holland, J., Thomson, R. and Henderson, S. (2006) *Qualitative Longitudinal Research: A Discussion Paper*. London: London South Bank University. www.lsbu.ac.uk/__data/assets/pdf_file/0019/9370/qualitative-longitudinal-research-families-working-paper.pdf (accessed 21 September 2017).

Jellinek, L. (1997) 'Displaced by modernity: The saga of a Jakarta street-trader's family from the 1940s to the 1990s', in J. Gugler (ed.), *Cities in the Developing World: Issues, Theory and Policy*. Oxford: Oxford University Press, pp. 139–55.

Lynd, R.S. and Lynd, H.M. (1937) *Middletown in Transition: A Study in Cultural Conflicts*. New York: Harcourt Brace.

Miller, T. (2015) 'Going back: "Stalking", talking and researcher responsibilities in qualitative longitudinal research', *International Journal of Social Research Methodology*, 18(3): 293–305.

Moser, C.O.N. (2009) *Ordinary Families, Extraordinary Lives: Assets and Poverty Reduction in Guayaquil, 1978–2004*. Washington, DC: The Brookings Institution.

Neale, B. and Flowerdew, J. (2003) 'Time, texture and childhood: The contours of longitudinal qualitative research', *International Journal of Social Research Methodology*, 6(3): 189–99.

Perlman, J.E. (2004) 'Marginality: From myth to reality in the favelas of Rio de Janeiro, 1969-2002', in A. Roy and N. AlSayyad (eds), *Urban Informality: Transnational Perspectives from the Middle East, Latin America, and South Asia*. Lanham, MD: Lexington Books, pp. 105–46.

(Continued)

Perlman, J.E. (2010) *Favela: Four Decades of Living on the Edge in Rio de Janeiro*. Oxford: Oxford University Press.

Pieterse, E. (2011) 'Grasping the unknowable: Coming to grips with African urbanisms', *Social Dynamics*, 37(1): 5–23.

Rigg, J. and Salamanca, A. (2015) 'The devil in the detail: Interpreting livelihood turbulence from a 25-year panel study from Thailand', *Area*, 27(3): 296–304.

Ruspini, E. (1999) 'Longitudinal research and the analysis of social change', *Quality and Quantity*, 33: 219–27.

Ruspini, E. (2002) *Introduction to Longitudinal Research*. London: Routledge.

Taylor, R. (2015) 'Beyond anonymity: Temporality and the production of knowledge in a qualitative longitudinal study', *International Journal of Social Research Methodology*, 18(3): 281–92.

Thomson, R. and Holland, J. (2003) 'Hindsight, foresight and insight: The challenges of longitudinal qualitative research', *International Journal of Social Research Methodology*, 6(3): 233–44.

Thomson, R. and McLeod, J. (2015) 'New frontiers in qualitative longitudinal research: An agenda for research', *International Journal of Social Research Methodology*, 18(3): 243–50.

UN (2016) *The Sustainable Development Goals Report 2016*. https://unstats.un.org/sdgs/report/2016/Overview/ (accessed 21 September 2017).

Ward, P.M. (2012) '"A patrimony for the children": Low-income homeownership and housing (im)mobility in Latin American cities', *Annals of the Association of American Geographers*, 102(6): 1489–1510.

Whyte, W.F. (1943) *Street Corner Society: The Social Structure of an Italian Slum*. Chicago: Chicago University Press.

15

HISTORICAL APPROACHES TO RESEARCHING THE GLOBAL URBAN

Mariana Dantas and Emma Hart

Why take a historical approach to researching the global urban?

Historians have long acknowledged that the movement and exchange of people, goods, ideas, and practices around the world dates back to ancient times and has since created interconnected global trends and developments (Abu-Lughod, 1991; Braudel, 1979 [1981–84]; Darwin, 2007). This understanding of human history has helped to produce research efforts focused not on empires or nations but seas and oceans, networks built by trade or intellectual exchanges, and supra-national, identity-based communities. It has also supported the rise of the rich field of world history, with its often macro-perspective on globalized and globalizing events and processes that have defined human experiences over time (Osterhammel, 2014; Pomeranz, 2000). These historians of course recognize that the more current process of globalization has its own idiosyncrasies, mostly related to technological and financial developments specific to the late twentieth and early twenty-first centuries. They nonetheless reject any sense that we live in an exceptional era of global connectivity, and highlight patterns in past global contexts that illuminate certain global phenomena in our present.

Urban historians, though, have yet to fully embrace the methods and analytical potential of the global or world history approach. Certain tendencies and trends in both the fields of urban history and urban studies help to explain why. As Pierre-Yves Saunier and Shane Ewen have recently argued, urban history has remained too focused on the production of city biographies (Saunier and Ewen, 2008). Its emphasis on studies of a particular city's past has prevented the adoption of a broader historical approach that favours paying attention to the interplay between urban spaces and communities and global economic, political, or cultural forces. To be sure, studies of commercial Renaissance cities, European imperial metropolises, or urban seats of colonial governments elsewhere in the world carefully consider how these urban centres and their populations were shaped by trading networks, the politics of conquest, and the culture of empires. The consideration of external contexts, however, usually serves the narrow explanatory purpose of helping to reconstruct the historical trajectory of a given urban environment at a given time.

Conversely, scholars in the field of urban studies more broadly, who have avidly explored the connection between globalization and urbanization, tend to restrict their forays into the past to the last half century. Saskia Sassen's (1991) framing of the concept of the global city has influenced that tendency in particular. The work of Sassen, Manuel Castells, and others has aimed to correct analyses of globalization that tended to overlook the relevance of localities to globalizing processes (Abu-Lughod, 1999; Brenner, 2004; Castells, 1996; Friedmann, 2002). Their work thus centres the investigation of globalization on cities, but it has also defined the global city as a site that concentrates services and industries which support contemporary global capitalism. Their efforts, moreover, have disproportionally focused on cities like New York, London, and Tokyo, identifying them as having the specific characteristics that make them global. And while it has inspired studies of other locations, their work has also supported the notion that cities form an urban network that is organized hierarchically based on the centrality of each urban centre to global economic, cultural, and political processes (Taylor, 2004; Taylor et al. 2011; Taylor and Derudder, Chapter 3). Recently, scholars have embarked on efforts to complicate the idea of the global city across both time and space. Endeavouring to embed cities, and the connections between them, in their local contexts, some critics have challenged the idea of the 'stateless' global city that floats free from its immediate environment (Therborn, 2011). By extending their explorations back in time, moreover, geographers have begun to unearth the deepest roots of contemporary urban networks that are the product of centuries-long processes of elaboration (Taylor et al., 2010; Taylor, 2013). This work has both highlighted the utility of taking a historical approach to global urban issues, while also revealing the need for a greater engagement by historians with this process.

Fortunately, some historians have recently risen to the challenge of linking the global and urban in a historical context. In their recent edited volume *Another Global City*, historians Pierre-Yves Saunier and Shane Ewen make a pitch for the relevance of urban history to our 'understanding of one of the most salient anxieties of today's world' (Saunier and Ewen, 2008: 2). In particular, they explore the importance of urban history to studies of globalization. To that effect, they take us back to the nineteenth-century urban municipal movement to demonstrate that tensions between national and city governments, and the municipalization of political and economic negotiations that drive global interactions and policymaking, date back two centuries. They further show that the struggle for, and the exercise of, municipal autonomy in issues as varied as regulation of immigration, infrastructure investment, and financial dealings with domestic and foreign actors has unfolded unevenly over time and frequently relied more on knowledge disseminated through urban networks than within nation-states. Their book reveals, therefore, that studies of cities in the past offer historical precedents to issues and concerns that interest scholars of and policymakers in cities today. More importantly, though, it explains how cities have, since the early nineteenth century, shaped negotiations between local, national, and international actors over the financial, political, and social role urban governments and institutions play in the promotion and management of global exchanges.

Efforts by historians like Saunier and Ewen push urban history beyond the biographical study of cities and beyond a mere articulation of the relationship between context (the rise of the nation-state, in this case) and local experience (cities' struggle for autonomy). Instead, they strive to answer the more interesting question of how cities produce globalization, or more specifically how they produce global and globalizing dynamics, practices, and cultures. Another important work that has taken us in that direction is by urban historian Carl Nightingale. In his global history of urban segregation, Nightingale (2012) gives a global context to some cities' efforts to separate populations which were deemed racially distinct and confine them to distinct sections within the urban geography; inevitably causing inequality, discrimination and disenfranchisement of one population by another. Again, Nightingale's work does not seek to trace the historical trajectory of an urban phenomenon in a particular city. He does not attempt either to explain segregation as a local response by colonial and postcolonial elites to economic, political, and cultural forces – internal and external – that were facilitating the growth and empowerment of non-white, non-elite urban groups, and thus threatening white supremacy. Instead, Nightingale treats segregation as a global phenomenon, the product of real estate investments, cultural and social ideas, and political strategies exchanged by interconnected cities around the world.

The study of cities, therefore, can offer more than a synthesis or explanation of causality of a global phenomenon. By engaging with the city as an agent of global history, urban historians can answer the question of how cities inform practices and processes that shape human experiences globally, as well as locally. This global approach to urban history, moreover, should not limit historical inquiry to the past two centuries. For instance, if one considers the age of European empires, it seems fruitful to consider the role cities played in the development of political, economic, social, and cultural institutions that favoured European interests and ambitions. The urban environment and populations of cities as diverse as the mining towns of Portugal's colony of Brazil, or the Atlantic ports of British North America, for instance, had to grapple with similar challenges as they negotiated their place within existing and changing global contexts. Expected to serve imperial economic pursuits while also supporting the needs and goals of their local population, they had to strike a balance between the economic and financial demands of local and global actors in order to make themselves relevant and viable (Bicalho, 2003; Fonseca, 2003; Matson, 1998; Prado, 2015). Reliant upon a labour force largely comprising voluntary and involuntary immigrants as well as slaves, these cities had to forge a culture of labour and population control (legal and otherwise) that nevertheless allowed for enough freedom of mobility and initiative to make these workers effective and profitable. Populated on the one hand by a small political white elite that drew justifications for its pre-eminence from its imperial connections, and on the other by a diverse middling and labour class that made their own claims on urban spaces and practices, these cities developed a geography of power and privilege that supported an unequal socio-economic and political hierarchy while creating spaces of belonging for all (Dantas, 2008; Hart, 2010).

The history of colonial towns of the Americas, as well as the history of nineteenth-century municipalities or twentieth-century segregated cities, can address important intellectual debates about the nature, trajectory, and outcomes of globalization. Indeed, a global urban history that is at once chronologically comprehensive, intrinsically comparative, and reliant on diligent archival-based research can add texture, nuance, and breadth to the fields of world history, global studies, and urban studies, and enhance critical analyses of globalization.

Challenges of taking a historical approach to researching the global urban

Before it can achieve its full potential as a field of inquiry, global urban history has to resolve the tension between urban historians' tendency to favour thick descriptions of a particular city's history and the panoramic approach the study of global history demands. Historians are trained to rely heavily on a discernible set of archival or otherwise curated sources, whether text-based or not. Their careful collection, examination, and analysis of documents on which they base their work enables them to produce rich and dense accounts and interpretations of the past. Their efforts afford them the confidence to draw conclusions and propose new narratives. Conversely, it also makes them unwilling to extend their observations, interpretations, and conclusions beyond their selected object of study, much less to propose in broader terms patterns or models that might elucidate the historical role cities have played in global processes. The emphasis on understanding the specificity of the context, locality and people one is investigating in order to avoid generalizations that might undermine one's research results can be overemphasized among historians (Carp, 2009; Nash, 1979; Walker, 2008). The resulting scholarship can consequently seem insular and irrelevant to research questions and intellectual debates that are external to that field, time period, or geographical region.

Another tension that still affects urban historians attempting a global approach is their almost instinctive tendency to use the study of the past to explain progressive trajectories in a city's history, rather than exploring that history's diverse connections to its global context. Teleological uses of historical studies can sometimes be hard to resist because they offer neat and seemingly logical linear explanations for predictable outcomes. Studies of port cities, for instance, may tend to emphasize the formation of merchant communities, credit practices, or maritime industries that were shaped by external investments, migrations, or technology. Such historical developments, while helping to insert a particular case study within a broader global context, are emphasized because of their obvious relevance to the known outcome being considered: the rise of an urban port (Knight and Liss, 1991; O'Flanagan, 2008). Unfortunately, their investigation for the purpose of reconstructing a particular linear narrative of the city forces the investigator to overlook their relationship to other urban contingencies, to urban realities more broadly, and to global practices and processes even more generally. The history of that specific city's transformation into an imperial, international, or global port may emerge from such narrative, but its relevance as part of an urban network that framed certain opportunities or limitations for global economic, financial, or demographic exchanges might be obscured.

Investigations of cities' relevance as agents of globalization similarly suffer from the strong tendency within the field of urban history to remain rooted in the nation-state. Most urban historians, because of their focus on thick descriptions and emphasis on explanatory trajectories, seek the context required to explain and interpret their observations in national – or imperial – histories (Arrom, 2001; Carp, 2009). There are practical reasons for doing so. Exploring historical contingencies within a national or imperial context to make sense of one's evidentiary sources may seem a less daunting exercise than seeking for context beyond that framework. The assumption is that equipped with knowledge of one's case study one also possesses the required literacy to understand or speculate about the broader political, cultural, or demographic environment with which a city engages. Additionally, looking beyond national or imperial boundaries can require a different set of language and intellectual skills, as well as research experience, to navigate different archives, scholarly traditions, and literatures. These challenges can thus dissuade scholars from favouring comparisons with other cities, and from exploring historical relationships between cities and global processes. They can also encourage further the more comfortable approach of tying a city's historical trajectory to fluctuations in the fortunes of their respective nations.

Techniques for doing historical research into the global urban

Despite the challenge it poses, urban history's emphasis on archival research, thick descriptions, and careful contextualization of distinct practices and processes has much to offer to studies of global phenomena in the past and present. For instance, historians have paired their dedication to empirical evidence, collected from archives and other curated documentation, with an analytical approach that owes much to critical theory. That combination has produced a rich description of cities as the product of the interplay between human society, institutions, and urban geographies. Urban histories have in this sense helped to explain the formation of gender and racial dynamics, voting practices, economic investments, and cultural disseminations which, in turn, have influenced a city's and, more broadly, country's political, social, and economic trajectory. Moreover, urban historians have continuously promoted a creative approach to archives, successfully retrieving a narrative about the city from collections that may initially seem more suitable to studies in economic, social or intellectual history (Carvalho, 2013; Dorsey, 2002; Guy, 1991; Michney, 2017; Osorio, 2008).

This creative and critical approach can similarly help to address questions concerning the global urban past. Drawing from our own research, we propose two examples. In one case, documents that relate to the religious brotherhoods in the mining towns of colonial Brazil, which have commonly been used to write the religious and social history of colonial populations, can reveal much about the ways Africans and their descendants, as members of brotherhoods, shaped the physical layout and cultural uses of urban spaces (Dantas, 2009; Kiddy, 2007; Scarano, 1976; Voigt, 2016). More broadly, these documents connect the colonial Brazilian towns to the African Diaspora, and to the role cities played in framing the terms of that global demographic and cultural exchange. Our second case centres on two port cities in the English-speaking Atlantic of the eighteenth century, Glasgow and Charleston. On opposite sides of the ocean, these two urban spaces have not previously been considered together (Devine, 1975; Hart, 2010). Yet, by paying close attention to varying uses of space across two continents we can uncover the ways in which the growing number of inhabitants involved in the global economy interacted with those who moved through the city in local circuits.

The historian's methods will, nevertheless, have to be supplemented with new methodological approaches before more successful forays into global urban history can be achieved. In particular, historians need to embrace comparisons more readily. To be sure, urban histories have often drawn small comparisons between their main object of study and another or other cities. These comparisons, however, tend to be rather timid, and to favour the identification of similarities or differences that ultimately serve to reinforce the author's understanding of the particular trajectory the city under examination experienced. Consequently, these evaluations stop short from exploring cities as agents of global processes whose coordinated experiences shape broader practices and patterns. Such an approach can prove more fruitful to doing global urban history. Similarly, urban historians may need to embrace more readily a multi-scale approach – what Carl Nightingale has referred to as a diascalar approach – in their exploration of historical contexts (Kenny and Madgin, 2015). While most historians agree that it is necessary to insert their case study in a regional or national context, there is less of a tendency to consider different contextual frameworks. Using an international, transnational, urban network, or other types of geographies may prove more relevant to the understanding of global phenomena, like migration, dissemination of cultural notions, and rise of social or economic practices, than referring to a national or regional context. Furthermore, it becomes important to examine the dialogue between local and broader contexts, and to understand how the trajectory of a practice or process on the scale of the city both informs and is informed by similar practices and processes on larger scales.

The adoption of these different methodological approaches poses, nonetheless, an important practical challenge to urban historians, whose commitment to archival research and thick descriptions remains an asset. Pursuing comparisons and a 'diascalar approach' demands, after all, research in different archives and careful examination of distinct historical contexts across various geographical and even chronological spans. It can be a daunting task for a single scholar. An important part of future global urban history efforts, therefore, will be collaboration between researchers and fields. Over the past few years, such collaborations have emerged among historians of both the modern and early modern era. Taking the form of research networks, blogs (such as https://globalurbanhistory.com/) and publications, these varied ventures mark a new era of cooperation between historians working not only on different cities, but also on different historical eras and continents. A number of these projects have also seen historians collaborating with scholars in the social sciences (Farías and Bender, 2010; Kenny and Madgin, 2015; Sandoval-Strausz and Kwak, 2018). Scholars' growing willingness to team up in pursuit of realizing a global framework for their work must now be harnessed to produce a coherent field that can demonstrate the centrality of the historical perspective to global urban studies.

Case studies of historical research into the global urban

With a view to demonstrating the utility of a historical approach to global urban issues, we will now present two case studies that elucidate its benefits. As historians working on the pre-1850 era, we will draw our

(Continued)

examples from this period and, we hope, will illustrate the importance of taking a long view into the past. Furthermore, by selecting case studies from cities in North America and South America, we elide traditional national and imperial frameworks to highlight a global-urban process that emerged beyond many of the borders customarily imposed by scholars.

In the eighteenth century in the Portuguese colony of Brazil, urban centres quickly emerged in the backlands of the territory's south-eastern region in response to the discovery of gold and rise of a local mining industry. Hamlets that formed near mining sites, along commercial routes, or by a church were incorporated as towns and gained a municipal government, a district government, courts, and became parish seats. The establishment of such a complex institutional structure aimed to facilitate imperial government and tax collection. It also attracted a large population of Portuguese and other migrants who swarmed to the region in hopes of seeking their fortunes. And yet, most of the region's population were enslaved Africans and their Brazilian-born descendants who were forcefully brought to Minas Gerais (as the mining district became known) to work on the extraction of gold. As these men's and women's labour enriched colonial and metropolitan coffers, it also supported local production of food and other commodities, sustaining urban life, connecting rural places of production to urban markets, and facilitating local commercial and financial exchanges (Bergad, 2006; Fonseca, 2003).

The profitable exploitation of slaves' labour required the consolidation of a local culture, legal and otherwise, that supported the complete subjugation of African descendants to the economic interests and claims of social and political superiority of white colonists. That culture slowly took shape as town governments strove to regulate slaves' mobility, their individual and collective activities, and their use of urban space. Local laws were created to establish curfews for slaves, make it illegal and punishable for them to organize gatherings and cultural events, and force them to carry written passes when labouring away from their owners' surveillance. The inconsistent enforcement of these laws, however, reveals the ambiguous and complex relationship colonial towns had with their most underprivileged inhabitants. Slaves were essential to the urban economy: they supported the mining industry on which all other economic endeavours relied, and they provided the labour for a wide range of urban activities, from public jobs like paving streets and cleaning water canals to private enterprises like bread-making and butchering. The viability of urban life could be compromised by the excessive curbing of their movements, activities, and even initiatives (Dantas, 2008).

Slaves also proved to be a necessary evil, from the perspective of their free and white fellow urban dwellers, through their formation of religious brotherhoods. These associations were widespread in the

Portuguese empire and served several social and community purposes: they marked an individual's belonging to a select collective; they provided funerary services and pooled resources to help families affected by the sickness or death of a member; they organized festivities that articulated the association and its members' claim to urban spaces to a place within the fabric of the urban community. Slaves quickly embraced that Portuguese cultural practice, forming their own brotherhoods. Their organization into distinct religious associations was supported by the Portuguese Crown and the Church, both of whom believed that the formation of slave brotherhoods would make better Christians and servants of that population (Scarano, 1976). Municipal governments and free members of urban communities, however, often questioned the freedoms slaves appeared to enjoy or attempted to claim as members of religious brotherhoods. These urban bodies complained that black brotherhoods encouraged arrogance among slaves, challenged white authority, and morally corrupted their religious and cultural traditions (Dantas, 2009). But once in a while even these critics could not deny that certain slave brotherhoods had served the interest of their towns by paving streets in the vicinity of their churches, helping to maintain waterways, properly disposing of the dead, providing for the sick, and helping to shoulder the costs of local and community celebrations. It was not only through their labour that slaves helped to make colonial towns, and the elites and other free members of their urban environment could not help but be aware of that fact.

The complicated relationship colonial towns had with their slave population was a reality that owed its origins to the globalizing world in which those towns emerged and thrived. The towns of Minas Gerais were a product of gold mining, an economy that was inexorably intertwined with Portuguese imperial ambitions and commercial trading in the Atlantic and Indian Oceans, and further beyond in the South China Sea. These towns' gold output quickly helped to intensify Portuguese and English trade and in time capitalize the credit market that supported British industrialization. And the labour demands of the mining economy reinvigorated the slave trade from West and Central Africa to colonial Brazil, leading to the breakdown of some African communities as well as the economic, social, and political reorientation and rise of indigenous societies in present day Guinea-Bissau, Benin, Nigeria, and Angola. Gold from Minas Gerais thus tied closer together the economic production, political priorities, and social organization of sites and peoples from far off continents and seas. Those exchanges helped to reinforce certain global forces, such as concentration of capital and

(Continued)

commercial influence by European elites, and the naturalization of African and black slavery (Brown, 2012). But lest we forget, those Minas Gerais towns, by supporting the extraction, collection, processing, and taxation of gold, and by legislating, repressing, and accommodating its enslaved and free African-descending residents, were instrumental to the development of those global and globalizing realities.

Shifting location, but not century, we find ourselves on the waterfront of Glasgow and Charleston, two cities that became intimately connected by their involvement in the economy of Britain's Atlantic empire. Indeed, it was the trade in enslaved Africans, British manufactures, and American agricultural crops that enriched the growing populations of both places and helped them become some of the most dynamic cities in the English-speaking world of the era. Historians have quantified the impact of these emerging long-distance connections. Charleston's population – leaping from hundreds to thousands in a few decades – was composed of roughly half Europeans and half enslaved Africans, a direct result of the slave trade that brought the latter to work on the region's rice and indigo plantations. Glasgow's population grew dramatically too, swelled by additional tradespeople who arrived to service its wealthy tobacco and sugar merchants or to work in a linen industry spurred on by American demand (Coclanis, 1989; Devine, 1975). Those city merchants who were the maestros of global trade amassed sizeable fortunes, becoming among the richest men not only in their home towns, but in their regions and countries.

As in Minas Gerais' cities, therefore, global connections concentrated capital and wealth in the hands of free white male elites. And, like their Global South counterparts, these men of capital were enmeshed daily in the complex negotiations and relationships that arose when their ambitions and aspirations as global elites met with the city's other inhabitants. Such clashes were often expressed in the construction and use of space in these rapidly expanding cities. In late eighteenth-century Glasgow, new townscapes of luxurious commerce came into conflict with spaces of local trade. Owners of stores selling expensive imports on the newly built St Andrews square sought to banish the poultry market from within its confines. Storekeepers complained that the market men and women, with their chickens, eggs, and farm produce, kicked up dust that ruined their pricey exotic goods and asked for these local dealers to be relocated away from the prestige spaces of the Georgian city. The dispute ended up in court, which ruled that the rights of local people to trade in this official market should be unimpeded, especially when the rainy Scottish weather meant that dust was at best an incidental problem. In eighteenth-century Glasgow, therefore, globally driven consumerism was already embedded in the cityscape, yet authorities were still willing to support local farmers who had long inhabited the urban commercial landscape.

The tensions between an elite created by global capital and 'others' was replicated in Charleston, a major city on the other side of Britain's Atlantic. Certainly, the enslavement of so many African Charlestonians produced particular urban pressures. However, this dynamic was one element in a complex interplay of the global and the local, which manifested itself daily at the city's bustling waterfront. Each wharf, owned by an elite merchant, was the point at which Charleston was connected to the global forces that created it. Indian fabrics, Africans, and British manufactures were delivered to the wharf, while locally grown rice was dispatched from it. British customs officials attempted to collect duties on these goods so that the Crown might receive its cut of the profit. At the same time, enslaved Africans, tradespeople, and sailors used wharves as marketplaces, selling food and services, and even for socializing. Tensions regularly arose between merchant owner, Crown official, and non-elite inhabitants as they each sought to assert their economic interest at the waterfront. While merchants undoubtedly held the majority of the power, they were not able to wield it without constant negotiation with other traders and officials who, although they had conflicting interests, made a fundamental contribution to the wharf as an engine of the globalizing economy. Getting ships to and from the wharf necessitated the employment of a pilot, who might well be a free African. Preparing a ship for departure required the services of local manufacturers, food suppliers, and labourers, who needed to equip the vessel if it was to embark on time for European markets. Overall, Charleston's waterfront spaces contained global and local commercial circuits that needed to intersect if they were to function.

Together, these two case studies reveal the ways in which early modern cities were vital focal points for the global currents that emerged before 1850. In this era, it was difficult to differentiate between a Global North and Global South, as cities across the hemispheres emerged as concentrations of capital, inequality, and the crossroads of cultures. Already, though, the city was not merely a backdrop for these processes but was instead the instigator of complex interplays between global and local dynamics that often produced tensions and flows that, arguably, are still visible today.

Reflections on doing historical research into the global urban

As Pierre-Yves Saunier has stressed, the historical approach to the global urban has often remained 'at most . . . a heuristic tool to explain variation in the fate of specific global cities and to account for their global features' (Saunier and Ewen, 2008: 6). Perhaps the most important thing that historians have learned over the brief life of global urban history as a sub-field is that this is not enough. We must do more than narrate the ups and downs of the global experience in individual cities. While documenting the global process in an urban context is important, it is even more critical to elucidate the ways in which cities always have been 'the creations and the creators of connections' (Nightingale, 2016). Recognizing and documenting these connections, historians are then in a position to use their archival base to theorize their dynamics in a way that incorporates the rich insights of the discipline. Global urban history can, in this manner, emphasize therefore how the global urban maintains consistencies over time and space. On a practical level, pursuing such ambitions will require that historians try harder to speak to each other across the chronological and geographical boundaries that have customarily separated them. Additionally, we should embrace collaboration, both with other historians and with social scientists. Finally, historians need to share more readily insights that can reveal the deep and tangled character of the conundrums that face scholars and planners in the contemporary globalized city. As the saying goes, forewarned is forearmed. In order to 'get cities right' (Nightingale, 2016) you have to know how and where they went wrong. Global urban history is surely well qualified to provide that information.

References

Abu-Lughod, J.L. (1991) *Before European Hegemony: The World System A.D. 1250-1350*. New York: Oxford University Press.

Abu-Lughod, J.L. (1999) *New York, Chicago, Los Angeles: America's Global Cities*. Minneapolis, MN: University of Minnesota Press.

Arrom, S.M. (2001) *Containing the Poor: The Mexico City Poor House, 1774-1871*. Durham, NC: Duke University Press.

Bergad, L.W. (2006) *Slavery and the Demographic and Economic History of Minas Gerais, Brazil, 1720-1888*. Cambridge: Cambridge University Press.

Bicalho, M.F. (2003) *A Cidade e o Império: o Rio de Janeiro no século XVIII*. Rio de Janeiro: Civilização Brasileira.

Braudel, F. (1979 [1981-84]) *Civilization and Capitalism, 15th-18th Century*. 3 Vols. Transl. S. Reynolds. London: Collins.

Brenner, N. (2004) *New State Spaces: Urban Governance and the Rescaling of Statehood*. New York: Oxford University Press.

Brown, K.W. (2012) *A History of Mining in Latin America: From the Colonial Era to the Present*. Albuquerque, NM: University of New Mexico Press.

Carp, B. (2009) *Rebels Rising: Cities and the American Revolution*. New York: Oxford University Press.

Carvalho, B. (2013) *Porous City: A Cultural History of Rio de Janeiro*. Liverpool: Liverpool University Press.

Castells, M. (1996) *The Rise of the Network Society*. Oxford: Blackwell.

Coclanis, P.A. (1989) *The Shadow of a Dream: Economic Life and Death in the South Carolina Low Country, 1670–1920*. New York: Oxford University Press.

Dantas, M.L.R. (2008) *Black Townsmen: Urban Slavery and Freedom in the Eighteenth-Century Americas*. New York: Palgrave Macmillan.

Dantas, M.L.R. (2009) 'Humble slaves and loyal vassals: Free Africans and their descendants in eighteenth-century Minas Gerais, Brazil', in A.B. Fisher and M.D. O'Hara (eds), *Imperial Subjects: Race and Identity in Colonial Latin America*. Durham, NC: Duke University Press, pp. 115–40.

Darwin, J. (2007) *After Tamerlane: The Rise and Fall of Global Empires 1400–2000*. London: Allen Lane.

Devine, T.M. (1975) *The Tobacco Lords: A Study of the Tobacco Merchants of Glasgow and their Trading Activities, c.1740–90*. Edinburgh: Donald.

Dorsey, B. (2002) *Reforming Men and Women: Gender in the Antebellum City*. Ithaca, NY: Cornell University Press.

Farías, I. and Bender, T. (eds) (2010) *Urban Assemblages: How Actor-Network Theory Changes Urban Studies*. London: Routledge.

Fonseca, C.D. (2003) *Des Terres aux Villes de l'Or: Pouvoirs et territoires urbains au Minas Gerais (Brésil, XVIIIe siécle)*. Paris: Centre Culturel Calouste Gulbenkian.

Friedmann, J. (2002) *The Prospect of Cities*. Minneapolis, MN: University of Minnesota Press.

Guy, D.J. (1991) *Sex and Danger in Buenos Aires: Prostitution, Family, and Nation in Argentina*. Lincoln, NE: University of Nebraska Press.

Hart, E. (2010) *Building Charleston: Town and Society in the Eighteenth-Century British Atlantic World*. Charlottesville, VA: University of Virginia Press.

Kenny, N. and Madgin, R. (eds) (2015) *Cities Beyond Borders: Comparative and Transnational Approaches to Urban History*. Farnham: Ashgate.

Kiddy, E.W. (2007) *Blacks of the Rosary: Memory and History in Minas Gerais, Brazil*. University Park, PA: Pennsylvania State University Press.

Knight, F.W. and Liss, P.K. (eds) (1991) *Atlantic Port Cities: Economy, Culture, and Society in the Atlantic World, 1650–1850*. Knoxville, TN: University of Tennessee Press.

Matson, C. (1998) *Merchants and Empire: Trading in Colonial New York*. Baltimore, MD: Johns Hopkins University Press.

Michney, T.M. (2017) *Surrogate Suburbs: Black Upward Mobility and Neighborhood Change in Cleveland, 1900–1980*. Chapel Hill, NC: University of North Carolina Press.

Nash, G.B. (1979) *The Urban Crucible: Social Change, Political Consciousness, and the Origins of the American Revolution*. Cambridge, MA: Harvard University Press.

Nightingale, C.H. (2012) *Segregation: A Global History of Divided Cities*. Chicago: University of Chicago Press.

(Continued)

Nightingale, C.H. (2016) '"World history needs more urban mess": A conversation with Carl H. Nightingale', *Global Urban History* blog https://globalurbanhistory.com/2016/08/08/rare-is-the-messy-stuff-of-urban-history-a-conversation-with-carl-h-nightingale (accessed 21 September 2017).

O'Flanagan, P. (2008) *Port Cities of Atlantic Iberia, c. 1500–1900*. Aldershot: Ashgate.

Osorio, A.B. (2008) *Inventing Lima: Baroque Modernity in Peru's South Sea Metropolis*. New York: Palgrave Macmillan.

Osterhammel, J. (2014) *The Transformation of the World: A Global History of the Nineteenth Century*. Princeton, NJ: Princeton University Press.

Pomeranz, K. (2000) *The Great Divergence: China, Europe, and the Making of the Modern World Economy*. Princeton, NJ: Princeton University Press.

Prado, F. (2015) *Edge of Empire: Atlantic Networks and Revolution in Bourbon Río de la Plata*. Oakland, CA: University of California Press.

Sandoval-Strausz, A.K. and Kwak, N.H. (eds) (2018) *Making Cities Global: The Transnational Turn in Urban History*. Philadelphia, PA: University of Pennsylvania Press.

Sassen, S. (1991) *The Global City: New York, London, Tokyo*. Princeton, NJ: Princeton University Press.

Saunier, P-Y. and Ewen, S. (eds) (2008) *Another Global City: Historical Explorations into the Transnational Municipal Moment, 1850–2000*. New York: Palgrave Macmillan.

Scarano, J. (1976) *Devoção e Escravidão: a irmandade de Nossa Senhora do Rosário dos Pretos no Distrito Diamantino no século XVIII*. São Paulo: Companhia Editora Nacional.

Taylor, P.J. (2004) *World City Network: A Global Urban Analysis*. London: Routledge.

Taylor, P.J. (2013) *Extraordinary Cities: Millennia of Moral Syndromes, World-Systems and City/State Relations*. Cheltenham: Edward Elgar.

Taylor, P.J. and Derudder, B. (2018) 'Exploring the world city network', in J. Harrison and M. Hoyler (eds), *Doing Global Urban Research*. London: Sage, pp. 34–51.

Taylor, P.J., Firth, A., Hoyler, M. and Smith, D. (2010) 'Explosive city growth in the modern world-system: An initial inventory derived from urban demographic changes', *Urban Geography*, 31(7): 865–84.

Taylor, P.J., Ni, P., Derudder, B., Hoyler, M., Huang, J. and Witlox, F. (eds) (2011) *Global Urban Analysis: A Survey of Cities in Globalization*. London: Earthscan.

Therborn, G. (2011) 'End of a paradigm: The current crisis and the idea of stateless cities', *Environment and Planning A*, 43(2): 272–85.

Voigt, L. (2016) *Spectacular Wealth: The Festivals of Colonial South American Mining Towns*. Austin, TX: University of Texas Press.

Walker, C.F. (2008) *Shaky Colonialism: The 1746 Earthquake-Tsunami in Lima, Peru, and its Long Aftermath*. Durham, NC: Duke University Press.

16

ADVANCING GLOBAL URBAN RESEARCH

Michael Hoyler and John Harrison

Urban research is increasingly global in its outlook, therefore as urban researchers we must intuitively know what global urban research is, when we are doing it, why we are doing it and how we are doing it. We began this book by critically addressing this basic proposition, because to our mind this is often not the case (Harrison and Hoyler, Chapter 1). Despite the emergence of a growing body of critical work aimed at theorizing the global urban, our chief concern is that there remains a notable silence surrounding the practice of doing global urban research. The contribution of this book has been to open up this particular black box by presenting insights into the opportunities and challenges, techniques and tools, theories and case studies which enable the *doing* of global urban research. But, as with any such endeavour, the end point is never a resolution; rather it presents us with a series of reflections and further questions. In this concluding chapter we offer some of our thoughts – you will no doubt have your own too – about how we can go about doing global urban research.

One of the main unresolved challenges that arise out of this book is what does and does not constitute global urban research. Let us be clear that in posing this concern, we do not seek to judge, let alone police, urban studies by suggesting this or that research is, or is not, global urban research. Our point is more well-intentioned. What this book does is to raise a concern that we do not often stop to think and to reflect on what it is that makes our research, and more particularly our research practice, part of an increasingly globalized urban study. In the following paragraphs, we identify three distinct but overlapping scalar approaches to researching the global urban that emerge from the chapters of this book, and point to five evolving trends advancing global urban research today.

First there are *macro-level approaches* to doing global urban research, where urban analysis is undertaken at a truly global scale. Perhaps unsurprisingly, this macro-level approach towards producing a global study of the urban has a tendency towards techniques which prioritize revealing global patterns and visualizing global urban processes, using analytical and cartographic strategies which are clearly evident in the chapters on planetary urbanization and exploring the world city network. A distinctive element of macro-level approaches is that the research is conducted remotely and at a distance from the objects of study. By engaging with the urban at the global scale, macro-level approaches help to make sense of urban complexity, revealing and rendering intelligible the dynamics and flows structuring global capitalist expansion.

Then there are those *meso-level approaches* which have at their core a comparative element. These emerge, to some extent, from the macro-level analyses which point towards the geographical unevenness of globalized urbanization. Meso-level approaches begin to allow for differential engagements with the global urban depending on researchers' own vantage point, frame of study, biography, and historical moment the research is conceived, conducted, and committed to print. One consequence has been the increased division that has come to characterize today's more globalized urban studies. Emphasis has been on difference and diversity in the global urban, with the formation of distinct research camps based on theoretical approach (political economy/postcolonial), object of study (global cities/ordinary cities), geography (northern/southern, Euro-America/postcolony) and emphasis (universality/particularity). Such had been the splintering that Jamie Peck recently argued it was placing cities beyond compare (Peck, 2015). However, through calls for 'engaged pluralism' (Barnes and Sheppard, 2010) and a newfound desire among urban scholars to seek out potential common ground rather than claim incommensurability (Brenner, 2017; Bunnell, 2016; Hoyler and Harrison, 2017; van Meeteren et al., 2016a, 2016b), rigorous comparative analysis is positioned as central to ensuring meso-level approaches are a constructive, rather than destructive, force in developing new knowledge and understandings of the global urban (see Gough, 2012; Robinson and Roy, 2016).

Finally there are the *micro-level approaches* to doing global urban research. This involves studying the impact of global processes and relations on particular locations, as well as tracing the influence of specific locations in the wider world beyond city and hinterland. It is important to remember that the element of originality in these studies is not simply the location. In this book we see examples that range from researching the impacts of a particular global urban 'event', such as the Olympic Games, on a host city (Gaffney et al., Chapter 9), through to the ongoing impacts of a specific global urban 'process', such as gentrification, on particular cities (Shin, Chapter 10). Having said that it is not the location which gives these micro-level approaches their original contribution, the location does often provide the impetus for global urban research. Take the example of researching global urban policy mobility, where Cristina Temenos and Kevin Ward's research (Chapter 5) begins with a place – in their case Manchester – to demonstrate how it features 'elsewhere' within global urban policy discourse (and this is also the case for – often neglected – smaller cities (Bunnell et al., 2017)). The point with micro-level approaches is they might be local in their origin, and often the research might be conducted in situ, yet they are not necessarily any less global in their scope (Massey, 2007).

Of course, there are overlaps and complementarities between these approaches, rather than scalar purity – for example, planetary urban research does not require a macro-level approach (see Schmid (2014) and Brenner and Katsikis (2014) for examples of doing planetary urban research in Switzerland and the Mediterranean respectively) – but reflecting on the book in this way illustrates our main point that there is not a singular approach to doing global urban research (nor should there be). To further emphasize this argument we end the book by highlighting five emergent trends in doing global urban research.

The first of these is a trend towards more *agency-centric approaches* to doing global urban research. At one level, agency-focused research is already a central pillar of global urban research. Who can forget the classic accounts from the 1990s and 2000s, for example, detailing the rapid ascendancy of transnational elites and transnational firms in structuring and managing global networks vis-à-vis the supposed declining power structures of the territorial state and its weakened ability to orchestrate economic and social life in globalization. But, at another level, we are witnessing divergence in the range of actors and practices included as objects in the study of global urban research (Hoyler et al., 2018). In this book, we see the two extremes. In Chapter 6, Donald McNeill and Andrea Pollio demonstrate the opportunities and challenges presented by focusing on the role and impact of profiteers – in their case, IBM and Uber – as global urbanists. In contrast, David Wachsmuth (Chapter 11) uses profiteering – in his case the real estate boom in Vancouver – as a backdrop against which to uncover the role and impact of non-profiteering groups (local residents, community leaders, social activists) to problematize who has the right to the city, and who it is that grants those rights. If you are thinking about an agency-centric approach to researching the global urban the obvious starting point to begin designing your project is to ask a 'who' question (Who are the global urbanists? Who are the global city makers? Who is managing this global urban network?) to help identify the actor(s) you want to focus your research on. From here you can formulate a series of questions that narrow down and shape your research project. Questions that begin with 'what' and 'where' will help you define the scale and scope of their agentic role in the global urban, while those starting with 'how' will allow you to uncover the strategies and mechanisms that enable the actor(s) to fulfil this role, and 'why' questions will help to unpack their motivations and interests.

The second trend centres on *historical approaches* to researching the global urban. Here we interpret 'historical' in a more than literal way because what we are referring to are approaches which not only include a strong spatial element, but also a strong temporal component. Not surprisingly this can present significant challenges to undergraduate and graduate students because of the time-limited nature of their projects. Nevertheless, it is important to note that what might start out as research where space dominates time, as research careers and interests develop, space and time can often become more equal partners in the research story that is told. This is arguably true of three approaches adopted by contributors to this book. Firstly, studies of global mega-events have a cyclical nature; for example, the four-year cycles between Olympic Games or the World Cups in football, rugby union and cricket (Gaffney et al., Chapter 9; Lauermann, Chapter 8). Secondly, the 'GaWC approach' outlined in the chapter on exploring the world city network is an example of research which began in the late 1990s as a spatial exercise aimed at exploring the world city network, but the repeating of this exercise has seen it morph into a longitudinal study with time-series data for 2000, 2004, 2008, 2010, 2012 and 2016, to the point where the story of GaWC research is as much about change over time as it is about patterns across space. What you begin to see here is that longitudinal research is not uniform, but – as Katherine Gough (Chapter 14: 197) notes – it can take on differing forms ranging from 'continuous research in the same society over a number of years; re-studies that take place periodically either at regular or irregular intervals in "waves"; or return to a place/people after an extended period of time has elapsed'. Her third approach is an example of precisely this variation, with one longitudinal study of 30 enterprises in Accra, Ghana, being repeated annually for ten years, while another study of Pereira, Colombia, has been more sporadic with research undertaken in 1986/7 (an initial one-off study for Gough's PhD), 1997, 2010, and 2016. The final approach in this book is the most explicitly historical in its design. This recognizes that urban historians have yet to fully embrace the methods and analytical potential of global or world history approaches but so too, perhaps, have urban studies scholars overlooked the methods and analytical potential of urban history in their approach to global urban research (Dantas and Hart, Chapter 15).

Despite some remaining focus on disciplinary specificity, a third trend in global urban research is the increasing tendency to embrace *diverse philosophical and disciplinary approaches*. Given the nature of urban theory-making in contemporary global urban studies, you may be forgiven for thinking that until recently global urban research has been inspired by very different – often apparently incommensurable – meta-theoretical and analytical frameworks, namely political economy or postcolonial approaches, northern or southern urbanism, critical realism or post-structuralist thought. Through calls for 'engaged pluralism' and rigorous comparativism the contours of a more progressive future for global urban research is being mapped out – though as with many of these points it remains easier said than done – but the truth is global urban research has always been more pluralistic than has been outwardly projected (Hoyler and Harrison, 2017). In one of many illustrations of this, we only need consider Linda Peake's (2016) quest for feminism and the global urban, or Skelton and Gough's (2013) endeavours to consider the im/mobile urban geographies of young people in a time of globalized urbanization.

Alongside philosophical and disciplinary diversity we also identify a trend towards *engagement with different regional contexts*. In the literature we see this most clearly in papers outlining the need to rethink global urbanism through the contextual lenses of Africa (Parnell and Pieterse, 2016), Southern urbanism (Schindler, 2017), and China (Wu, 2016) to name but three recent examples. Underpinning this trend is a more fundamental argument for the decentring of global urban research (Leitner and Sheppard, 2016). When encountering global urban research there is much to choose from, but it is important to bear in mind how scientific interest in certain places/peoples/processes is as uneven as the geographies of globalization itself. Take this book as an example. By necessity it is selective, a partial take on approaches to doing global urban research: certain topics are included, others are missing; certain countries and cities are highlighted, many more are never mentioned; certain disciplines are drawn upon, but certainly not all; some methods and methodological techniques are identified by contributors, alternatives are not present. The point being is that there is no right or wrong way to do global urban research. Yes, there are places/peoples/processes which are more/less prominent in global urban debates, but the call has to be for research which is driven by your intellectual curiosity far more than by what is currently (or worse still, formerly) fashionable.

A fifth distinctive feature of global urban research is the growth in *collaborative approaches*. This is significant because trends three and four both emphasise 'diversity' and 'difference', while the chapter as a whole characterizes global urban research according to multiple approaches. From our vantage point in Loughborough, it is worth remembering at this point Peter Taylor's final comments when arguing the need for a global study to solve, what he saw as, the empirical/methodological problem of doing global urban research:

> *Conclusion as invitation*: [. . .] I do not think that social scientists have fully appreciated the implications of globalization for their research practices. Some sizeable segment of research effort is required [. . .]. I think I have proposed a methodology that meets our data needs and have also provided the necessary theoretical context for the study. Of course, this is not the only way of proceeding with investigation of the topic and debate on the matter is welcomed. (Taylor, 1997: 331)

Twenty years on there is no denying that a sizeable segment of research effort has occurred, multiple ways of proceeding have been proposed, and although debate on the matter has not always been welcomed by some over this time, strong and robust debate has deepened knowledge and advanced understanding of the global urban. More importantly, the current state of global urban research suggests the spirit of open 'invitation' is reflected in opportunities for dialogue as well as debate among urban researchers approaching the global urban from different vantage points, perspectives, and traditions (Robinson et al., 2016). One important aspect of this is the undeniable growth in collaborative research practices and networks. It is one thing to have engaged pluralism in theory – and our theories – but it is another to have engaged pluralism in practice – and our practices (Hoyler and Harrison, 2017). As such, it is heartening to see an increasing number of invitations for researchers from across the broad spectrum of global urban research to engage in open dialogue. This was the origins of this book, and the preceding conference, which we deliberately pitched as 'doing global urban research' (as opposed to say 'doing global cities research'). It is striking to us how many of the contributors to this book are themselves part of newly forged ('global') research networks working across multiple disciplines, contexts and sites. Indeed, it is exactly this which has brought us to this point, because within our own context of GaWC, its expansion has been characterized by a transition from a single discipline (Geography) and single location (Loughborough) research group to an interdisciplinary and international research network. Whereas 20 years ago most urban research would have been done by individuals and research groups – making the task of undertaking a global study 'daunting' (Taylor, 1997: 331) – the establishment of research networks is providing more opportunities for urban researchers to engage in dialogue and debate than ever before.

If these are the trends and aspirations for global urban research going forward, then we hope this book will serve as the guide to what is involved and, perhaps more than this, provide insights into what is possible. Of course, how you approach doing global urban research is for you to determine. And this is our point. We have been very deliberate in the book to not set limits on what is or is not global urban research. Nor are we telling you how to do global urban research. We have not even tried to convince you that you must become researchers of the global urban – though we do hope you will have been inspired and encouraged by the many different possibilities of doing global urban research.

References

Barnes, T.J. and Sheppard, E. (2010) '"Nothing includes everything": Towards engaged pluralism in Anglophone economic geography', *Progress in Human Geography*, 34(2): 193–214.

Brenner, N. (2017) 'Debating planetary urbanization: For an engaged pluralism', *Working Paper*, Urban Theory Lab, Harvard GSD Available from www.urbantheorylab.net/publications/debating-planetary-urbanization-for-an-engaged-pluralism (accessed 21 September 2017).

Brenner, N. and Katsikis, N. (2014) 'Is the Mediterranean urban?', in N. Brenner (ed.), *Implosions/Explosions: Towards a Study of Planetary Urbanization*. Berlin: Jovis, pp. 428–59.

Bunnell, T. (2016) 'Conventionally partial critique', *Dialogues in Human Geography*, 6(3): 282–6.

Bunnell, T., Padawangi, R. and Thompson, E.C. (2017) 'The politics of learning from a small city: Solo as translocal model and political launch pad', *Regional Studies*, doi: 10.1080/00343404.2017.1298087.

Dantas, M. and Hart, E. (2018) 'Historical approaches to researching the global urban', in J. Harrison and M. Hoyler (eds), *Doing Global Urban Research*. London: Sage, pp. 211–24.

Gaffney, C., Wolfe, S.D. and Müller, M. (2018) 'Scrutinizing global mega-events', in J. Harrison and M. Hoyler (eds), *Doing Global Urban Research*. London: Sage, pp. 125–37.

Gough, K.V. (2012) 'Reflections on conducting urban comparison', *Urban Geography*, 33(6): 866–78.

Gough, K.V. (2018) 'Doing longitudinal urban research', in J. Harrison and M. Hoyler (eds), *Doing Global Urban Research*. London: Sage, pp. 196–210.

Harrison, J. and Hoyler, M. (2018) 'Making sense of the global urban', in J. Harrison and M. Hoyler (eds), *Doing Global Urban Research*. London: Sage, pp. 1–11.

Hoyler, M. and Harrison, J. (2017) 'Global cities research and urban theory making', *Environment and Planning A*, 49(12): 2853–8.

Hoyler, M., Parnreiter, C. and Watson, A. (eds) (2018) *Global City Makers: Economic Actors and Practices in the World City Network*. Cheltenham: Edward Elgar.

Lauermann, J. (2018) 'Evaluating global urban sustainability', in J. Harrison and M. Hoyler (eds), *Doing Global Urban Research*. London: Sage, pp. 110–24.

Leitner, H. and Sheppard, E. (2016) 'Provincializing critical urban theory: Extending the ecosystem of possibilities', *International Journal of Urban and Regional Research*, 40(1): 228–35.

Massey, D. (2007) *World City*. Cambridge: Polity.

McNeill, D. and Pollio, A. (2018) 'Tracking the global urbanists', in J. Harrison and M. Hoyler (eds), *Doing Global Urban Research*. London: Sage, pp. 81–95.

Parnell, S. and Pieterse, E. (2016) 'Translational global praxis: Rethinking methods and modes of African urban research', *International Journal of Urban and Regional Research*, 40(1): 236–46.

Peake, L. (2016) 'The twenty-first-century quest for feminism and the global urban', *International Journal of Urban and Regional Research*, 40(1): 219–27.

Peck, J. (2015) 'Cities beyond compare?', *Regional Studies*, 49(1): 160–82.

Robinson, J. and Roy, A. (2016) 'Debate on global urbanisms and the nature of urban theory', *International Journal of Urban and Regional Research*, 40(1): 181–6.

(Continued)

Robinson, J., Scott, A.J. and Taylor, P.J. (2016) *Working, Housing: Urbanizing.* Cham: Springer.

Schindler, S. (2017) 'Towards a paradigm of Southern urbanism', *City*, 21(1): 47–64.

Schmid, C. (2014) 'A typology of urban Switzerland', in N. Brenner (ed.), *Implosions/Explosions: Towards a Study of Planetary Urbanization*. Berlin: Jovis, pp. 398–427.

Shin, H.B. (2018) 'Studying global gentrifications', in J. Harrison and M. Hoyler (eds), *Doing Global Urban Research*. London: Sage, pp. 138–52.

Skelton, T. and Gough, K.V. (2013) 'Introduction: Young people's im/mobile urban geographies', *Urban Studies*, 50(3): 455-66.

Taylor P.J. (1997) 'Hierarchical tendencies amongst world cities: a global research proposal', *Cities*, 14(6): 323–32.

Temenos, C. and Ward, K. (2018) 'Examining global urban policy mobilities', in J. Harrison and M. Hoyler (eds), *Doing Global Urban Research*. London: Sage, pp. 66–80.

Van Meeteren, M., Derudder, B. and Bassens, D. (2016a) 'Can the straw man speak? An engagement with postcolonial critiques of "global cities research"', *Dialogues in Human Geography*, 6(3): 247–67.

Van Meeteren, M., Bassens, D. and Derudder, B. (2016b) 'Doing global urban studies: on the need for engaged pluralism, frame switching, and methodological cross-fertilization', *Dialogues in Human Geography*, 6(3): 296–301.

Wachsmuth, D. (2018) 'Researching the global right to the city', in J. Harrison and M. Hoyler (eds), *Doing Global Urban Research*. London: Sage, pp. 153–68.

Wu, F. (2016) 'Emerging Chinese cities: Implications for global urban studies', *The Professional Geographer*, 68(2), 338–48.

INDEX